Charles

The Untold Story

ROSS BENSON

CHARLES
THE UNTOLD STORY

St. Martin's Press
New York

ISBN 0-312-10950-4

First published in Great Britain by Victor Gollancz.

First U.S. Edition: April 1994
10 9 8 7 6 5 4 3 2 1

Acknowledgement

I would like to thank all those who, for the best of reasons and in their different ways, helped me with this book.

Prelude

When Princess Diana announced in December 1993 that she could not take it anymore, that she had had enough, that life in the royal goldfish bowl had become a hideous strain which she could bear no longer and that she fully intended to retire from public life, there was one person who fervently hoped she was telling the truth. Her husband.

For month after mortifying month, Prince Charles had been upstaged by his wife, the woman he had grown to detest, and it was driving him to distraction. As he complained to friends and members of his staff, *he* is the next king of England. He is royal by birth while Diana is only royal by marriage; it is therefore her duty—indeed her patriotic obligation—to defer to him, just as he must defer to his mother, the Queen.

But that is exactly what Diana was refusing to do. She enjoyed the limelight. It reinforced her fragile sense of her own identity. At the same time, her enormous popularity made it very hard for the royal family to move publicly against her. Diana was no Fergie, to be shouted at and ordered to behave.

It was becoming increasingly plain, though, that matters could not continue along their present course. Charles, usually so meek and mild mannered, simply would not allow it.

Matters came to a screaming head in the first week of December, 1993. On Wednesday night Charles attended a gala performance by Placido Domingo at the Royal Opera House in London's Covent Garden. It was staged in aid of charity and

Charles, a keen fan of the opera, had been looking forward enormously to the event which he hoped would generate publicity (and therefore funds) for the Royal Opera House Trust.

This was exactly the kind of opportunity Diana had become so adept at exploiting. She did so again and she did so brilliantly. She chose that night to attend a rock concert held in support of World AIDS Day. The result was a foregone conclusion. The following morning's newspapers were full of the Diana story, while Charles's outing hardly warranted a mention.

The Prince lost his temper. Once again Diana had stolen all the publicity. It was finally more than he was prepared to tolerate. For eleven wretched years he had been subjected to her temper and tantrums. She had outshone him and out-manoeuvred him. Now she had humiliated him.

It was time, he declared, to put a stop to Diana's activities. In that he had the full support of his family. The Queen Mother objected to being in the same room as the young woman she once so assiduously promoted as a suitable bride for her favourite grandson.

Prince Philip, too, had turned against Diana. The previous December, when it had been announced that the Prince and Princess of Wales were to separate, Philip had declared, "She wants out—she can get out!" Diana, he had pronounced, should henceforth be banned from every royal occasion. She should not be allowed to continue to play the royal princess at charity events and state banquets. But only the Queen could enforce such an order. And the Queen could not bring herself to do so.

She was angry with Diana, just as she was with Fergie, for the way she had so wilfully walked out on her marriage and, in so doing, placed the royal family to crisis. As she remarked with more bitterness than wit to one of her household, "You take in two girls from broken homes and look how they repay you."

She was concerned about their mental and emotional health. On more than one occasion she remarked, "Of course, my poor daughters-in-law are both mad."

Fergie was not really the problem. Diana, the wife and mother of two future kings, most certainly was. Yet despite the promptings of her husband and her mother, the Queen refused to exert her regal authority and order her daughter-in-law to behave herself. For the simple reason that the Queen was frightened of Diana—frightened of the power she exerted over the media; frightened of the influence she had over her sons, William and Harry; most of all, frightened of the future which she sensed belonged to Diana.

It was Diana who topped the opinion polls with a popularity rating which was three times that of the Queen and the Queen Mother—and seven times more than Charles. Any move against her, especially at a time when the standing of the House of Windsor was at its lowest ebb this century, would be fraught with danger. It was Charles who was born to be king, but it was Diana who held the high ground of public esteem. It was Diana the crowds wanted to see, not Charles. It was Diana who appeared on the front pages of newspapers and magazines. In this biting internecine confrontation, headlines counted for more than bloodlines.

In effect, if not in regal face, Diana had hijacked the royal family. As one member of the Queen's staff bluntly put it, "When William is king, Diana will have won."

It was power without responsibility. To Charles being royal is an inescapable duty which he must fulfil, no matter what the personal cost. Diana, convinced of her right to put her own happiness before the well-being of an institution, chose to take a sledgehammer to the foundations of propriety on which the House of Windsor was built and, despite Charles's pleadings, insisted on walking out on her marriage. And she had got away with it.

This time, however, Diana had overplayed her hand. Charles had been goaded into action. And this time the Queen did not protect her.

Diana had been to see the Queen regularly since the formal

announcement of the separation. The meetings all ended the same way—with Diana in tears and complaining that no one liked her, that nobody understood her, that the world was against her. The Queen had tried to reassure her that this was patently not the case, but Diana, too wrapped up in her own plight, was not to be placated. But now even the Queen's patience had worn thin. She finally came round to her son's thinking and agreed that Diana, the loose cannon on the deck of royalty, had to be brought under control.

In the time-honoured royal way it was left to someone else to do the Queen and Prince Charles's dirty work for them. The Queen's Private Secretary, Sir Robert Fellowes, was assigned the unpleasant task of informing Diana that she was no longer required on royal duty. It was a most painful duty to carry out—for by brutal coincidence, Fellowes happens to be Diana's own brother-in-law.

Diana would have liked to refuse, but she did not dare. The Royal Family make dangerous enemies, and Diana is terrified that they might try to take away her sons, William and Harry, by going to court to prove that she is mentally unstable. The Royal Family would consider such a drastic move only if Diana decided to set up home outside of England, and even then only with the greatest reluctance. The situation was nonetheless still fraught enough for Diana to opt for a tactical retreat rather than a full frontal confrontation.

Only time will tell whether Diana has really left the world's stage for good. The manner of her going suggests that she has not. As both the Queen and Sir Robert Fellowes pointed out in the strongest possible terms, calling a press conference to announce her "retirement" was not the best way of convincing the public that she really meant to quit public life. Diana, however, insisted on making her exit in her own way—which meant as publicly as possible.

The Queen Mother was most upset by the events that led to the separation of Charles and Diana and the bitter in-fighting that ensued. She was particularly disturbed at the way Diana, after the breakdown of her marriage, had set about usurping the Royal Family. Time and again she would ask, "Why didn't Charles do something to stop her?"

The answer to that question, as the Queen Mother well knew, lay with Charles himself and the way he had been brought up. He had been trained to be king. He had not been taught how to deal with a woman like Diana Spencer.

Chapter One

Prince Charles was born on 14 November 1948, son of Princess Elizabeth and the recently ennobled Duke of Edinburgh. He was abandoned by his parents shortly afterwards, or so it would much later seem to millions of his mother's subjects.

He was not without affection. He was cared for by a pampering retinue of nannies and under-nannies and nursery maids and he had a grandmother who doted on him. The love of his mother and father, however, like his food and clothing in those austere post-war years, was severely rationed. It had to be fitted in between their official duties. Even when time and duty permitted, the emotional needs of the little Prince were not always paramount on their agenda.

'I am going to be mother to my child, not its nurse,' Princess Elizabeth declared shortly before her son was born.

In the event it was the Scots-born Nanny Helen Lightbody who assumed both roles in Charles's formative early years. She arrived at Buckingham Palace two days before Charles's first Christmas and stayed with him until he went off to school eight years later. She would have stayed longer had she not fallen foul of Prince Philip.

It was 'Mrs' Lightbody – she was actually unmarried but in the titled world of the Royal Family the senior nanny is always known by the honorific of Mrs – who had day to day charge of his needs. And not just of the practical kind.

'Charles absolutely adored her,' recalled Eileen Parker whose husband, Mike, was Prince Philip's equerry at the time. It was Mrs Lightbody who got him up in the morning and gave him his last goodnight kiss.

In this nanny-orientated world, Mother remained a distant figure. As the romantic novelist, Dame Barbara Cartland, step-grandmother of Diana, Princess of Wales, observed: 'Mummy was a remote and glamorous figure who came to kiss you goodnight, smelling of lavender and dressed for dinner. Prince Charles worshipped his mother, but from afar.' Too far, as it transpired, for a 'normal' mother-and-son relationship to develop. They were simply not together often enough or long enough and when they were a wedge of formality came between them, although according to the authorized accounts of Charles's early years, the Princess made it a point of maternal honour to build her routine around his young life.

Charles and his sister, born twenty-one months later, were got up at seven, washed, dressed and given their breakfast by Nanny Lightbody and another Scots woman, Miss Mabel Anderson, who cared for Princess Anne. They then played in their nursery until they were taken downstairs to spend half an hour with their mother and their father, if he should happen to be around. They did not see their parents again until after tea, when the Princess would venture up to the nursery floor, duty permitting, for bath-time when she would spend another half-hour with her offspring. She was said to take especial delight in playing with Charles as he splashed about with his toy submarine and plastic ducks. The apparently informal family idyll was somewhat spoilt, however, by everyone having to stand when the Princess walked into the bathroom. And rather than roll up her sleeves to join in the play, she would sit on a gilt chair, often eating a light supper which a footman had brought in for her on a tray.

'She was always very formal with them. To my knowledge she never bathed the children; Nanny did all that,' Mrs Parker said.

Philip was even more aloof. 'He was very severe on both of them,' said Mrs Parker. And on Charles in particular. He

11

tolerated Charles but he was not a noticeably loving father. 'I think Charles was frightened of him,' Mrs Parker said.

He was not a tactile father. Very much a 'man's man', he had little time for the petticoat world of the nursery – or, indeed, for any of the other formalities of Palace life. He did not spend much time with his children. When he did, their meetings were brief and brusque.

Charles – shy, diffident, always in need of reassurance – did not respond well to his father's truculence. 'He became very quiet when Philip was around; he was not confident with him,' Mrs Parker observed.

When she became pregnant, Elizabeth, like all expectant mothers, devoted much thought to how she would like her son to be brought up. 'Normal' was the word she used. 'I want my children to live ordinary lives,' she insisted. But normal and ordinary were exactly what the Royal Family was not. Nor had they been notable characteristics of Philip's upbringing. Both he and Elizabeth were the products of distinctly abnormal backgrounds, which had its inevitable effect on the way that they in turn approached parenthood.

The future Queen, like all her immediate relations, had been raised by nannies, that self-sacrificing caste of hard-working, usually Scottish women from modest backgrounds who were charged with the responsibility of turning out well-mannered, well-behaved princes and princesses. Some were brutal in their methods – Elizabeth's father, George VI, and his brothers were abused, possibly even sexually, by one nursery maid – but most were kind and affectionate surrogate mothers who loved their charges and whose only practical reward (the Royal Family has never been generous with wages) was the hugs and kisses they received in return.

Elizabeth was looked after by Clara Knight, who had been nanny to the Princess's own mother and her brother David Bowes Lyon, and later to the children of their elder sister, Lady Elphinstone. Known as Alah – a childish derivation of Clara –

she adhered to a strict, no-nonsense routine where everything had its set time and place.

Elizabeth's contact with her father and mother was carefully prescribed. She saw them in the morning and the evening and that was about it. The Duke and Duchess of York, as they then were, were determined that she should not be subjected to the rigours and rejections that had made the Duke's own childhood an unmitigated misery, but that did not extend to building their lives around their daughter. When she was only nine months old, for instance, her mother left her in the care of her nanny while she joined her husband on a six-month tour of Australia.

Elizabeth was fond of her grandfather, George V, but frightened of her grandmother, the unbending, indomitable Queen Mary of whom Princess Margaret once remarked, 'She didn't like children and made no sort of effort with them.'

Her education was slapdash. 'I often had the feeling that the Duke and Duchess . . . were not over-concerned with the higher education of their daughters,' their governess, Marion Crawford, recorded.

The only true objective of a well-brought-up lady's childhood, her mother insisted, echoing the pre-feminist opinions of the age, was to provide a fund of pleasant memories to 'store up against the days that might come and, later, a happy marriage'. That did not include mathematics. As Queen Mary pointed out – wrongly, as it happened – Elizabeth would never have to worry about the household accounts.

Manners, on the other hand, were of vital importance. She was taught to curtsey and to say please and thank you. Queen Mary put it succinctly. 'Teach the child not to fidget!' she imperiously ordered Alah. The nanny dutifully obliged, bribing Elizabeth with biscuits to control her bladder.

It was a lonely upbringing. Her real friends were not other children who she rarely met but her collection of model horses. The high point of her day, as her governess recalled, was waiting, her nose pressed against the window of the house at

145 Piccadilly where the Yorks first lived, for the brewer's dray drawn by two horses to pass by.

It produced a self-contained woman with a deep sense of duty but one too inhibited ever to allow her feelings to show. Not even the birth of Charles could break down her barrier of emotionally incapacitating reserve. She loved her son. As Godfrey Talbot, the BBC's court correspondent from 1948 to 1969, observed: 'The Princess adored baby Charles. She was forever popping in and out of the nursery to see him. If anyone wanted to find her that was the place to look.'

Yet however much she may have wanted to, she never found it easy to hug him. Indeed, she found it nigh impossible to cuddle him at all. She had no first-hand experience of the kind of warm physical contact most people take for granted and was unable to give her son the palpable affection she herself had never enjoyed but which it was soon obvious that Charles craved.

Philip was not the man to pick up this emotional slack. Tough and determinedly independent, he had been brought up to fend for himself in a way that left little room for other people. 'When I was only a year old I had to leave my family and, since I was eight years old, I've always been at school,' he explained shortly before his judicious marriage to the heir to the throne. 'First Paris, then Baden, then Gordonstoun, then the Navy since I was seventeen.'

That stark outline left out the nuances that went to make him the man he became.

Of part Danish but mainly German origin, he was born a prince of Greece on 10 June 1921, on the island of Corfu on the dining-room table of a house called Mon Repos which had no gas, electricity or running hot water.

It was a wretched beginning – 'They did not live like royals – we had a few untrained peasant girls to help and two unwashed footmen,' their housekeeper recalled – and it was downhill from there. The following year Philip's father, Prince Andrew, an officer in the Greek army fighting a war with Turkey, had disobeyed orders, been charged with treason and condemned to death. Only the intercession of George V, who had personally intervened to ensure that the Tsar of Russia and his family were refused asylum in Britain and was now faced with the unpalatable prospect of the execution of another first cousin – and one who coincidentally also had a wife, four daughters and a son – saved him from the firing squad. The cruiser HMS *Calypso* was dispatched to bring Andrew and his family away to safety. Not to England, however: the King's sense of familial loyalty did not extend to supporting his impoverished relations out of his own purse as he would have had to have done if they had arrived on his sovereign territory.

Instead the family joined that wandering band of royal rejects that populated Europe after the First World War. They made their base in Paris, first in an apartment, then in a lodge owned by the rich wife of one of Philip's Greek uncles. It was a dispiriting existence, with funds always in short supply. Prince Andrew, a weak, effeminate man, took to the café life before finally leaving his family and wafting off to Monte Carlo where he set up home with a widowed actress.

When Philip was ten years old his mother, Alice, sister of the future Earl Mountbatten of Burma and once described as 'the prettiest princess in Europe', had a nervous breakdown. He had never been able to communicate easily with her; she was deaf and conversation was conducted in sign language. Now he couldn't communicate with her at all. After prolonged stays in a succession of Swiss sanatoriums, she became a nun and founded her own order, the Christian Sisterhood of Martha and Mary. At the same time his four older sisters all married and left home, and Philip was now effectively an orphan.

He was taken under the wing of his maternal uncle George, the second Marquess of Milford Haven, whose wife, Nadejda, had been accused in court of being the lesbian lover of heiress Gloria Vanderbilt during her battle for her daughter, the original 'poor little rich girl', also named Gloria. On Milford Haven's instigation, Philip was sent to Cheam prep school outside London. Then, on the insistence of his German relations, he went to Salem, the school founded in 1920 by Prince Max of Baden, the last chancellor of Imperial Germany and father-in-law of Philip's sister, Theodora.

There he fell under the influence of Kurt Hahn, the radical Jewish thinker to whom Prince Max had entrusted the task of training the new generation of Germans to save their nation from the failings of the old. Hahn's views were to leave as profound an impression on the young dispossessed Prince as they would later on his son.

Drawing on the teachings of Plato and Lord Baden-Powell, founder of the Boy Scout movement, Hahn believed in physical endeavour, self-reliance and community service. The new Germany, however, preferred a firmer solution to its ills than the one proffered by Hahn and his mentor. Prince Max idealistically exhorted: 'Let us train soldiers who are at the same time lovers of peace.' His successor in the Reichstag, Adolf Hitler, preferred soldiers who loved war. When Hahn challenged the Nazi party – 'It is a question now in Germany of its Christian morality, its reputation, its soldierly honour; Salem cannot remain neutral,' he wrote to the school's old boys. 'I call on all members of the Salem Association who are active in the SA or SS to terminate their allegiance either to Hitler or to Salem' – he was arrested.

Released following the protest of, among others, the British prime minister Ramsay MacDonald, he moved to England and then to Scotland where in 1934 he founded Gordonstoun on the windswept shores of the Moray Firth. Philip followed him there and rose to be head boy.

He was still a rootless German princeling without money or obvious prospects. But he was handsome and possessed of what Hahn called his 'undefeatable spirit'. Gordonstoun suited him. Hahn's teachings brought a philosophic order to his life, while the school's emphasis on rugged outdoor activity gave him the opportunity to show off his athletic prowess. He learnt to sail, played cricket and excelled at athletics. He left no academic impression, but that was no handicap at a school which placed little emphasis on scholastic achievement.

'I wouldn't have missed the experience for anything,' he said. Most importantly, the disruptions of his youth appeared to have been condemned to the recesses of memory. 'People talk about a normal upbringing,' he once said. 'What is a normal upbringing?' His own childhood, he insisted, was 'not necessarily particularly unhappy'.

The scars were there, however, and it did not take much to inflame them. Self-reliant by nature and necessity, he had little intuitive sympathy for anyone less capable than himself. Sometimes fair-minded, he was more frequently rude and intolerant. Denied the emotional continuity of a settled family life, he had constructed a protective persona of vigorous independence which took slight account of others, his own son included. 'There was always the Gordonstoun thing,' said Eileen Parker. 'It was his guiding precept.'

There were aspects of Hahn's teachings that Charles would eventually embrace, most particularly the commitment to community service. His father's muscular interpretation of the doctrine cast a fearful shadow over his early life, however. Like his grandfather, George VI, and his great-grandfather, George V, he suffered from knock knees and had to wear orthopaedic shoes to correct his flat feet. He was 'chesty' like his mother and suffered unduly from colds. His hearty father made no concessions to his son's infirmity.

The Parkers' daughter, Julie, born a month after the Prince, would often come from playing with Charles and ask her parents, 'Why is Prince Philip cross with Charles? Why isn't he nice to him?' Philip's method of teaching his son to swim, for instance, was simple and to the point. Over his sobbing objections, Charles would be dragged into the Buckingham Palace swimming pool. Sometimes he would be thrown in. On one occasion Nanny Lightbody objected to the treatment being meted out to her three-year-old charge, on the diplomatic grounds that he was 'chesty'. Philip replied, 'It's ridiculous to make such a fuss of him. There's nothing wrong with him!' In the screaming child went.

As Nanny had worried, Charles duly came down with a cold. She was furious but even that determined Scotswoman shied away from a direct confrontation with the always irascible Philip. 'The trouble is I can only say so much,' she complained angrily.

It was with an understandable sense of trepidation, therefore, that Charles would await his father's barked command ordering him into his presence. But if it reverberated loudly in his imagination, it featured less resoundingly in reality. Right from the outset of his marriage Philip established what became a lifetime's habit of being absent from his home for long periods and Charles saw very little of his father from one year to the next. He was rarely around, even at Christmas, and the first of his son's birthday parties he attended was his fourth.

His relationship with his young wife was also conducted from a distance for much of the time. On the instigation of Dickie Mountbatten, who had assumed the paternal role in his nephew's life following the death in 1938 of his brother, George Milford Haven, Philip had joined the Navy.

Philip has always tried to underplay the role Mountbatten assumed in his life. 'I don't think anyone thinks I had a father,' he once complained. 'Most people think that Dickie is my father anyway.' It was Mountbatten, none the less, who talked Philip out of joining the RAF and persuaded him to follow family tradition and make a career in the Royal Navy. It was a wise choice, as it turned out. Philip's grandfather, the first Marquess of Milford Haven, had risen to be First Sea Lord. The son of a morganatic marriage between Prince Alexander of Hesse and the penniless Countess Julia Hauke, whose grandfather had been a private in Napoleon's Grand Army, he had been forced to resign by the wave of anti-German feeling that followed the outbreak of the First World War. His son, Dickie, dedicated his career to expunging that blot on the family name and by hard work and a talent that almost matched his self-aggrandizement, rose in time to the rank his father had had to relinquish.

Philip, too, showed a noticeable aptitude for the job. He won the coveted King's Dirk for being the best cadet at Dartmouth. He became one of the youngest lieutenants in the Second World War, despite the handicap of not being a British subject. He was brave, efficient, and quickly earned a reputation for being what one of his petty officers called 'a strict disciplinarian'. It was ability harnessed to intense ambition, and a significant number of his contemporaries believed that he was destined to maintain his family's tradition.

Admiral of the Fleet Lord Lewin, Chief of the Defence Staff during the 1982 Falklands War, served with Philip as a midshipman and later commanded the royal yacht *Britannia*. He firmly believes that had Philip remained in the Navy, he, and not Lewin, would have been First Sea Lord.

There was another and more tangible prize in view, however. The nightclub singer Hélène Cordet has known Philip since his childhood and remains one of his closest confidantes. Her brother Jan, looking back to those days in exile in Paris, recalled that Philip always knew where he was going. 'Some day I'll be an important man – a king even!' he would boast. By the time he joined the battleship HMS *Ramillies* in 1940 he had adjusted his sights. As he told Vice Admiral Harold Tom Baillie-Grohman: 'My Uncle Dickie has ideas for me; he thinks I could marry Princess Elizabeth.'

Philip had met the Princess in 1939 when she had paid a visit with her father to the Royal Naval College, Dartmouth. He was eighteen, she thirteen. His manner, Elizabeth's governess remarked, was 'rather offhand'. The Princess, however, was smitten.

As a collateral member of the Royal Family, Philip was regularly invited to Windsor Castle and, later, to Balmoral. It was there that her fondness for the dashing officer with the 'looks of a Viking' developed into infatuation. She was young for her years, and while she had been taught that essential royal skill of making small talk with anyone she happened to be seated next to, she had no experience of dealing with members of the opposite sex of around her own age. Sheltered and chaperoned, she had been shielded from the normal emotional entanglements of adolescence. Philip was the first man she had got to know – and then only because his royal connections enabled him to slip under the protective wire strung around the heir to the throne by the King and his courtiers.

The old guard quickly took exception to the 'bumptious' interloper, who didn't even have a surname yet, who had so taken the Princess's fancy. Daphne du Maurier's husband, Lieutenant General Sir Frederick 'Boy' Browning, the hero of the battle for Arnhem and the first comptroller of Elizabeth's Household, heartily disliked him. Her sister, Princess Margaret, did not get on with him. Her mother had never got on with his Uncle Dickie – 'We always took Dickie with a pinch of salt,' was one of her kinder remarks – and wondered at the wisdom of allowing Elizabeth to marry into such a nakedly ambitious family.

Even the King, ailing in health and anxious to see his eldest daughter safely married, had doubts as to Philip's suitability. In 1947 he insisted that Elizabeth accompany him on a tour of South Africa where she celebrated her twenty-first birthday. Ostensibly the trip was arranged to give her time to think matters over. In fact, the King was hopeful that distance would bring the romance to an end.

Some of the objections to him speak more of the stifling protocol of the Palace than they do of Philip. One complaint was about the way he blatantly ignored court etiquette, which decreed that when the Princess wished to dance an equerry should invite a young man to be her partner. From the outset, the forthright Philip, who by then had learnt how to get his way with young women, brazenly took it upon himself to invite Elizabeth to dance with him.

Others were more consequential. Philip was not a British subject and though he had fought well in the Royal Navy in the Mediterranean and Pacific theatres of war and been mentioned in dispatches, his Teutonic origins were no recommendation in the aftermath of the Second World War when anti-German feeling was again running high. His royal bloodline was impressive but set against that was the potentially embarrassing fact that he had absolutely no money. A newspaper poll taken at the time revealed that 40 per cent of respondents were against the match.

Elizabeth and the man she loved were determined to overcome these political and constitutional complications, however. As he was obliged to, Philip renounced his hereditary right to the Greek throne and the title of prince that went with it, assumed the surname of Mountbatten, took the oath of allegiance as a subject of George VI, and formally asked the King for his daughter's hand in marriage. The King gave his approval and Elizabeth accepted with alacrity.

It was a more deferential age and little mention was made of the expedient way in which Philip had so hastily exchanged the Greek Orthodox faith of his upbringing for the Anglicanism he was now required to profess, and none at all of the wartime activities of his German relations, some of whose support for Hitler had extended to serving in the SS. Britain, locked in the despairing recession that followed the end of the war, was looking for something to celebrate and the wedding at Westminster Abbey on 20 November 1947 was a glorious, lavish defiance of the nation's economic ills.

Almost exactly one year later when Princess Elizabeth gave birth to a son, the Union Jacks were again raised, a resounding forty-one-gun salute fired in the baby's honour, and the fountains in Trafalgar Square floodlit blue for a boy.

The birth that foggy night in November 1948 was not an easy one. The official bulletin pinned to the gates of Buckingham Palace announced that 'Her Royal Highness and her son are doing well.' It was later revealed that she had been given a pain-killing anaesthetic. It is commonly supposed that the 7 pounds 6 ounces (3.34 kilogram) boy was delivered by forceps. In fact he was born by Caesarean section but such was the prudishness of the age that this was never officially disclosed. Even her friends were not informed. 'Breast-feeding', as one of Elizabeth's confidantes remembered, 'was never spoken of.' Pregnancy, and especially a royal pregnancy, was a condition that polite society feigned not to notice. In another indication of contemporary attitudes, Philip did not attend his wife during her confinement (not that he would have wanted to). Neither, for the first time in more than a century, did the Home Secretary. A few weeks before the birth the King had issued the formal announcement that this archaic custom, dating from the reign of James II when his wife, Mary of Modena, had been accused of deceptively producing a changeling son to ensure the succession, was to be discontinued.

When labour started Philip was shooed out of Buckingham Palace's Buhl Room, once a part of the children's quarters but which had been converted into a surgical theatre for an operation on the arteries of the King's legs. Philip retreated to the squash courts for a fast game with Mike Parker, before bounding back up the stairs again to hold his first-born, still wearing his sporting flannels and open-necked shirt and sweating with exertion.

His wife was still drugged and did not come to for some minutes more. Elizabeth would later say that her husband's face was the last she saw before she slipped under the anaesthetic and the first when she came round again. She had seen little of him during the early months of her pregnancy: Philip contracted German measles and had to be kept apart from his expectant wife. She would see even less of him in the months and years to come. Those problems, however, lay in the future and for the moment the royal couple was a reassuring picture of marital contentment. And by producing a son, Elizabeth had fulfilled her essential duty, which was to provide an heir.

The Princess, who had taken a matter-of-fact approach to her pregnancy ('After all, that's what we are made for,' she said), was beguiled by what she had produced. 'I still find it difficult to believe I have a baby of my own,' she remarked. In the long human tradition, she set about searching for family resemblances in his features. His hands attracted her attention. They were, she said, rather large, 'but fine with long fingers'. Philip declared that his son looked like a plum pudding.

That he was a prince was taken for granted – so much for granted, that he almost was not one. He could trace his lineage back to Alfred the Great. By royal oversight, he almost started on his preordained progress towards the throne as the Earl of Merioneth without even a Royal Highness before his name.

Under the royal warrant issued by George V in 1917, the title of prince was limited to the children of a sovereign and his sons. Daughters were not taken into account. George VI had made Philip a Royal Highness when he created him a duke in 1947. But though the King always addressed him by his Greek title of prince, Philip was not one in the eyes of the rest of the country until 1957. That meant that his son was only entitled to use the secondary title of Merioneth which went with the dukedom of Edinburgh. The monarch still retained the power to grant titles as he saw fit, however, and five days before his grandson was born he issued letters patent conferring on all children born of the Edinburghs the title of prince or princess and the right to be addressed as His or Her Royal Highness.

Considerable surprise was expressed when it was announced that the name of Charles was to go with the baby's royal handles. Was this a conscious effort on the part of Elizabeth and her husband to revive the Stuart names which had not been used by the Royal Family in almost three hundred years? The royal courtiers insisted it was not. Charles and later Anne just happened to be the names their parents liked best. It was simply a coincidence that one of the most popular films at the time was *Bonnie Prince Charlie* which starred the always urbane David

Niven, a friend of Philip and a member of the small circle of like-minded men who accompanied the newly married Duke on his bachelor forays late into the night.

The Queen chose not to acknowledge her husband's escapades. She referred to his circle as 'Philip's funny friends'. When he was so late home one night that he had to climb in over the locked gates of Clarence House where they were living her only remark was, 'Serves him right.'

The Palace courtiers did not take such a benevolent view. They complained that he was getting involved with the 'wrong sort' and objected to what Eileen Parker called 'his apparent desire to continue bachelor friendships'.

Along with Niven, who began his Hollywood career sharing a house with the notorious Errol Flynn, the Philip Set included Baron, the society photographer who, as Mrs Parker noted, 'was hardly known as a model of sexual propriety in the gossip columns, nor in the drawing rooms of Mayfair or Belgravia'. Another friend was Prince Alfonso von Hohenlohe, the founder of the Marbella club who in 1955 created an international scandal by marrying Fiat chief Gianni Agnelli's fifteen-year-old niece, Princess Ira von Fürstenberg.

They formed what they called the Thursday Club which met for long lunches at Wheeler's restaurant in Soho. In the evening they would often retire to the flat in Grosvenor Square, Mayfair, belonging to the third Marquess of Milford Haven, Philip's best man and a notorious womanizer who had a long affair with the Hungarian-born actress Eva Bartok and who may indeed have been the father of her daughter, Deanna. As one of Philip's own royal relations put it bluntly: 'He was back to his old ways within a year of his marriage.'

A veil of discretion was drawn over these nocturnal romps. It was kept in place by firm legal action. One woman friend who worked as a waitress at Fortnum and Mason made the mistake of talking too openly about him. She told a friend how fond she was of Philip, how well she got on with him and 'What an awful life he leads; he's like a caged animal.' The conversation was overheard and reported to the Palace. Farrer's, the firm of solicitors that acts for the Royal Family, was called into action the following day. Statements were taken. The woman was not seen at Fortnum's again.

In part Philip's wilful disregard for the conventions demanded by his position as consort of the future Queen could be put down to his increasing sense of frustration at the situation in which he found himself (but one which, in truth, was substantially of his own making – no one could have forced him to marry Elizabeth). He was made to give up the red convertible sports car which he used to drive himself to Windsor (more than once by way of ditch and fence) during his courting days and replace it with a more dignified family vehicle. His efforts to play a significant role in his wife's public affairs were firmly discouraged. When he started to fly helicopters he was ordered to appear before the newly re-elected prime minister, Winston Churchill, who kept him standing for several minutes, like a naughty schoolboy brought before the headmaster, before asking, 'Is your objective the destruction of the whole of the Royal Family?'

He was even denied the right to call his children by his own, albeit only recently acquired, surname. When Philip married Elizabeth, his Uncle Dickie boasted that the Mountbattens were now the reigning family. The remark was brought to the attention of the Government which, with the full backing of Queen Mary, declared that they would remain Windsors, as George V had decreed when he had changed the family's name from Saxe-Coburg-Gotha in 1917 (provoking the Kaiser to joke that henceforth Shakespeare's play would be known as *The Merry Wives of Saxe-Coburg*).

'I feel like a bloody amoeba,' Philip protested impotently.

But if marriage had deprived him of his independence, it had given him what he had always lacked: a home. The newly-weds were allotted Clarence House, which the Red Cross occupied as their London headquarters during the war, now the London residence of the Queen Mother. It was in need of extensive repairs and alterations, including the installation of electricity, to bring it up to royal standard. The Government voted £50,000 for its refurbishment (about £900,000 in 1993, a financial indication of how attitudes towards the Royal Family have changed in the intervening years).

In the upper-class manner of the times, the Princess and her husband took separate bedrooms. She chose red curtains and bed covers. His dressing room was a replica of a ship's cabin. The nursery was on the top floor and was decorated with modern blue and white plastic furniture mixed with a few odd pieces carried over from Elizabeth's own childhood.

The couple also had the use of Windlesham Moor near Bagshot as their country home. Built in 1914 of whitewashed bricks, it stood in thirty-seven landscaped acres. For a man who reputedly only had two shillings and sixpence (12.5p) in the bank when he married the future Queen, Philip had come a long way very quickly.

It was soon clear, however, that he had no intention of settling into the cosy, claustrophobic domesticity of royal life. He insisted on pursuing his naval career. He detested what he called 'loose ends. Either I stay in the Navy and work, or I retire on half-pay and give my full time to the other things I now have to do.' He chose to stay, and was based at the Admiralty when Charles was born. He then attended a staff course at the Royal Naval College in Greenwich and within a year was back in the Mediterranean as second-in-command of the destroyer HMS *Chequers*.

So began the traumatic series of separations from his parents that were to blight Charles's young life. It established a pattern that has carried through into his own adulthood – with all its dire consequences.

It was not, of course, unusual for children of aristocratic families to be placed in the care of nannies. Indeed, at the turn of the twentieth century one child in ten was being brought up by someone other than its own mother or father. But even when judged by the standards of the time, Philip and Elizabeth saw remarkably little of their offspring. The declining health of George VI compelled the Princess to assume more of the royal workload. Her accession to the throne upon her father's death from cancer in 1952 moved her family out of Clarence House into the impersonal vastness of Buckingham Palace and resulted in her seeing even less of Charles and Anne.

'From the moment the King died the Queen didn't have a minute to spare,' observed Godfrey Talbot. 'She immediately had to take over the responsibilities of State. She had been trained since the cradle by her father that duty came before everything, including family. She reluctantly had to abandon her children and they virtually didn't see their parents for months on end.'

It was to the overall care of the new Queen Mother that Charles was now entrusted for several months of each year. She herself had not been the most attentive of mothers but the grand-motherly role – of love without the parental responsibility – suited her and Charles responded with all the enthusiasm of a neglected puppy.

'My grandmother has been the most wonderful example of fun, laughter, infinite security and, above all else, exquisite taste,' Charles would later declare. 'She belongs to that priceless brand of human beings whose greatest gift is to enhance life for others through their own effervescent enthusiasm for life.' She was, said Talbot, a tender shoulder to cry on. 'During the first years of the Queen's reign the Queen Mother was both mother and father,' he observed.

But if the distancing from her son was the consequence of her royal duty, the new Queen was not always as reluctant to be parted from Charles as the old court correspondent suggested. In August 1950, Elizabeth had given birth to Princess Anne. Four months later she joined her husband for a holiday in Malta, leaving her son and baby daughter to spend Christmas at Sand-ringham in the company of the ailing King, his queen, and, of course, the nannies. Elizabeth felt she needed the break: she was run down and, as one courtier recalled with language more forthright than she could ever have brought herself to use, 'in agony from breast-feeding'. She also wanted to see the husband of whom she saw so little. The habit of separation was being established early.

Her long absences at least gave Charles the chance to get to know his only surviving grandfather, if only just: his one recollection of the last British emperor of India is of someone much bigger than himself sitting beside him on a sofa while his third birthday photograph was being taken. More importantly, it allowed the King to spend time with the boy who was born to succeed him. George enjoyed watching his grandson learning to walk with the assistance of Jumbo, a blue elephant on wheels, and playing with his menagerie of stuffed animals. And he delighted in seeing him ride his white tricycle down the corridors of Sandringham shouting, 'Fire, fire!'

'Charles is too sweet, stumping around the room,' the King recorded.

Even the ramrod-backed Queen Mary unbent a little when Charles was with her. He had to bow to her when he was ushered in to Marlborough House where she had resided since the death of George V, and Gan-Gan, as he called her, was still an intimidating presence. But she let her great-grandson play with her collection of jade, a treat she had denied her children and grandchildren.

Philip took a more detached view of his son. He did not attend six of Charles's first eight birthdays. If he happened to be in London he rarely visited his children, even if his wife was away on official business.

Nor was he welcome when he did venture into the nursery. The staff there, led by Nanny Lightbody, disliked his dictatorial manner and what they saw as his bullying methods of childrearing. They 'ganged up on him' and went out of their way to protect their charges, and Charles in particular, from their father.

'Nanny Lightbody saw through him,' one member of the Palace household recalled. She tried to avoid a direct confrontation with her employer but was never in any great hurry to carry out all of his instructions. Philip, for instance, wanted his son playing out of doors, regardless of the weather. Nanny, wary of Charles's 'chesty' condition, would declare to Miss Anderson and Catherine Peebles, the spry Scots woman in her mid-forties who was employed as his governess when he was five years old: 'I'm not going to let him do that. I'm not going to have the responsibility. His father wants him to do it but I'm not allowing it: the Queen wouldn't like it.'

For all the pomp and palaces, it was not an ideal environment for a little boy whose most noticeable characteristic, as everyone remarked, was his 'sensitivity'. He needed encouragement. 'He was very responsive to kindness but if you shouted at him he would draw back into his shell and you would be able to do nothing with him,' Miss Peebles observed. He was always very subdued in the presence of his father whose demands he found so hard to live up to and whose caustic dismissal of his childish qualms only served further to undermine his already delicate sense of self-worth. Those long separations from his mother also had a noticeable effect on him. He found them, Talbot noted, 'very upsetting and bewildering'.

His more robust, independent sister, on the other hand, quickly learned to take them in her stride but, then, everything Anne did was marked by a self-reliance Charles could never match. The sibling rivalry between the Prince and his younger sister was intense and often ended in fisticuffs, with Charles all too often emerging the loser. 'He was never as boisterous or as noisy as Princess Anne,' Mabel Anderson noted. 'She had a much stronger, more extrovert personality. She didn't exactly push him aside but she was certainly a more forceful child.' Miss Anderson was being diplomatic. As Princess Anne herself said, 'We fought like cats and dogs!'

'There were terrible scenes,' said Mrs Parker who used to

entertain the children at her home in Kensington. 'Anne would boss Charles. She would take command of things.' Anything he had she was sure to want and he was constantly being bundled off his tricycle and out of his blue pedal car. When they were older Philip gave them each a pair of boxing gloves. Such was the ferocity of their battles that he soon had to take them away again, with Anne, a much better athlete than her brother, emerging with pugilistic honour.

She was a better sailor than he was (he suffered from seasickness) and quickly proved herself a better rider. 'Not being nearly as brave as my sister, which very often happens, I rather got put off,' Charles meekly explained.

Most of the time the two got on well, but no boy likes to be outshone by a younger sister and Charles was no exception. It was an affront to his youthful dignity that was compounded by his having to compete against her in public, while the attitude of his father only exacerbated the problem. Because he was the heir to the throne, Charles inevitably commanded the greatest attention. Anne accepted that. Her qualities, however, were of a kind that were bound to appeal to her father and he made it patently obvious to everyone, including his susceptible son, that he favoured Anne. 'He always had more fun with Anne,' Eileen Parker observed.

It was Anne who teased the soldiers by walking backwards and forwards in front of them, so forcing them to present arms at every circuit. Charles, more polite and more fearful of Nanny's displeasure, was content just to imitate their march. And it was Anne who was confident enough to break out of the cocoon of their royal position. She was always eager to get out and mix – at Madame Vacani's dancing classes, at the occasional children's party they were allowed to attend. Charles was always more reticent. 'If there were other children there he would cling to Nanny Lightbody,' Mrs Parker recalled.

Nowhere was the difference more keenly observed between the son born to be king and the daughter their father believed would have made a better monarch than in the way they responded to love and attention. Anne objected to being kissed and cuddled and would push people away if they tried to embrace her. Charles was just the opposite. 'He was always asking me if he could kiss my daughter, Julie,' said Mrs Parker. 'Then he would ask, "Can I kiss her mama?"'

The Parkers, mother and daughter, obliged. His own mother was dramatically less forthcoming. She rarely kissed him. Indeed, Charles himself once remarked that he has no recollection of his mother embracing him after he started school. He wept profusely when his mother left for her tours but such shows of emotion were firmly discouraged. Kept at arm's length, he was placed in emotional quarantine. He was destined to remain there.

Chapter Two

Charles did not display an early aptitude for school work. He was what his governess would call a 'plodder'. That did not matter, not then, not very much when he was older, because education, in the narrow academic sense, was never the most important part of his royal training. The objective was not any number of highbrow qualifications. He was there for the single purpose of being moulded, by discipline and example, to fit the role of constitutional monarch that was his by birthright.

'I've learnt the way a monkey learns – by watching his parents,' Charles said.

His father agreed. His children, he said, 'do on-the-job training, and learn the trade, or business, or craft, just from being with us and watching us function, and seeing the whole organization around us'. It was an example that taught Charles how to carry himself in public with the confidence expected of a future king. It was not one that would furnish him with the skills needed for dealing with private predicaments.

The Queen once remarked, 'I have been trained since childhood never to show emotion in public.' It is a royal habit that spills over into their private lives. Like his mother, Charles is adept at communicating with people on a superficial level – at official receptions and factory openings, on impromptu walkabouts and at State dinners. But, like his mother, he is less able to handle himself in personal situations, when the shield of protective formality is no longer in place. Emotions had to be repressed. It was drilled into him that appearances had to be maintained at all costs.

Even the contents of his letters had to be carefully considered: what, it was pointed out to him, if his informal thoughts contained in a missive to a friend or relation were somehow swept into the archives, to be unearthed by some future historian and confused with national affairs? The thought 'oppressed' him. So did its corollary. For no matter how he felt, regardless of his own wishes, whatever his mood, Charles was made to conform. In his own interests. In the interests of the monarchy. By one of the contradictions inherent in his position, it was only in matters educational, the one area where most of his contemporaries were subjected to the strictest discipline, that he was allowed to progress at his own pace, free from undue fear of being punished for any failure or transgression.

By the age of five he could tell the time. He took piano lessons and showed some aptitude for music. He looked to have inherited his father's talent with a paintbrush though it was still too early to be certain. But although he soon learnt to write his name, he had difficulty with his writing and reading and still depended on others to read him the tales of Beatrix Potter and the adventures of Babar the elephant, which were his favourites. And despite being able to count to a hundred, the complexities of arithmetic remained an incomprehensible foreign language to him, as they would for the rest of his life.

Neither his mother nor his father was concerned. 'Look,' Philip told his son, 'I'm only going to bother if you're permanently bottom.' The Queen concurred. Her rule for her son's education was 'No forcing'. Charles, she said, must be allowed to progress at his own pace, no matter how slow.

The woman employed to begin Charles's education was Glasgow-born Catherine Peebles, who had no formal teacher's training but who came on the personal recommendation of the Duchess of Kent, whose younger children, Princess Alexandra and Prince Michael, she had looked after. In a world where who you know is more important than what you know, that was reference enough. She was small, dark-haired and shrewd in her appraisal of her young pupil. Charles, she said, 'liked being amused, rather than amusing himself'.

Somewhat unusually for a time when the cane and the strap were deemed vital adjuncts to the learning process, Mispy (as in Miss P and as Charles soon called her) took note of her employer's instruction and, rather than bully him into learning, preferred to make the subjects as interesting as possible. To develop his understanding of geography, she installed in the Buckingham Palace schoolroom, which overlooked Constitution Hill, a large globe on which Charles could follow his parents' world tours. To fire his interest in history, she prepared a series of studies entitled 'children in history'.

As heir to what was still the largest empire in the world, Charles's place in history was already assured. And history, as one of his schoolmasters would later point out, was the story of his forebears. He was related to Henry VIII and to each of his six wives, was descended twenty-two times over from Mary Queen of Scots and counted King Canute and Vlad the Impaler, the model for Dracula, amongst his more remote ancestors. The Duke of Wellington and Charles Darwin appear in his family tree, as, more exotically, does Musa ibn Naseir, an Arab sheik born in Mecca in 660. Through Alfred the Great he traces his line back to Woden, the chief god of the Norsemen. They were heady bloodlines that came together in one self-effacing boy who, deprived of his parents' company, was now to be denied the companionship of others of his own age.

That was the Queen's decision. Charles, she decided, was too timid to go to school. By royal tradition, other children were brought in to join princes and princesses at their lessons in the Palace schoolroom; the Queen, however, was of the firm opinion that Charles would gain the greatest benefit from being taught alone. Even Anne was not allowed into the classroom.

Charles himself would later argue that his mother had done

the right thing. Miss Peebles was not so certain. She came to regard her pupil as a 'vague child', or, as another courtier summed it up, 'a child who still had only a vague relationship to the external world'.

It was a relationship governed by the protocols of the position into which he had been born. His parents, and Philip in particular, tried to shield him from the privilege that was his by right of birth. They ruled that he was to be addressed as plain Charles by the Palace staff until he was eighteen, after which he would be known as Prince Charles. They also insisted that he be properly disciplined.

Like his grandfather, George VI, whose rages, according to members of the Royal Household, sometimes ended in violence towards his wife, Charles was prone to sudden flares of temper. When that happened he was slapped across the back of his legs or his backside. In extreme cases he was confined to his bedroom for the rest of the day, a punishment he disliked much more than the occasional spanking.

His misdemeanours were always of the most minor sort. He would forget to thank the engine driver of the royal train that took the family to Sandringham. He once stuck out his tongue at the crowd waiting outside Buckingham Palace. Occasionally he would leave off the 'Mr' when he was addressing Sergeant Kelly, the detective who guarded him. He had heard his parents do just that, but in those far-off days when the concept of children being seen and not heard was still popular and the rod was rarely spared, youngsters were expected to do as they were told and not imitate their elders. Charles was duly chastized.

A number of letters were received at the Palace, urging that these beatings should be discontinued. They were politely answered by one of the ladies-in-waiting – and ignored. The Royal Family is nothing if not traditional, always strolling a step behind the fashion, and Charles continued to be spanked, though not frequently. He did not need to be. The most biddable of children, he usually did as he was told. He was eager to please and more than one observer has pointed out the poignancy of the sight of the young Prince forever saying please and thank you, even to his menagerie of mice and hamsters as he urged them to perform their repertoire of simple tricks.

There was, however, no doubting that he was not as other boys. Nor, in final truth, was he ever intended to be. He was born to be a monarch and was raised with that sole objective in mind.

Soldiers saluted when he walked past. He witnessed the humble postures people adopted in the presence of his parents. When he visited Madame Tussaud's waxworks he saw the effigies of his parents. He was becoming aware of the interest in his family and in himself. When he went to church, he heard prayers said for his mother, his family, for himself.

'I wish they prayed for other boys too,' he remarked. (His sister took a more lighthearted view. When the minister at Sandringham gravely invited everyone to pray for the Duke of Cornwall, she called out, to the stifled amusement of the congregation, 'The Duke of Cornflakes'.)

Charles was four years old when his mother was crowned Queen. He attended the Coronation, dressed in a white silk suit and with his hair neatly brilliantined for the occasion by Nanny Lightbody. Because he was so young, the Duke of Cornwall, and head of the peerage as he now was, only attended part of the service, and on the good chance that he was unlikely to mount a rebellion against his mother, was excused taking the oath of allegiance. It proved too much for his young mind and his recollection of the day is confused and indefinite.

The fact that the proceedings focused on his mother did leave its impression, though, as did the tumultuous reception with which the vast crowd gathered in the Mall greeted the Queen and her family when they stepped out on to the Buckingham Palace balcony. It was a foretaste of the attention that would dog him for the rest of his life.

36

When he was a baby, Nanny Lightbody had been able to take him out of Clarence House for uninterrupted walks in his pram through St James's Park. One nanny pushing a pram looked very much like another and no one took any particular notice of them. It was one such outing that provided Charles with his first memory, of looking down the pram's long length at a pair of white hands pushing him along.

As he grew older, those strolls through London's parks had to be discontinued. Photographs of the chubby prince were starting to appear regularly in the newspapers; he was beginning to be recognized and crowds of onlookers now followed him when he ventured outside the Palace gates. The royal-watching industry was in its inception and the Royal Family objected to the intrusion. It was deemed important that Charles should get out and about as much as possible and educational visits – to the zoo, to the museums, to Madame Tussaud's and the Planetarium next door, and, most exciting of all, down into the London Underground – now formed an important part of the curriculum Mispy had arranged for him. To try to ensure that these excursions could be carried out peacefully, the Queen's press secretary, Sir Richard Colville, took the unprecedented step of writing to the Fleet Street editors.

'The Queen trusts,' Colville wrote in his letter dated 11 April 1955, with unconscious irony, that 'His Royal Highness' will be able to enjoy his trips 'in the same way as other children without the embarrassment of constant publicity'. Colville also requested that those charged with looking after the Prince 'should be spared undue publicity, which can so seriously interrupt their normal lives'.

And so they were, up to a point. The press, however, had discovered that the Royal Family, and the royal children in particular, generated circulation. They were a touch of class in a distinctly drab decade. And unlike film stars or that new and developing phenomenon, the pop singer, it was the apparent ordinariness that people chose to see under the crowns and raiments of their regality that was the lodestone of their popularity. There was nothing new in this. Since the high empire of Victoria's later years, the Royal Family had been presented as an idealized personification of everything that was deemed right with Britain. For many millions it represented the family, fidelity, constancy, tradition and glorious heritage. In its children lay the hope for the future.

A price inevitably had to be paid for such uncritical popularity, however, and it was exacted in the coinage of the Royal Family's privacy. When the Queen was a little girl and lived at 145 Piccadilly, Queen Mary had been able to call by and take her for an open carriage ride through the streets of Mayfair. She had been able to walk unmolested through Hyde Park. She had no real need for bodyguards; her royal status was protection enough in that respectful age. Now everyone felt entitled to a sprinkling of the star dust, if only vicariously acquired via the conduit of newspapers and magazines.

It was not a development the Royal Family chose to embrace. Reserved, used to being treated with deference, discreet, they found the demands of the modern media intrusive and vulgar. They sought refuge behind the high walls of their palaces and country houses. That in turn only fuelled the public's interest in their privileged but absurdly over-glamorized lives. The compact between subject and ruler was starting to strain.

Charles's education was a means employed to try to bridge the widening gulf between the security of what had been and the uncertainty of what lay ahead. If the Queen had had her way he would have continued to be educated at home in the traditional royal manner. Her husband had decidedly different ideas. He was insistent that, once the most elementary period of his education under Miss Peebles had been completed, Charles would be sent away to school. 'The Queen and I want Charles to go to school with other boys of his generation and learn to live with other children, and to absorb from childhood the discipline

38

imposed by education with others,' Prince Philip explained on a visit to the United States in 1956.

Given the benefit of hindsight and taking into account the social changes that have taken place in the intervening years, it is difficult to see what other decision the Queen and Philip could have arrived at. At the time, though, it was regarded as a daring break from royal tradition. It did not meet with the approval of the Palace old guard, most of whom had come to dislike Philip's decisions on a point of principle. The Queen, wary of something she had never experienced, continued to harbour reservations and, when anything went wrong, as it quickly did, was the first to argue that the experiment should be terminated.

For Charles it was yet another traumatic disruption. Other boys go to school. Most settle in after a few days. Charles belonged to that sad minority who find themselves on the outside of that sometimes cruellest of groupings, the society of little boys, because he was different. But then different, as Philip pointed out in an unguarded moment, was what Charles and his sibling would always be.

'There's always this idea about treating them exactly like other children,' he said. 'It's all very well to say they're treated the same as everybody else, but it's impossible.'

No matter how hard he tried to mingle, Charles always stood out. He had never had to fend for himself, never learnt how to fight his corner, had never travelled on a bus and been into a shop, and knew nothing of money, except that his mother's head appeared on the coins. He had never had the opportunity to learn how to make friends. He would inevitably be singled out by the teachers, but also, and more disconcertingly, by his con- temporaries who would all be told by their parents to treat the pudgy newcomer like anyone else, thereby ensuring that they did not.

The first stage of the experiment went reasonably well, though. On 28 January 1957, Prince Charles became the first heir to the British throne ever to go to school when, at 9.15 that morning, a black Ford Zephyr driven by one of the royal chauffeurs delivered him to Hill House, the pre-preparatory school in Hans Place, Knightsbridge, run by Colonel Henry Townsend.

He had been led up to it gently. A tutor was employed to give him the male companionship that his father, who had left the Navy when his wife acceded to the throne but was still too busy to devote much time to his family, did not. (Philip spent these important five months of Charles's life in the southern hemisphere aboard the royal yacht *Britannia*). The tutor's name was Michael Farebrother and he was a thirty-six-year-old former Guards officer and headmaster of St Peter's School, Seaford. Christmas was spent at Sandringham and Farebrother played football with Charles, went bicycle and pony riding with him, and accompanied him on expeditions to Brancaster beach.

More importantly, he had to explain to the eight-year-old soon-to-be student what to expect when he found himself no longer in the centre of a world dominated by nannies and governess, but one among 120 boisterous boys.

To prepare him further, it had been arranged for Charles to join his future classmates the previous November on their crocodile walks to the playing fields at the Duke of York barracks on Chelsea's King's Road for afternoons of football.

Inevitably the press had been on hand to record his arrival. Despite the best efforts of the Palace staff to smuggle him in unnoticed, he was quickly recognized because of his velvet collared overcoat, a proto-example of which two years earlier had earned him a place on the *Tailor and Cutter*'s list of the world's best-dressed men. (The magazine, not surprisingly, is no longer published.) When the press's attentions persisted into the New Year when Charles finally joined the school, Colville again contacted the newspaper editors and the reporters were pulled off the assignment, for the time being.

Charles seems to have been reasonably happy at Hill House, a friendly, well-run school for children of the well-to-do and diplomats. Townsend was an Oxford Blue at football, president of the university athletic club, and a top-class skier. His wife was a former theatre sister to Sir John Weir who had assisted at Charles's birth, a recommendation in itself. And if they had been concerned by the responsibility of providing the Prince with his first step up the educational ladder, they were none the less flattered to be chosen and had done their best to make his stay there as pleasant as possible.

The situation was more obtuse on the academic front. The school's motto, borrowed from Plutarch, was 'A boy's mind is not a vessel to be filled, but a fire to be kindled.' It took a lot of blowing to get Charles going. He was, as Townsend noted politely in his first report, 'tremendously observant'. The rest of the report, with the exception of history ('Loves the subject') was very average. As the Queen observed, her son was a 'slow developer'.

It was the same story on the sports field. Those conventional games of boyhood, cricket and football, did not appeal: Charles, by nature and nurture, was not a team player. And while he quite enjoyed running and wrestling and even the rough and tumble of the playground – or so his official biographers insisted – he much preferred the comfort and safety of the palace he was driven home to every afternoon. Now even that lifeline of security was about to be broken. Charles, his father had decided, was to be sent away to boarding school.

When it had first been decided that the heir to the throne was going to break from royal convention and be educated, not at home but at school, a number of Labour politicians had vociferously demanded that he be sent to the nearest primary run by the council. That was never going to happen. The Queen had only reluctantly agreed to allow the boy she considered delicate and timorous to be subjected to the rigours of a private schooling. She had no intention of permitting him to have his mettle tested in the public educational sector. Princess Anne would later send her own children to a local village school but in the 1950s the class barrier was still firmly in position and the Queen's advisers

41

argued, with some logic, that Charles would have less chance of receiving an 'ordinary' education at a state school where the children of 'the postman or the plumber', as one courtier phrased it, would undoubtedly treat him with more obsequious deference than would the offspring of the upper middle class and the aristocracy. It was to boarding school, therefore, that Charles was sent. It was the start of his long, excruciating march in his father's always too large footsteps.

The Queen, anxious to do what was best for her son, invited the headmasters of a number of potentially suitable preparatory schools for the informal luncheons at Buckingham Palace that she instituted in the summer of 1956 as a method of meeting people she otherwise might not have encountered. None of those teachers presented as good a case for their establishments as did Philip for his and without the Queen ever having met its joint headmasters, it was decided that Charles would be sent to the school where his father had begun his English education. It was the British way. As Philip explained: 'When Charles first went to school one of the problems we were confronted with was, "How do you select a prep school?" In the end he went to Cheam, where I had been. But this is something better under-stood in this country than almost anything else – that people very frequently do what their fathers have done. People say, "Oh, he has gone because his father went," and there is no further argument.'

Philip had been sent to Cheam by his uncle, George Milford Haven, who had been sent there himself for no other reason than that his own father, the First Sea Lord forced out of office during the First World War, had once been impressed by the good manners of two Cheam-educated midshipmen. His aca-demic record there was mediocre but he shone on the sports field, winning diving competitions and the hurdles, coming equal first in the high jump. He was goalkeeper in the First XI football team, and played in the cricket team. He had enjoyed himself there.

Charles hated it. The Queen remembered him literally 'shuddering' with terror on the journey there. For nights after she left him he cried himself to sleep – quietly, into his pillow, hopeful that no one would hear him – in his wooden bed which, as his mother had observed before she left him, was too hard to jump on. The memory still hurts; it was, he said many years later, the unhappiest time of his life.

He was only eight years old. 'He felt family separation very deeply,' Mabel Anderson said. 'He dreaded going away to school.' He was used to the coddled security of the matriarchal Palace society of nannies and nursery maids: suddenly he was on his own, one of twelve lowly new boys in a school of one hundred pupils.

The best way of dealing with that trauma, as generations of British schoolboys before him had quickly learnt, was to make oneself as inconspicuous as possible. He tried – 'He was very quiet,' one teacher recalled – but that option was never really open to him. His card was marked even before he arrived for the beginning of the September term in 1957, when the joint headmasters, Peter Beck and Mark Wheeler, wrote to the other parents that 'It is the wish of the Queen and Prince Philip that there shall be no alteration in the way the school is run and that Prince Charles shall be treated as the other boys.' It would be helpful, they continued, if parents would explain that to their sons.

They no doubt did. And in case any of them still failed to recognize the new boy who was receiving such extraordinary attention, and had his own bodyguard hovering in attendance, the fawning attitude of the masters soon had him pointed out; while his fellow pupils were allowed to call him Charles, it had been decided that they had to call him Prince Charles. His situation was exacerbated the following July when his mother grandly announced on television that she was making her son Prince of Wales and a Knight of the Garter.

By then Charles had managed to settle into the routine of

school life. It had not been easy. He had been bullied; some of the senior boys carved his name in the back of a pew in the local church in the hope that Charles would get the blame. The anecdotes that survive from that unhappy period present a picture of a sad but open-hearted little boy. He was always dutiful: one night a master found him up late past his bedtime, finishing his odd jobs. Warned that Matron would be angry, he replied, 'I can't help that, I must do my duties.'

Above all else, he was lonely. He eventually made the acquaintance of a couple of his classmates and the headmaster's daughter, Mary Beck. His dearest companion, though, was probably the teddy bear he had brought to school with him. For though he was the centre of attention, he was denied the friendship of what he called 'the nicest boys' who did not wish to appear to be sucking up, a problem that would beset him throughout his schooldays and beyond, until he was old enough to retreat behind the protective wall of his position and only mix with those he chose to, not those with whom chance – at school, university, or in the Navy – had thrown him in contact.

He had to be forced to make any friends at all; the mathematics master, David Muir, who had been delegated to keep a watchful eye on the Prince, recalled seeing him standing apart from the general throng of boys, bewildered and frightened. Muir had to take him in hand and introduce him to some of the others. Shyness, Charles later observed, drawing from his own pitiable experience at that time, 'is often a disability ... It isn't only those who are confined to a wheelchair who are disabled.'

His misery had been compounded by the spate of stories about him that appeared in the newspapers which created an atmosphere of suspicion at the school. Everything from the length of his hair, worn, it was noted, on the overlong side, to his ability on the football field – excellent, was the rose-tinted consensus – was duly recorded in the prints. Some of the items were gross exaggerations. Others were accurate enough to suggest that either pupils, masters or visiting tradesmen had succumbed to the temptation of Fleet Street's financial blandishments. When Cecil Cox, the Harrods barber employed to keep the boys' hair in trim, was quoted as saying that he had seen one of the seniors hold Charles's head under a cold tap, Philip exploded, 'Even the school barber is in the pay of the newspapers!'

Once again Sir Richard Colville went into action. At the end of Charles's first term he called the newspaper editors into Buckingham Palace and told them, courteously but authoritatively, that if this intrusion did not cease, Charles would be removed from school and educated privately, and that they, the newspapers, would be left to bear the responsibility for so disrupting the education of the future king.

After that things quietened down and Charles was able to get on with what for him was the always difficult matter of trying to fit in with his schoolmates, without having his every hiccup recorded in the newspapers delivered to the school each morning. There was no escaping the burden of his position, however. On 26 July 1958, as the end of his first full school year approached, the Queen broadcast a message at the Commonwealth Games in Cardiff. She would have delivered the speech herself but for a bout of sinus trouble and it was her pre-recorded voice that Charles and some of the other boys were invited into the headmaster's study to hear.

The Queen's voice declared: 'The British Empire and Commonwealth Games in the capital, together with all the other activities of the Festival of Wales, have made this a memorable year for the Principality. I have therefore decided to mark it further by an act which will, I hope, give as much pleasure to all Welshmen as it does to me. I intend to create my son, Charles, Prince of Wales today. When he is grown up I will present him to you at Caernarvon.'

With that title came a host of others. In the year Harry Webb renamed himself Cliff Richard, Charles became his Royal Highness Prince Charles Philip Arthur George, Prince of Wales and Earl of Chester, Duke of Cornwall, Duke of Rothesay, Earl of

45

Carrick, Lord of the Isles and Baron Renfrew, Prince and Great Steward of Scotland, Knight Companion of the Most Noble Order of the Garter. He was nine years and eight months old.

The Queen came to regard that pronouncement, dropped on to an unsuspecting child, as one of the 'few mistakes' she made in Charles's upbringing. Peter Beck remembered the outward look of trepidation on his face. Charles recalled the inner turmoil. 'I remember being acutely embarrassed when it was announced,' he said. 'I heard a marvellous great cheer coming from the stadium in Cardiff, and I think for a little boy of nine it was rather bewildering. All the others turned and looked at me in amazement.'

The normal, ordinary childhood his parents had once professed to place such great store in had been laid to inevitable rest, its requiem the sound of the thirty thousand Welsh voices gathered in the stadium singing out across a nation's airwaves 'God Bless the Prince of Wales'. It was, Charles recollected, the moment when the 'great sense of embarrassment' he felt at being who he was crystallized into a sense of foreboding at what he presciently labelled his 'awful fate'.

The grandiosity of his destiny did not spare him the mundanity of the immediate. He still had to polish his own shoes and make his own bed and wait on the older boys. Nor did it spare him the teasings of his contemporaries. He was a trifle overweight for his age, a fact his contemporaries were quick to point out. 'Oh, get *off* me, Fatty,' shouted the unfortunate boy who found himself pinned down by the Prince of Wales in a rugby scrum. Upset by such remarks, Charles started exercising in the school gymnasium, working out on the rings and the parallel bars. It was the start of a lifelong obsession with his weight which eventually turned into vanity touched by faddism.

But if effort and exercise would slim him down and keep him fit into middle age, no amount of practice or training was ever going to make a true athlete out of him. He was eventually made captain of the First XI football team but that was a nod more towards his title than his talent. The team lost every match that season. The goal tally was four for, and eighty-two against. Even the *Cheam School Chronicle*, which went out of its way to see the better side of the performance of any pupil, never mind that of its future sovereign, felt moved to report, 'Prince Charles seldom drove himself as hard as his ability and position demanded.'

Fortunately for the boy's always fragile sense of self-worth there were some more tangible achievements to show for his four years at Cheam. His piano playing improved and he sang in the choir. He was encouraged to develop his interest in painting and drawing and exhibit the results in the school art exhibitions. He took up carpentry and earned a commendation for a piece entitled, 'Gallows and Stocks'.

He also discovered a talent for acting. As an infant he had been fond of dressing up, rifling the clothes box in the Buckingham Palace nursery and putting on, as one courtier remembered, 'high-heeled shoes and hats'. He also inherited his mother's fondness for charades. This nascent ability found its creative outlet at Cheam, once with amusing results.

Early in 1960 he understudied the boy cast as the future Richard III in a school abridgement of Shakespeare's play entitled *The Last Baron*. When the leading actor suddenly left the school, Charles stepped forward on the night to deliver, very much in the style of Laurence Olivier, such apposite lines as, 'Soon may I ascend the Throne'.

The play was staged on the evening of 19 February 1960. While Charles was on stage the headmaster entered to announce that the Queen had given birth to Prince Andrew.

Charles, we learn, was delighted by the arrival of a baby brother. 'This was a great event in the life of the Prince of Wales, still very much a home-loving boy with a highly developed sense of family,' recorded Dermot Morrah, Arundel Herald Extraordinary. Charles worried that Andrew would have no one to play with and told one member of the Household that the Queen would have to have yet another child. When he was back from school he was constantly popping into the nursery to hold and hug his brother. He went one better than the Queen did and helped the nannies bathe him. Indeed, school permitting, he probably saw as much if not more of Andrew than their mother did. And he certainly saw more of Andrew than he ever saw of his mother.

The Queen, always a stickler for good form, would not visit Cheam more often than other parents, which was about three times a term. Most of the other parents, though, managed to see somewhat more of their offspring in the holidays than the Queen ever did. The distance between Charles and his parents, ingrained in habit from birth onwards, was now the accepted formality.

Charles was invariably polite and solicitous when he was with his mother and father. He obediently wrote to them, enquiring as to their health, passing on trivial items of school news, obediently saying how much he missed them. There were no memorable displays of genuine, impulsive affection. When mother met son they did not kiss, they shook hands.

That had its predictable consequences and it was to Nanny Lightbody and Mispy and Mabel that Charles turned for affection. It was reciprocated. They, and not the distant woman who was the Queen before she was a mother, or his absentee father, were his real family. They were the ones who missed him when he went away to school almost as much as he missed them. Mispy, as Princess Anne recalled, 'virtually lost interest' when Charles was gone. The nursery, not the State rooms or his parents' quarters, was his real home.

He would always run up to Nanny Lightbody, Mispy and Mabel before he went to pay his respects to his parents. Charles himself once said that sometimes a whole day and night would pass before he went to see his mother or she asked to see him.

It was the nursery that had provided Charles with the only real love he would know. Even that sanctuary was not sacro-

48

sanct. Shortly after Charles went away to Cheam, Nanny Light-body's disagreements with Prince Philip came to a head aboard *Britannia*. When Charles came home at the end of term the surrogate mother he had loved so much had been summarily 'retired'.

Chapter Three

Prince Charles loathed Gordonstoun. He found it hard to adapt to its Spartan environment, to make friends, to rise to its hearty, outdoor demands. He was bullied. He was crushingly lonely for most of his time there. The wonder is that he survived with his sanity intact. It is no wonder that he was even more miserable at Gordonstoun than he had been at Cheam and spent his time dreaming of escape.

Gordonstoun, for its part, found it almost as difficult to adjust to him. Unlike the traditional British public school which relied on disciplined team games and its attendant spirit to bring the best out of its students, Kurt Hahn's foundation demanded greater individual responsibility. Every boy, he believed, should be trusted to discipline himself, with 'dishonour' and a deep sense of guilt, rather than a master's chastisement, providing the harshest punishment.

What that meant in practice was freedom which sometimes bordered on licence and Gordonstoun, for all its high-flown principles, had become something of an upper-class reformatory for boys who found the usual constraints of school life difficult to abide by. At the same time, its hardy reputation, which its association with Prince Philip had done so much to embellish, attracted those boys who relished its rugged challenge (or, in many cases, boys whose parents thought their sons would). There was more of the spirit of an adventure camp than an academic institution about the place. Now those liberties were drastically curtailed.

For Charles's protection, cobwebbed rules started to be enforced and new ones introduced, much to the chagrin of the four hundred boys already at the school. The local town of Elgin and even the village of Duffus, which guards the western entrance to Gordonstoun, were placed out of bounds. Smoking, in a school where corporal punishment had always been disavowed, became a caning offence. Drinking, while never previously condoned, now carried the threat of expulsion with it. Just as Britain was about to embark on the social revolution of the sixties, Gordonstoun was making a determined effort to stop the clock.

These changes were enacted by the headmaster, Robert Chew, who had a glass eye that wandered off in disconcerting directions, spoke with sub-Churchillian inflexions, had been at the school since its inception, and took a loyal subject's pride in the honour of having the heir to the throne under his educational wing. The changes had nothing to do with Charles but Charles was blamed and he was made to pay a cruel price.

Gordonstoun had strict anti-bullying rules. A certain amount of tormenting was written into the tradition of many schools in the guise of 'initiation rites', but it had no part in the educational creed expounded by Hahn, the Jew driven from Germany by the Nazis.

Even fagging, where the younger boys act as servants to the older ones, was prohibited on the grounds that it was a system open to abuse. Instead everyone had to take part in some form of service for the community as a whole. In the individual houses that meant sweeping the corridors or mopping out the shower room or, in Charles's case, emptying the dustbins. For the school as a whole it entailed participation in fire-fighting, mountain rescue, surf life saving or the coastguard service favoured by Charles. The point of these exercises was to instill a sense of community responsibility: 'to teach,' said Hahn, 'the protection of the weak, the recognition of the rights of the less fortunate, and the worth of a simple human life.'

Those fine principles provided only partial protection for the royal new boy who arrived to be 'incarcerated', as he put it, in 1962. Good intentions have a way of going askew in practice and radical educational theories, however worthy and well thought out, depend for their ultimate success on the response of those being experimented on. A goodly number of the boys who came under Hahn's influence gained from the experience, Charles among them; in 1987 he would call for compulsory community service to replace military National Service, which was abolished in Britain in 1960, and such Hahn-inspired notions figure increasingly in his private search for a solution to what he perceives as society's ills. While he was at Gordonstoun, however, he was more concerned with surviving the system than benefiting from it.

The muscular tradition of the school had wrought some brutal customs and enforcing them were some tough boys who, had their parents not been rich enough to pay fees which were a third higher than those charged by Eton, would probably have ended their educational careers in prison rather than at a public school.

One coterie of ruffians resident at Hopeman Lodge hanged the cat belonging to their housemaster, Major 'Hebbie' Downton, in retaliation for his attempt to curb their unruly behaviour. At another house the seniors made a practice of greeting new boys by taking a pair of pliers to their arms and twisting until the flesh tore open. In all the houses boys were regularly trussed up in one of the wicker laundry baskets and left under the cold shower, sometimes for hours.

Charles was spared those extremes of persecution. There were too many watchful eyes looking over him, including his detective, Donald Green, and his housemaster, Bob Whitby, who made it absolutely clear to the other boys under his authority that anyone caught bullying the heir to the throne would be expelled. The school had already taken a precaution of limiting the intake of pupils in Charles's year to allow the masters more time to concentrate on their royal charge.

Whitby added his own security measure by making Windmill Lodge off limits to boys from other houses. As in any school, the boys tended to draw their friends from their own houses. There had never been any restriction on inter-house social visits, however, until Whitby chose to turn Windmill into what one contemporary from nearby Bruce House called 'Colditz – except there no one was allowed in.' It was all part of the headmaster's and housemaster's effort to shield the Prince from the harsher aspects of life at Gordonstoun.

The Gordonstoun of Charles's time was not as tough as some legend suggests. The Gulf Stream makes its climate warmer than its position on the map indicates; in a marshy dip behind the sea cliffs edging the Moray Firth, it is protected from the colder torrents of wind which sometimes sweep down from the Arctic. The summers can be hot with long, warm evenings in that northerly latitude stretching towards midnight. The cold showers in the 1960s were never more than a quick run-through and were always preceded by much longer hot ones. The early-morning run was no more than a forty- or fifty-yard jog up the road and then only if it was not raining, which it was more often than not. But it was still tough enough.

Gordonstoun was divided into seven houses. Charles's, Windmill Lodge, was a low stone and timber building, little more than a glorified Portakabin with only the most basic accommodation. The boys slept in hard wooden beds in dormitories of fourteen. The windows were kept open throughout the night, which meant that those closest to them were likely to wake up with blankets rain-soaked or, in winter, covered with a light sprinkling of snow. There was no privacy during the day, nowhere comfortable to sit. Only the senior A level students had their own studies. Everyone else crammed into common rooms which had no carpet or curtains.

Toughest of all for the young Prince to bear was the attitude of the other boys. He was immediately picked upon, 'maliciously, cruelly, and without respite', as one fellow newcomer recalled.

53

Some of the problems he encountered were no more and no worse than those faced by any other new boy. There was, for instance, the ritual of the Evening Uniform.

The hierarchical structure at Gordonstoun is based on the Training Plan, that list of daily community chores and physical exercises everyone was duty bound to complete (but always under some supervision; even the idealistic Hahn had come to recognize that human nature is not infallible and that there is sometimes a need for the guiding hand of authority). It progressed from the Junior Training Plan, through the Senior Training Plan, White Stripe or junior prefect, Colour Bearer Candidate, up to Colour Bearer, the Gordonstonian equivalent of prefect and eventually, to Guardian or head boy, who in theory if not in practice, was supposed to share equal power with the headmaster.

At the bottom of the pile was the New Boy who had no training plan, was told what to do, checked to make sure he had done it, and singled out by the clothes he had to wear. In the evening everyone changed into light grey sweaters and shorts except for the New Boys who had to stay in the dark blue daytime wear. It was with pride and relief that, at the end of his first term barring misdemeanours, the New Boy was awarded his first Training Plan and the evening uniform that went with it.

He was never able to wear it on the first night, however, for as soon as he had changed into grey he was grabbed by boys from the year above 'who were always the worst', and dunked in a cold bath. As soon as he had changed into his one set of back-up clothes he was dunked again and so was forced to spend the rest of the evening in his day clothes. The indignity of arriving at dinner wearing the despised blue was more painful than any bruises sustained in the battle to keep out of the water.

It was his attachment to uniforms and the status they confer that made the incident of the cherry brandy so wounding to Charles. As his great-great-great grandmother, Queen Victoria, observed, 'Dress is a trifling matter but it gives also the outward

54

sign from which people in general can and often do judge upon the inward state of mind and feeling of a person.'

Towards the end of his first year Charles joined the school *Pinta* on an expedition through the Western Isles. They stopped at Stornoway on the Isle of Lewis, and Charles and four other boys were deposited at the Crown Hotel while Donald Green went to buy tickets for an afternoon performance of a Jayne Mansfield film. But the *Pinta* had been recognized and a crowd quickly gathered to peer in through the window at its royal crew member.

Charles, deeply embarrassed by the people staring in at him and pointing, beat a retreat. 'I thought, "I can't bear this any more" and went off somewhere else,' he recalled. 'The only other place was the bar. Having never been into a bar before, the first thing I thought of doing was having a drink, of course. And being terrified, not knowing what to do, I said the first drink that came into my head, which happened to be cherry brandy, because I'd drunk it before when it was cold out shooting.'

Drink was one of the great attractions of these annual Outward Bound-style expeditions when the boys were let out of school and off the leash. Those who went on the *Pinta* would try and slip away at every port of call for a surreptitious pint in a pub if they looked old enough to pass the landlord's cursory inspection, while the younger boys would plead with their older companions to buy them a drink at an off-licence (vodka was greatly favoured, in the mistaken belief that it left no tell-tale smell on the breath). Those who went on the orienteering expeditions made sure that their route passed several amenable watering holes and the hills were alive with the sight of masters attempting to round up their drunken flock.

Charles had not got past his first sip before, as he said, 'the whole world exploded around my ears'. It was to his immense misfortune that the incident was witnessed by twenty-two-year-old Frances Thornton, a freelance journalist to whom the Prince afterwards referred as 'that dreadful woman'. The story made the front page of most British newspapers. It cost Green his job. Buckingham Palace, in a harbinger of worse *faux pas* to come, chose officially to deny the incident only to have to confirm it the following day.

Charles was devastated by the reaction and mortified by the punishment meted out to him. Under the new stricter rules which his own arrival had caused to be augmented, this minor misdemeanour was considered an offence so heinous that it had to be dealt with by the headmaster himself. As this was Charles's first serious misdeed, expulsion was not considered (not that it ever would have been, given who he was, no matter how many cherry brandies might have been consumed), and Chew, in his scholarly wisdom, decided against beating the heir to the throne, which was the usual punishment for boys guilty of such a misdemeanour. Instead Charles was reduced to the rank of New Boy.

Such demotions were fairly common occurrences. Most boys took them in their stride. Charles did not. He had been brought up to have a profound sense of his own status and all the symbols that went with it, and he acutely resented the indignity of losing his training plan. He had been pushed right back to where he had started.

It was, so the Queen and her courtiers sagely told each other, a salutary lesson in the public responsibilities and restraints his royal position entailed. Charles did not see it that way. 'I wanted to pack my bags and go to Siberia,' he recalled. It was an affront to his dignity. He felt, he said, that he had been very harshly treated. As Morrah, the Arundel Herald Extraordinary, noted all of five years later, 'When he speaks of it, his eyes have a look of pain, even of repressed anger.'

But if incidents like that could be dismissed as one of those injustices all public schoolboys feel themselves subjected to at some time or other, there were other, more painful, situations Charles had to face which carried the mark of genuine discrimination. And for all their efforts, there was only so much his 'minders' could do to shield him.

There was no one for him to shelter behind, for example, when he played sport. As a youngster he had acquired the sporting skills befitting a prince. He had learnt to ride soon after he could walk and at the age of ten had taken his pony to a meet of the West Norfolk Foxhounds. He shot his first grouse when he was ten, his first stag at thirteen. He had learnt to fish and derived a spiritual pleasure from casting his line into the lochs and rivers around Balmoral. 'I can pray when I'm fishing but I can't fish in church,' he said.

The physical requirements of team games, however, proved beyond him. He had been bad at soccer. He was worse at rugby which was the code of football played at Gordonstoun. Lacking mobility, turn of speed or any noticeable ball sense, he was placed in the second row – 'The worst place in the scrum,' as he observed. He never made one of the school teams. Instead he was confined to playing in the house matches and he found those hard enough.

'It was a point of honour to make physical contact with the Prince of Wales – and the more violently the better,' one of his antagonists recalled. The playing fields of Gordonstoun left Charles battered and bruised and looking like a remnant of Napoleon's Old Guard after their defeat at Waterloo by the graduates of the playing fields of Eton where the Queen Mother had been so anxious for her grandson to go. He quickly came to dread games and rather than getting stuck in would move as far away from the action as possible, a despondent figure with his hands clasped behind his back in a pose more suited to the garden at Buckingham Palace than a rugby pitch.

His contemporaries' off-field attitude towards him wounded him in a different, more painful way. Gordonstoun was a school that made a cult out of egalitarianism. The use of titles was prohibited. People were judged on what they were rather than who they were and that was the way that Hahn and millions of others in the Britain of the 1960s believed it should be. The 14th Earl of Home, the old Etonian Sir Alec Douglas-Home, was being replaced in Number 10 Downing Street by the grammar-school-educated Harold Wilson. The aristocracy and its attendants were being shouldered aside to make room for the meritocracy of Liverpudlian rock stars, East End actors, and the entrepreneurial talents of the 'self-made man'.

Even 'Charley's aunt', as Princess Margaret once called herself, had entered into the Bohemian spirit of this new age, adopting its fashions and mores and partying in Chelsea with its leading lights like the Beatles. It was the era of irreverent informality and John Lennon addressed her as Priceless Margarine.

In that remote north-eastern corner of Scotland where Charles was sequestered the current of change flowed more sluggishly. Charles was still very much the privileged Prince. Not in name – everyone was instructed to call him 'Charles' – but at a school where everyone, foreign princes included, were addressed by their surnames, that was title enough. While others had to see out a whole term without an exeat – in the days before mass air travel Morayshire was too far away for most parents to journey to for a weekend – Charles was regularly allowed home to Balmoral. Or so his contemporaries chose to tell themselves. To many boys of his own age, a number of whom had been held back a year to accommodate his privileged progress, Charles was a convenient scapegoat for the restrictions to which they were subjected. And to a teenager in the sixties, those restraints were infuriating and frustrating in the extreme.

Within a few years his sister, Anne, would be dancing on the stage of a West End theatre with the naked cast of the musical *Hair*. But hair, which people everywhere else were growing, had to be worn short at Gordonstoun and on the last day of term Chew would sometimes go to the extraordinary length of rounding up boys whose locks he deemed to be too long and personally driving them fully twenty miles to the local barber in Elgin to be shorn.

Chew's attitude towards sex was equally inflexible. So it was at most British public schools, which were still a decade away from introducing co-education. At Gordonstoun, however, this determinedly asexual stance was underpinned by Hahn's own pronouncements on the subject which had the ring of a moral crusade. Juvenal's belief that a healthy mind requires a healthy body had been one of Hahn's inspirations, as had the teaching of Plato. It was the example of Lord Baden-Powell, though, that had encouraged Hahn to develop his system of 'simple physical training, expedition training and rescue service training' as the correctives to what he saw as an increasingly 'sick civilization'.

Like the Chief Scout, who on discovering that performing his conjugal duties gave him a headache had moved his bed out of the marital bedroom on to the balcony outside, the founder of Gordonstoun had a distaste bordering on fear of anything sexual. One of Baden-Powell's aims was to save his acolytes from the perils of the 'solitary vice' (and any other kind) by a programme of vigorous outdoor activity. Hahn, who never married and was regarded by many of the masters he recruited as a latent homosexual, likewise aspired 'to kindle on the threshold of puberty non-poisonous passions which act as guardians during the dangerous years'.

With Chew's assistance he largely succeeded. There was little homosexuality at Gordonstoun – despite later rumours to the contrary, no one made any advances on the Prince of Wales. But there was very little heterosexuality either and the school gave the Prince no experience of dealing with women. Quite the contrary: to keep the royal virtue intact the usual sources of female companionship had been carefully closed off.

There was almost no fraternization with any of the neighbouring girls' schools. Upon Charles's arrival the number of parental visits allowed in a year had been severely reduced, so limiting the opportunities for meeting younger sisters. The maids who worked in the kitchens were imported from the Gallic-speaking Outer Hebrides and were kept strictly segregated from the boys. The only recourse was to climb on to a bicycle, break school bounds and cycle those twenty miles to Pete's Café beside the park in Elgin. There the more adventurous boys, absurdly conspicuous in their short trousers and black duffel coats, could have a cup of coffee, smoke an illicit cigarette and meet the girls from the local academy. Over the years a number of passionate romances were spawned under these unpromising conditions. None involved Charles.

As the incident of the cherry brandy had shown, however, even a prince could sometimes venture off the narrow path of youthful righteousness. It was not his last brush with authority.

During the election campaign of 1964 which swept the patriarchal Tories from office and replaced them with the Labour government of Harold Wilson, the school conducted its own mock election. Charles, lacking the second sight to foresee that one day the party would challenge the political homogeny of the United Kingdom, enthusiastically supported the Scottish Nationalists. At the urging of others, and with the aid of crampons, he climbed a tree to hoist a Nationalist flag, an excess of factionalist enthusiasm which earned him a 'punishment drill'.

For minor peccadillos Gordonstoun punished its miscreants by sending them on 'silent walks' for a quarter, half or three-quarters of an hour during which they were expected to reflect on their wrongdoing. The penalty for more severe breaches of discipline was 'punishment drill', a supervised run of up to two hours round and round the south lawn of Gordonstoun House. It was tiring, though not always as tiring as it was intended to be. For there were bushes at the far end of the lawn and in the short evenings of spring and autumn it was soon dark enough for the boys to take it in turns to peel off and hide behind them for a circuit or two, out of sight of the bored supervising master. Charles was made to do a number of punishment drills. He took advantage of the shrubbery on several of those occasions.

But if he was not the complete goody-goody, his sporadic scrimmages with authority were not of the kind to mark him out as one of the 'shades', as the boys who went to Pete's Café were known. He never visited the place. He never expressed an interest in doing so and the 'shades' did not invite him to join them on their unauthorized expeditions. But, then, Charles was rarely invited by the other boys to join in any of their informal activities, illicit or otherwise.

'Publicity', the Palace had appealed, 'singles out his Royal Highness as different in the eyes of all other boys of the school.' But so did the actions of those who so vocally declared that he was to be treated without favour.

Towards the end of Charles's time at Gordonstoun three of his sixth form classmates, including the son of the school bursar, arrived in London at the beginning of one holiday. They telephoned Buckingham Palace and asked (more, it must be said, in jest than out of any deep sense of friendship) if they could call by. The matter was reported back to the school and they were gated when they returned the following term. In the end, actions like that only succeeded in drawing unwelcome attention to Charles and the sad result was that the Prince, too locked into his position, too timid to break out of his isolation, was ostracized for much of his time at Gordonstoun.

He was a member of what one of his school contemporaries called 'the last generation of old-fashioned children who were brought up without psychiatrists'. There was nowhere for him to hide his loneliness and every day he had it confirmed in the most public and painful way. It was a quarter of a mile's walk from Windmill Lodge to Gordonstoun House where everyone ate their meals. Charles would have liked to have joined the groups of boys strolling down in the morning and back up again in the evening. But if he was invited once he was rarely invited to do so again. For as soon as anyone started to talk to Charles he was accused of 'sucking up'. A crowd would quickly gather behind them to boo and hiss. Boys from other houses would join in and Charles and his companion could find themselves being followed by up to thirty boys, all making a loud slurping noise.

This peer pressure was too much for most boys to tolerate and they would soon drop away to rejoin their own friends, leaving Charles feeling more alone than he had done when he started out. Even those who in other circumstances might have been expected to befriend the Prince were wary of associating with him. His own cousin, Earl Mountbatten of Burma's grandson Norton Knatchbull who was in the same house but the year above, preferred the company of friends in his own year.

The Marquess of Huntley's dashing nephew, Geordie Gordon, whose forebear had built Gordonstoun House, was in the same class as Charles and resident in nearby Altyre. He valiantly accompanied the Prince, forlornly wrapped in a duffel coat that always seemed two sizes too large for him, on several occasions. But the abuse eventually got to him, too.

It was bullying of the cruellest kind and after a while it became self-generating. A boy taking pity on Charles would take the risk of engaging him in conversation. Charles, by now convinced that anyone who spoke to him was only setting him up for another bout of harassment, would refuse to answer. The boy would take offence at what he was quick to interpret as a princely snub, and would rejoin the baiting crowd. And so it went on, without respite, year after year. On the eve of his departure for Australia at the age of seventeen, Charles was still having to run that gauntlet.

Looking back at his time at Gordonstoun he recalled: 'I had this schoolboy dream that I was going to escape and hide in the forest, in a place where no one could find me, so I wouldn't have to go back to school. I hated the institution, just as I hated leaving home. When you lead a perfectly agreeable existence you don't want to go back to cold showers at seven in the morning and a quick run before breakfast.' And you certainly do not want to go back to face yet another lonely walk pursued by a pack of boys making clamorous slurping noises.

Dr Hahn himself had nursed considerable doubts as to whether his school was really suitable for Charles, and the Queen Mother soon had reason to be particularly concerned with the effect the place was having on him. 'He is a very gentle boy with a very

Family group at Balmoral, 1951. 'Charles is so *sweet*,' said King George VI. (*AP*)

Charles celebrating his second birthday with Nanny Lightbody when it was still possible for a Royal to cross St James's Park unmolested. (*AP*)

Charles, not yet four, takes a princely lead ahead of his mother and sister.
(*Topham*)

Housemaster Bob Whitby (on Prince Philip's right) and headmaster Robert Chew greet Charles on his first day at Gordonstoun. He had reason to be apprehensive. (*PA/Topham*)

The 'informal prince' rehearsing a student revue at Trinity College, Cambridge, 1969. (*Hulton Deutsch*)

Mountbatten and his honorary grandson at Brands Hatch, 1968.
(*Hulton Deutsch*)

kind heart which I think is the essence of everything,' she said. At Gordonstoun it could be a positive disadvantage, and if she had been allowed her way, Charles would not have gone there.

The Bowes Lyons are an Etonian family and the Queen Mother is an honorary Old Etonian. The College has a centuries-long tradition of dealing with the offspring of the great, unlike Gordonstoun which was then barely three decades old and was better equipped, as one housemaster of the time put it, to look after the 'laird's idiot son' than the sovereign's heir. Eton also happened to be just a short stroll across the bridge over the river Thames from Windsor Castle. That was a disadvantage as far as Prince Philip and the Queen were concerned. Eton is an integral part of the town and the boys go about their business through its streets, past the snapping cameras of the gawping day trippers who were already starting to arrive by the coachload to view this bastion of educational privilege. The presence of the Prince of Wales, it was felt, would only accelerate what the College and the Royal Family alike had some reason to regard as a discomforting trend in mass tourism.

But if not Eton then where? An informal 'think tank' was set up. It included the Queen Mother, the Dean of Windsor, and Earl Mountbatten. They consulted Charles, who expressed a preference for Charterhouse where some of the friends he had finally made at Cheam were going.

Prince Philip brought these discussions, which he regarded as a waste of time, to an end by ruling that what was good enough for him was good enough for his son and that Gordonstoun it was going to be. The Queen was only twenty-five years old when her father had died and was initially overwhelmed by the responsibility of the position he bequeathed her. As she struggled to come to terms with the burden of office, Philip had taken charge of mapping out their children's educational futures. In the cases of Anne, Andrew and, surprisingly, Edward, he got it more or less right. His first-born, on the other hand, had ample cause to lament his father's choice of school. As Dermot Morrah noted, 'In effect the decision meant an attempt to mould him in his father's image to which . . . he did not naturally approximate.'

Charles himself said that what he had heard about the place 'sounded pretty gruesome'. But Philip, who had a dislike bordering on contempt for the British Establishment and many of its élitist institutions, was not for the turning. He felt that Gordonstoun's fresher and ostensibly more rounded approach to education was more suited to the latter part of the twentieth century than that offered by any of the longer established schools. He was also very aware of his son's shyness and tendency towards self-effacement, and was of the opinion that his *alma mater*, with its emphasis on self-reliance, would make Charles more 'self-assertive'.

There was also the security advantage. If he went to Eton 'every time you hiccup you'll have the whole of the national press on your shoulders. If you go to the north of Scotland you'll be out of sight,' he explained. Any pursuing newspaper reporter was 'going to have to think twice before taking an aeroplane to get up there'.

As the cherry brandy incident proved, the press was quite capable of getting its stories, regardless of distance. And those verbal keel-haulings with their accompanying sucking sound that Charles had to endure on his walks to and from Windmill Lodge, were more likely to undermine his self-confidence than build it up.

The choice of housemaster had not helped matters. Bob Whitby was intimidating and self-opinionated. He took a gleeful delight in shouting at the cowering new boys assigned to his house and took Philip's directive to treat Charles like everyone else literally when it came to barking instructions of his own. If he sometimes warmed to his charges as they grew older, inviting them into his own quarters for coffee and discussions (history was his subject, coffee the schoolboy nectar signalling approaching manhood), there were still a lot of boys who never overcame the sense of dread at his presence which he had so fiercely instilled in them.

Never less than pedantic in his enforcement of rules, Whitby was especially severe with Charles, pulling him up for every minor violation. And by insisting that the Prince dress according to the letter of the regulations, he ultimately ended up making him look ridiculous in the eyes of his contemporaries. The school insisted that its 'boys', no matter how old or well developed, always had to wear short trousers and long socks. The local youths were not slow to make mockery at the sight of fully grown young men, some as old as nineteen, displaying their knees. Most Gordonstoun boys took that in their stride and, in the way of small communities, made a style out of embarrassing necessity. The ideal look was African bush ranger not District Commissioner and it was achieved by shrinking the socks until they only came up to mid-calf, and at the same time not replacing the shorts which started off so baggy and got shorter and tighter as they were grown into, then out of.

Charles was not allowed such sartorial idiosyncrasies. Others somehow got away with old clothes and the minor display of individuality they represented; Charles always looked like a new boy, for ever doomed to wear new clothes that always looked too big for him. It was then that he learnt how to wear the kilt which was allowed as an alternative to shorts in the evening; better a kilt than those ludicrous baggy shorts that Whitby made him affect.

The sight of Charles, hunched, frightened, out of place, was enough to make even Whitby's gruffness waver on occasion, however. One weekend Charles had been to visit the Queen Mother at Birkhall, her white Queen Anne mansion on the Balmoral estate. He was late back and missed Sunday chapel. It was the kind of misdemeanour that was capable of drawing out the worst of Whitby's temper but on this occasion he chose to overlook the incident. That may not have been unconnected, of course, with the Queen Mother having telephoned personally to offer her apologies for bringing him back late ('You know what grannies are like,' she said) but, even so, Charles had cause to be grateful for that moment of unexpected leniency on Whitby's part. Gating was the usual punishment for lateness of this kind, which no amount of parental pleading could overturn. Had the housemaster chosen to apply it in this case Charles would not have been able to visit Balmoral again that term.

That would have been a grievous loss to the Prince, who had come to regard Birkhall as what he called 'a unique haven of cosiness and character' and much preferred its homely comforts to the grander setting of the castle itself. He had learnt to fish in the whisky-brown water of the river Muick which flows at the bottom of the house's sloping garden. He had come to regard it as a sanctuary from the stresses of a school at which he was never going to be happy. 'I am happier at home than anywhere else,' he once remarked and Birkhall, where the tea table always groaned with freshly baked scones and cakes, the garden was heavy with fruit and blooms and organically grown vegetables, and log fires kept everyone snug in winter, was the perfect repose. It provided him with what he desperately needed: as he put it, 'fun, laughter, warmth, infinite security'.

The Queen Mother was delighted to have her grandson to join her there for weekends when she came north for the fishing. What she would not do, however, was intervene on his behalf, as he pleaded with her to do, and try to persuade his father to take him away from Gordonstoun. He was there and there he was going to stay. 'At least he hasn't run away yet,' Prince Philip replied when asked how his son was getting on there. That kind of escape was never an option for the schoolboy Prince. He was trapped; he had no choice except to get on with it and make of the situation what he could.

It is to his credit that he did just that. If the harassment he was forced to endure reinforced his sense of detachment, it also pushed him to develop those interests he could pursue at his own pace, in his own time, and by himself.

His interest in music strengthened. Shortly after he arrived a rumour swept the school that Philip had bought him a guitar, that instrument of adolescent rebellion. He had not. Charles's interest in pop music was minimal. It was more the classical that appealed to him, and after a brief wrestle with the bagpipes ('You're not going to play that thing around *my* house,' Whitby declared) he took up the trumpet before moving on to the cello.

'There was a wonderful German lady who had been there for years; she was there when my father was there. She kept turning round in the middle of the orchestra and saying, "Ach, ze trumpet, I cannot stand ze trumpet." So I decided to give it up.' Under the tutelage of Frau Lachman, who had come over from Germany with Hahn, he learnt to play the cello with passable proficiency.

Art, too, provided him with a means of expressing himself. His childhood interest in painting had been encouraged by his father who had 'shown me how to do it with oils' when he was only seven. Now, under the guidance of Bob Waddell, Gordonstoun's art master, he took up pottery. Waddell, more aesthetic and much better dressed than the usual run of tweed-clad hearties who made up the Gordonstoun teaching staff, took a conscientious interest in Charles's progress, continually checking to make sure that he had grasped the finer points of technique, correcting any minor mistakes. A frequent visitor to the salerooms of London, he would invite the Prince to view his purchases in his bachelor flat in the Round Square, a circular stable block built at the beginning of the eighteenth century by an owner who did not wish to be cornered by the devil and which now accommodated many of the school's classrooms, one of its houses, and a few apartments. Master and pupil became friendly and Waddell was able to provide some of the sensitive appreciation that Charles needed.

The Combined Cadet Force and the expeditions were other, if very different, outlets for Charles's frustrations. He joined the naval unit. When the weather was fine the boys were occasionally taken to sea in an old Royal Navy minesweeper and allowed to fire rifles at floating barrels. On rainy days Charles and his fellow cadets would climb into his detective's Land-Rover and drive to the nearby Fleet Air Arm base at Lossiemouth, supposedly for extra training but in fact to watch *Tom and Jerry* cartoons.

On a more taxing front, the Outward Bound-style excursions had given Charles the chance to test his physical mettle against the hard Scottish elements and, equally importantly, against the standards he was required to set himself. He had done well, better than many, including his father who was inclined to treat Princess Anne as the boy in the family, had expected. On one dangerous twenty-five-mile canoeing trip along the Morayshire coast from Findhorn to Hopeman he had been caught in a storm which threatened to drown him. When he made shore he was exhausted but exhilarated. It gave him a point of contact with Philip, who said that after he had undergone a similar ordeal on a Gordonstoun expedition: 'I was wet, cold, miserable, probably sick, and often scared stiff, but I wouldn't have missed the experience for anything.'

Charles gradually made friends. Not many and not among the boys in his own house. His closest confidant, Philip Bagnall, who hailed from East Africa, was in Round Square and that, because of Whitby's restrictions on visitors, kept contact between them to a minimum. But it was enough to cut the worst of his loneliness.

Most importantly, there was his acting. He was not the best actor in the school. That distinction belonged to David Gwillim who went on to play Henry V in the BBC's lavish series of all Shakespeare's plays which cast Laurence Olivier as King Lear. Both Gwillim and Charles were encouraged by Eric Anderson, then the house tutor at Bruce House, later the headmaster of Eton. He first recognized Gwillim's talents when he saw him miming in imitation of Rolling Stone Mick Jagger in an end-of-term house revue and promptly cast him as Pistol in the play that would later earn him such prominence on television.

Charles answered the audition call posted on the notice board and was impressive enough to be cast as the Duke of Exeter in Anderson's outdoor production in the middle of the Round Square of *Henry V*. It was not inverted snobbery, as is sometimes stated, that kept him out of a more important role. In Anderson's considered opinion, Charles was only 'the gifted amateur' compared to 'the very professional' Gwillim. He none the less played his part, Anderson said, 'as to the manner born', and the following year, with Gwillim gone and on his way to a career in acting, Charles was rewarded with the title role of *Macbeth* in the winter term before he left for Australia.

It was staged indoors at the Service Centre and Charles played the part of the tragic Scottish king led astray by a conniving woman with genuine distinction. It was as if he had an intuitive understanding of the weaknesses of a man manipulated by a scheming wife.

Something else caught the attention of the audience, which on one night included the Queen, and that was the confidence that radiated from the stage. This was Charles's finest moment at Gordonstoun. The awkward, shy, self-effacing young man had been left behind in the dressing room. In its place was a character, assured and poised and confident in its destiny.

It was as though only by playing someone else was Charles able to play himself.

Chapter Four

Charles had not wanted to go to Australia. It was yet another unwelcome disruption in his already disrupted youth. The idea of being uprooted and sent as far away as it was possible to be from home and family, simply did not appeal to this shy, conservative and essentially unadventurous young man. He disliked change, even if it was one he had only recently been dreaming about. After all those early miseries, he was at last settling in at Gordonstoun and the prospect of starting all over again revived his now well-embedded sense of insecurity.

What he heard of the country on the other side of the world was not encouraging. He sought the advice of the few Gordonstoun boys who had been there. They told him that the xenophobic outback mentality still reigned and foreigners, particularly from Britain, were treated with suspicion. They warned him to beware of the 'Pommie bashing' which rivalled Australian Rules as the national sport.

Yet by extraordinary good fortune and against all his expectations, Australia proved to be the happiest interlude of his young life. 'I took out a boy and I came home with a man,' said Prince Philip's equerry, Sir David Checketts, who was assigned to look after Charles.

In later years Charles would come to rail against the country and ceased to enjoy his visits there. 'All they talk about there is Aborigine rights,' he complained after one trip in the late eighties. His change of attitude might have been the consequence not of Aborigine rights but another touchy subject, which by then was starting to occupy Australian political conversation: republicanism and the threat of redundancy it carries for Charles. In 1966, however, the Antipodes were still staunchly loyal, the National Anthem was still sung with pride, and Charles was welcomed with open-hearted enthusiasm. He responded in kind. His time there, he said, was 'the most wonderful experience I've ever had'. He found the Australians he met open and unaffected. 'In Australia you are judged on how people see you and feel about you,' he said. 'There are no assumptions.'

That was not strictly true. Between the end of the Second World War and Charles's arrival, 1,334,407 Britons had emigrated to Australia. Many found the adjustment to life on the southern continent extremely difficult, not least because of the aggressive attitude that many native-born Australians adopted towards them. Independent, cocky, and used to speaking their minds in the most colourful of metaphors, they resented the haughty air of superiority assumed by these new arrivals from an increasingly distant mother country.

Charles was no ten-pound assisted passage 'migrant', however. He arrived at the personal invitation of the former prime minister and grand old man of Australian politics, Sir Robert Menzies. The Queen had agreed that Charles should have first-hand experience of the Commonwealth nations he would, one day, hopefully, reign over. It was Menzies, together with Philip, who had seen something of the country during the war, who persuaded her to choose Australia for this latest chapter in the royal experiment of Charles's education. Menzies, a member of Churchill's wartime Cabinet who had once been talked of as a future British premier, was a committed Anglophile who thrilled to the idea of entertaining the heir to the Crown he had so assiduously served. He was also a wily enough politician to turn the Queen's request for information to his own political advantage when, on a visit to Balmoral, she asked him to recommend a suitable school for Charles.

He suggested Geelong Church of England Grammar School in Victoria. That provoked an immediate chorus of protest in the Australian capital, Canberra. In a repeat of the Labour outcry that had greeted the announcement that Charles was going to be educated privately in Britain, Menzies' parliamentary opposition demanded to know why the Prince was going to a fee-paying school and not a state one. Menzies was at his most urbane when he replied that 'I should feel very sorry for the young Prince if he were at school in the middle of a crowded city in Australia.'

Far better, surely, to send him to Timbertops, Geelong's satellite school at the 'back of Bourke' in the mountains of the Great Dividing Range 200 miles outside Melbourne, where there would be no chance of 'people gazing at him, with people trying to get pictures of him'. Menzies would tolerate no accusation of bias in his choice because 'I was quite detached, personally, because I went to another school.'

Not everyone was convinced by that argument. Geelong was in Menzies' home state of Victoria and that, given the interstate rivalry rife in Australia, was certain to provoke the enmity of New South Wales where the grammar schools are older and naturally consider themselves to be on a socially more elevated plane. Menzies, it was widely believed, had pulled off a political flanker, with Charles cast in the role of innocent pawn.

Yet, for all his deviousness, Menzies had probably made the wisest choice. Charles certainly thought so. He 'absolutely adored' Timbertops. He arrived in Australia at the end of January 1966. He was pensive and not a little apprehensive and his first ten days, he recalled, were tense. He had to face the press who had been invited up to Timbertops to meet him on his first day. Even more embarrassingly, he had to get to know the other hundred-odd boys whose turn it was to leave the comfort of Geelong grammar itself for a term or two of 'character-building' in the outback and who had the disconcerting but typically Australian habit of asking any question that came into their heads, no matter how pointed.

But if Charles was taken aback by the apparent impertinence of their enquiries, Timbertops was not the place where even a prince could stand on ceremony. Dr Darling, a former headmaster of Geelong, had been much taken by the teachings of Hahn and had founded Timbertops as a place where those under his direction could learn the self-reliance of the early pioneers who, at great cost in lives, had opened up the Australian continent. This was Gordonstoun played for real and the boys were left to fend for themselves. If the wood was not chopped there was no fire and therefore no hot water. The routine was rugged and demanding but also liberating and Charles responded to the challenge.

'Almost everyone, masters and boys, enjoy themselves here,' he wrote in an article for the *Gordonstoun Record*. 'One never seems to stop running here and there for one minute of the day from 7.30 a.m. breakfast – and no morning run, though there's worse to follow – until the lights go out at 9.15 p.m., having had tea at the unearthly hour of 5.30 p.m. If you have done a cross-country run at 4.45 p.m. and arrived back at 5.05 p.m. it's difficult to persuade your stomach to accept food.'

During his first week, he recorded in a letter home, 'I was made to go out and chop logs on a hillside in boiling hot weather. I could hardly see my hands for blisters.' His daily chores included 'chopping and splitting wood, feeding the pigs, cleaning out fly-traps (which were revolting glass bowls seething with flies and very ancient meat), or picking up bits of paper around the School'.

He was taken to a sheep station where he attempted to help with the shearing. 'I made rather a mess of it,' he admitted, 'and left a somewhat shredded sheep.'

There were the weekend-long expeditions to be planned and undertaken through the endless, bottle-green bush 'where you can't see anything but gum-tree upon gum-tree', and a sharp eye always had to be kept for poisonous snakes, deadly spiders and all the other hazards of the outback. 'You virtually have to inspect every inch of the ground you hope to put your tent on in case there are any ants or other ghastly creatures. There is one species of an ant called Bull Ants which are three-quarters of an inch long and they bite like mad!'

On a more cerebral level the school took him and thirty other boys to the jungles of Papua New Guinea where they toured some missionary stations and met people whose pagan grand-parents had reputedly been headhunters and, so they were told, cannibals. Charles was touched by their generosity but also saddened by what he saw as a disappearing heritage, a theme which would come to concern him more and more in later years.

'I was given one or two presents by young people and when I asked if they had made them, they said their mothers or aunts had. No doubt, however, in the years to come, when there are new generations of Papuans, they will consider these ancient skills of no use,' he wrote, adding, with unconscious irony, 'But I expect there will be those who make souvenirs for tourists; or, if not, I hope a suitable amount of relics will be preserved for history.'

On that historical front, the trip provided the affirmation, if he needed one, of the still potent authority of the recently vanished British Empire and the totem power of its ruling family. When, on a trip up country, he arrived at a village 'the drums stopped and the whole village was assembled there and for some unknown reason they suddenly started to sing "God Save the Queen", and it was the most moving, touching thing I have ever experienced, I think, to see these people, miles from Britain, singing the National Anthem. And the tears practically rolled down my cheeks.'

There was spiritual inspiration, too. Charles had been con-firmed by the Archbishop of Canterbury, Dr Michael Ramsey, in the private chapel of Windsor Castle just before the Easter of the previous year. The ceremony had been notable for the lax attitude of Prince Philip who, it was noted, spent the entire service reading a book, much to the chagrin of the Archbishop who was heard to intone afterwards, 'Bloody rude, that's what I call it.'

Philip was not without faith. 'Without the chance of receiving the message of religious thought, the most well-meaning, energetic and intelligent human is really no more than a bumble-bee trapped in a bottle,' he once remarked. There had been times, though, when he had moved close to agnosticism, and ritualized religion of the kind exemplified by the Archbishop of Canterbury had little hold on a prince who had so nonchalantly changed denomination from Orthodox to Anglicanism to marry the future Queen.

Charles was more like his mother, who is a firm and convinced Christian. He took religion much more seriously than his father did and in the flush of faith following his confirmation, developed what observers called 'a genuine religious feeling' which involved taking holy communion several times a week.

As the future Supreme Governor of the Church, he will one day be required to pull together the competing and sometimes incompatible strands of High and Low that run through it, without showing favour to either. His private leaning, however, was away from the 'bells and smells' of the High, and towards the more austere form of worship postulated by the Protestant wing of his mother's Church. That was due in great part to the influence of the Reverend W. P. Young, holder of the Military Cross and the Distinguished Conduct Medal, who was Gordonstoun's Presbyterian minister. The school also had an Anglican clergyman. The Reverend Philip Crosfield was nicknamed 'Holy Joe' by the boys and might well have stepped out of the pages of Jane Austen. Young was cut from a different cloth. He had survived the trenches of the First World War and the creed he preached was stark and fallible and all the more human because of it. He would address the boys in their houses two or three times a term. One night his lesson was on the subject of forgiveness. He told how, while he was serving on the Western Front during the

First World War, the Germans had attacked his regiment with mustard gas. He said he had struggled to live up to Christ's teachings and how he had failed. In a soft and humble voice he confessed, 'I still cannot forgive them.'

The humility, the simplicity of Young's lessons made a profound impression on Charles. He encountered their primal echo in the rainforests of New Guinea where, for the first time, he encountered religion at work at grass root and hut level. It was, he recorded, 'fresh and sincere' compared to the formalized pomp of his own experience. He attended a service in the township of Dogura. 'Everyone was so eager to take part in the services, and the singing was almost deafening,' he wrote. 'One felt that it might almost be the original Church. Where Christianity is new, it must be much easier to enter into the whole spirit of it wholeheartedly, and it is rather wonderful that you can still go somewhere where this strikes you.'

The Very Reverend Robert Woods, who, as Dean of Windsor, was the Royal Family's personal religious adviser and as such had a unique insight into the welfare of their souls, regarded those months spent Down Under as the most formative in Charles's 'spiritual development'. It certainly set the tone – of forever looking to the simple, the primitive, whether with a poor sheep farmer on a croft in Scotland's Western Isles, or with Laurens van der Post in the stillness of Southern Africa's Kalahari desert – in what has become Charles's lifetime search for spiritual enlightenment. And while now not overtly religious, he still takes holy communion regularly with the vicar of Tetbury in the privacy of his ground-floor study at Highgrove.

There is more to kingship than metaphysical contemplation, as his father emphasized. 'If you are really going to have a monarchy ... the family has got to be in the public eye,' Philip observed. In Papua that involved attending the kind of ceremony that would soon form a regular part of his official life. On his last night there Charles was treated to an exhibition of dancing by feather-bedecked men and their scantily dressed women.

Entering into the spirit of the occasion, he ended the evening by performing a Highland reel.

Charles would find that aspect of his role the hardest to fulfil. Intensely private, always self-conscious, he did not like being put on show. 'I assure you it makes the heart sink, to have to make an awful exhibition of ourselves,' he said. To cover up the embarrassment he always felt, he had very early on developed that series of 'displacement activities', as sociologist Desmond Morris named them, which became so beloved by impressionists. He had acquired the habit as a very young boy, Eileen Parker recalled, of twisting his mouth up at the corner when he spoke. To that he added the mannerisms of constantly touching his cuff and, most famously, of walking with his hands behind his back (the fault, he joked, lay with his tailor who cut the sleeves of his suit so tight 'I can't get my hands in front').

By the time he arrived in the southern hemisphere, however, the little boy who had hung on to his nanny's legs in terror had learnt how to hide the more obvious signs of his discomfort. Australia confirmed the process and Checketts, who had moved into a farm 120 miles from Timbertops with his wife and family but was available to smooth out any problems, helped it along. Checketts had made Charles go and talk to the cheering reception when they landed at Port Moresby in New Guinea. He did the same again when towards the end of his antipodean sojourn, Charles paid a visit to Cairns, above the Tropic of Capricorn in Queensland. On his way back to Melbourne his aeroplane touched down at a small airport on the Gold Coast on Queensland's border with New South Wales. Charles shook hands with the local dignitaries and exchanged the usual pleasantries. After a short while he ran out of conversation. 'I can't stand here doing this all day,' he said.

'Then go and talk to the holidaymakers,' Checketts suggested, pointing at the crowds clustered behind the makeshift barricades. This was exactly the kind of situation Charles had always dreaded but on Checketts' prompting he walked across and started

77

shaking hands and asking the most basic of questions: 'Where are you from?' 'Are you here on holiday?' 'Are these your children?' In years to come the queries would be refined to the elementary 'Have you come far?'

The substance of the enquiry was always beside the point, though. It was the asking that mattered and the crowd at the airfield responded, as crowds all over the world have responded ever since, to the Prince's seeming interest in their affairs. Charles, in turn, drew comfort from the welcoming, obsequious smiles on the faces of the people to whom he spoke. He had discovered the power inherent in his position.

'Australia got me over my shyness,' he said.

Timbertops encouraged that welcome development. At Gordonstoun Charles was just another boy who, no matter what the school hierarchy might have wished, was not regarded by his peers as a natural leader.

The situation in Australia was different. There his status was assured, for instead of having to vie for position against boys of his own age, which was something he had never been very good at, he was placed in charge of a group much younger than himself. Boys were sent there from Geelong when they were fourteen or, at the latest, fifteen years old. Charles was seventeen when he arrived and was immediately placed in charge of a unit of fourteen juniors who, if they had any objections to being placed under the command of a 'Pommie' prince, were too young to do anything about it other than shout the occasional insult. By sending him into the bush, those whose responsibility it was to try to create a prince fit for the modern age ensured that he swam rather than sank in the sea of competition he would have encountered had he attended Geelong Grammar itself.

Many boys of seventeen would have chafed at being sent to live in a hut, dozens of miles of virgin bush away from the nearest girl. Others would have missed the companionship of their friends. Charles did neither. A slow developer, he had yet to show any interest in the opposite sex, while the absence of any

78

contemporaries other than Stuart Macgregor, the former head boy of Geelong who was studying for his university entrance, was a relief to a prince who got on far better with people younger or older than himself than he did with those of his own age. When he was asked if he wanted to extend his stay which had originally been planned for one term only, he readily agreed; he was in no hurry to return to Gordonstoun.

Gordonstoun, for the sake of its own reputation, was in no rush to have him back. Charles was due to sit his A level examinations that summer and there was no guarantee that he was going to pass. That was not going to affect the job prospects of a prince whose future was preordained but despite that (or more likely because of it) the Queen's advisers were most anxious to spare their sovereign's heir the ridicule of failure.

The choice of Gordonstoun had already raised doubts as to his academic prowess. Other public schools only accepted boys who had passed the Common Entrance exam. Gordonstoun, in keeping with Hahn's belief that there was more to a boy than an exam result, selected its future pupils on the results of its own, conspicuously less demanding written and oral exam. And while the boys did attend classes in between their sailing and climbing expeditions, no one ever accused the school of being a university production line.

That happened to suit Prince Philip who harboured a barely disguised contempt for higher education and cheerfully described himself as 'an uncultured polo-playing clot. I'm one of those stupid bums who never went to university – and I don't think it's done me any harm.' His advice to his eldest son reflected that anti-intellectual bias. 'Just stay in the middle, that's all I ask,' he said.

The trouble was that Charles was much closer to the bottom than he was to the middle. He had passed O levels in 1964 in English language and English literature, French, Latin, and history. He had failed physics and, inevitably, maths. He resat maths the following term and failed again – much to the embarrassment of the headmaster, Robert Chew, who had stepped in and person-ally tutored him for the exam. It was not an impressive academic track record and there was little sign of improvement when he moved up to the sixth form and started studying French and history for A level.

History proved a particular disappointment. It had always been his strongest subject, yet at the end of the first year he came second bottom in a class of fifteen in the mock A levels. The English history he was studying covered the period from the reign of Elizabeth I through to Charles I. 'Come on, Charles, you really have to do better than this,' Gordonstoun's history master, Robin Birley, admonished him during one lesson. 'This is, after all, the history of your family we're studying!'

Charles looked suitably sheepish. His work did not get better, however, and that term's break in Australia, where he was left to set his own schedule, free from supervision or guidance, all but ensured that history and most probably French as well would have been added to the list of his scholastic failures.

The solution was neatly to hand; while other boys took two years to prepare for their A level examinations, Charles would take three. It would afford him the extra study time he needed, while at the same time allowing him to enjoy another few months of independence in the outback before the restrictions inherent in his position closed in on him again. There was also the added advantage that by keeping Charles away from Gordonstoun until the others who had started there at the same time had left, the way would be cleared to the high offices that might otherwise have been denied him.

For the reputations of all concerned there was productive pur-pose therefore to that extra term spent in Australia. And when he did return the following autumn, Whitby duly appointed him House Helper (head of house). 'I knew people would accuse me of favouritism but too bad,' the housemaster said.

In Australia, Charles noted, 'Having a title and being a member of the upper classes, as often as not militates against you.' That was not the case in Britain, not even at Gordonstoun, despite its long tradition of egalitarianism. That it was vital that Charles should rise to the highest positions of authority had been clear right from the start of his education. The royal family depended for its position upon appearances and for Charles to be seen as a creditable heir to the throne, he had to show himself able to assume the mantle of authority.

In many ways Charles was worthy of the responsibility placed in him. He was honest, honourable, and hard-working. And if his judgement was sometimes a little flawed (he once tried to intervene on the behalf of two boys who were being expelled for holding up a local store with a rifle) he only erred on the side of compassion. But if he really was the right choice for the position of head of house there was one person who harboured the gravest of doubts: Charles himself.

Whitby insisted: 'I chose him because he was the outstanding candidate,' but even he was forced to concede, 'I don't think he ever believed that.'

That nagging sense that he was being promoted beyond his ability was underlined when, the following term, Robert Chew moved him up from House Helper of Windmill Lodge and made him Guardian. The terrified new boy who had been mocked and humiliated and followed by chanting crowds making disgusting noises at him had risen to be head of the whole school. The radical experiment in a prince's education had come to its conclusion with the subject sitting high on the top of the pile.

But what in truth had really been achieved? Gordonstoun may have been a 'prison of privilege' as Charles astutely observed, but he also believed that it had 'developed my will-power and self-control, helped me to discipline myself, not in the sense of making you bath in cold water, but in the Latin sense – giving shape and form and tidiness to your life'. And that, he insisted, 'is the most important thing an education can do'.

But at what cost? Royal children learn how to act 'royal' by imitating their parents, as both Charles and his father pointed out. 'What is much more difficult,' Philip said, 'is bringing them up as people.' That proved hardest of all in the case of Charles, who could never be allowed to forget that he was destined to be a king, with all of a king's responsibilities and constraints.

That he was better equipped to deal with ordinary people than any other prince in recent generations was generally acknowledged. Along the way, however, he had had to acquire a hard veneer of self-absorption to protect the vulnerability that had been such a mark of his young character but was now lost from sight.

If he still harboured lingering doubts about his true worth, the way he was always given the top jobs – from captain of the football eleven at Cheam through to the Guardianship of Gordonstoun – and the way his mediocre exam results would be enough to secure him a place at Cambridge provided the irrefutable evidence that the ordinary rules of life and its achievements did not apply to him. It had taught him to recognize the power of his position, to appreciate how, by extending a hand and asking the most banal of questions, he could command the affection of a crowd – and how, by simply turning his back and walking away, he could cut off anything that offended him as his detachment of equerries and bodyguards closed up behind him.

He had learnt how to keep his emotions in check, how always to present a brave face. But the little boy who had hung on to his nanny's legs still lurked under the surface. It was Mabel Anderson he had run to when he came home from Cheam. It was Miss Peebles he first telephoned when he returned home from Australia. The parental affection most children take for granted and which he needed more than most had been denied him, leaving a still resonating hollow in his life.

As with others brought up by servants, he found it easier to show affection to nannies and governesses than to his own family. And that, as events would prove, would have the direst consequences for the monarchy he had been born to inherit and for which all his training was supposed to prepare him.

Chapter Five

O n 1 July 1969, in fulfilment of his mother's promise which had caused him such embarrassment at Cheam eleven years before, Charles was invested as the twenty-first Prince of Wales at Caernarvon Castle. He was an undergraduate at Cambridge but first and foremost he was a prince and he was there to do his duty – for the pleasure of many, to the advantage of a few, and at some risk to himself.

The ceremony cost £200,000 of taxpayers' money. It was attended by 4000 'snobs and nonentities, flunkeys and lick-spittles', as the Welsh Nationalist MP Emrys Hughes unkindly described the important guests to the House of Commons. It was watched by an estimated worldwide television audience of 500 million.

The town around the castle had been decorated in a fetching mixture of yellow, blue and red paint provided free by a local firm. A giant Perspex canopy, weighing one ton and bearing the motif of the Prince of Wales's three feathers, kept the drizzle off the Queen who was wearing a yellow Norman Hartnell outfit cut a fashionable couple of inches above the knee, as she placed on her son's head a crown of 18-carat gold set with diamonds and emeralds made for him by the Goldsmiths' Company, girded him with a sword, placed a gold ring on his finger, and delivered a gold rod into his hand.

Charles solemnly swore the oath of loyalty he had been too young to take at the Coronation. 'I, Charles, Prince of Wales, do become your liege man of life and limb and of earthly worship, and faith and truth I will bear unto you to live and die against all manner of folk.' The moment for rebellion was past.

Then, weighted down with the regalia of his princely appointment, and praying that 'I don't get covered too much in egg and tomato', he addressed the crowd in Welsh.

It was, he told them, with 'a certain sense of pride and emotion that I have received these symbols of office, here in this magnificent fortress, where no one could fail to be stirred by its atmosphere of time-worn grandeur . . .'

To the fanatics who infiltrated the crowds that day the grimness of the ancient fortress stirred other emotions. They had come to Caernarvon, not to enjoy the colourful ritual designed by the Earl of Snowdon, and certainly not to praise the Prince who bore the name of their country. They had come to give literal interpretation to that part in the oath of allegiance which referred to dying. They had come to murder Charles.

Fifteen bombs had exploded at Welsh government buildings in the run-up to the Investiture. A parcel bomb had gone off at a post office in Cardiff the day before the ceremony. On the night before, two men had been killed attempting to plant a bomb on the railway line leading into the town.

As Charles was being driven into Caernarvon from the railway station in a horse-drawn carriage, another explosion was heard. Charles was sitting beside the Welsh Secretary George Thomas, the future Speaker of the House who became Viscount Tonypandy in 1983. 'What was that?' the Prince asked.

'Oh, a royal salute,' came the insouciantly spoken answer.

'Peculiar sort of royal salute,' Charles said.

'Peculiar sort of people up here,' Thomas replied. They were certainly not Thomas's sort. 'I am sure I speak for all Wales,' he declared, 'when I say the sooner these people are caught, the happier I shall feel. They represent no part of the Wales I know.' But Thomas, for all his decent words, knew as well as anyone just how real was the threat to the Prince's life.

Running in tandem with the historical process that brought Charles to Caernarvon that wet afternoon was a blood-stained sense of Welsh grievance. In 1282 Edward I had conquered the country and executed its prince, Llewellyn-ap-Gruffydd and built Caernarvon Castle with what Emrys Hughes insisted on calling 'Welsh slave labour'. He abolished Welsh nationhood. Then, after hanging, drawing and quartering Llewellyn's brother, David, he declared his son, Edward, the new Prince of Wales.

The Welsh, like the Irish, have long memories and for the next seven centuries succeeding English monarchs felt it prudent to invest their sons with the title so ruthlessly purloined in the safety of Westminster. It was not until the political expediencies of the twentieth century inspired George Lloyd George, MP for Caernarvon and future Prime Minister, to invent the Investiture in the interests of 'Anglo-Welsh unity' (not to mention his own political advancement), that a prince was made Prince of Wales in the principality itself. That dubious honour fell to David, the future Edward VIII and Duke of Windsor who, in 1911, was kitted out in a 'preposterous rig' which he feared would make him a laughing stock among his contemporaries. With all the 'tradition' Lloyd George had been able to invent, he was duly invested in what was in effect a 'mini-coronation'.

Keir Hardie, the first Labour member of Parliament, condemned the spectacle, fiercely declaring: 'The Investiture ceremony ought to make every Welshman who is patriotic blush with shame.' They didn't. Britain was in the full flush of imperial pride and Lloyd George's flamboyant gesture caught the mood of a country bursting with a sense of its importance and power.

The situation fifty-eight years later was very different. The Empire had gone, blown away by the wind of post-colonial change. Britain was in the throes of a severe depression and runaway inflation which, within five years, would see a nation that, less than half a century before, had been the richest on earth, suffer the indignity of having to call in the International Monetary Fund to help bail it out of its economic mess. Nationalism of the kind that had succeeded in severing Eire from the United Kingdom had crossed the sea and was gaining considerable support in Scotland and more particularly in Wales where the Free Welsh Army claimed links with the Provisional IRA. The pomp and ceremony were still on parade outside Buckingham Palace and at the State opening of Parliament but Britain no longer rested easy with itself. And underlining that discontent was a subtle shift in attitude towards the Royal Family which had so exemplified the nation's glory but, because of its outmoded grandeur and its adherence to what to many seemed an increasingly irrelevant tradition, was in peril of becoming, at best, a quaint anachronism, at worst the institution that symbolized that national decline.

Charles did not fully comprehend the significance of what was happening. Wearing a disguise, he once watched a student demonstration at Cambridge. He said afterwards: 'I wanted to see what they were like. I do try and understand what they are getting at, but I can't help feeling that a lot of it is purely for the sake of change, and for the sake of doing something to change things, which, from my point of view, is pointless.'

It was a foolish viewpoint for a prince to adopt, especially one who professed such an interest in history, long tracts of which are littered with the remains of dynasts who failed to adapt to shifting events. In 1969, however, it was still possible to pretend that, as Mrs Alexander proclaimed in her Victorian hymn to class order, 'All Things Bright and Beautiful', the rich man really was still in his castle, the poor man uncomplainingly at his gate. There was still a healthy residue of respect for the Royal Family. Many, indeed a majority of Britons still continued to look up to the Queen and her brood to provide an example of moral fortitude. The image was still intact. So settled was the Royal Family in its position that, as one contemporary commentator observed, the whole royal show was in 'danger of becoming a great, big, thundering bore'.

Only on the eccentric edges of the Celtic fringe was the monarchy genuinely disliked. That fringe, however, happened to include large parts of Wales and wise heads from all political parties had warned against subjecting Charles to the kind of abuse the Investiture was certain to generate. But it offered too convenient a diversion for the Labour government and its beleaguered prime minister, Harold Wilson, to pass up, despite the dangers entailed. Just as Lloyd George had made political capital out of the last Investiture, and Robert Menzies had turned Charles's time at Geelong to his own advantage, so Wilson wrung all the kudos he could out of the quasi-medieval pantomime.

Charles was less convinced than his mother's ministers of the value of it all. Using words which in a few years hence would be applied to the Royal Family itself he said: 'Spending £200,000 or £250,000 or whatever it is on an apparently useless ceremony ... does not get you positively anywhere, unless you think, "Oh, well, we shall get some return in tourism, or investment from interested Americans." My view of the situation is that if you are going to have a ceremony like this you should spend enough money to make it dignified, colourful and worthy of Britain. But you should not spend too much.'

The right-wing historian A. J. P. Taylor put it more forcefully. Echoing the sentiments of the left-wing Hardie, he called the Investiture 'a sordid plot to exploit Prince Charles'. But, then, Charles was there for the exploiting. The Investiture was part of his 'duty', which in a constitutional monarchy means following the advice of the ministers who ostensibly are there to serve the Crown. And that 'duty' had to be fulfilled, regardless of his own feelings on the subject.

Charles had never exercised any control over his own destiny and he was in no position to do so now. His life had been mapped out and was still under the control of others. Against his will and with disregard for his emotional needs, he had been wrenched from home and sent away to boarding school at the age of eight. He had been 'incarcerated' in Gordonstoun. While he was still there, the next stage of the programme had been decided upon.

On 22 December 1965, just before Charles flew to Australia, the Queen and Philip gave a dinner party at Buckingham Palace. The guests included the Prime Minister, Harold Wilson, the Archbishop of Canterbury, Earl Mountbatten of Burma, who was representing the armed forces, the Dean of Windsor, Sir Charles Wilson, chairman of the Committee of University Vice Chancellors, and the Queen's private secretary, Sir Michael Adeane. Noticeable by his absence was Charles, whose future it was they had gathered to discuss.

The deliberations carried on late into the night. The following morning Charles was informed of the committee's decision. It could not have been safer or more traditional. As Mountbatten explained it: 'Trinity College, like grandfather. Dartmouth like his father and grandfather, and then to sea in the Royal Navy, ending up with a command of his own.' And that was exactly the course Charles's life took.

'You cannot understand what it's like to have your whole life mapped out for you a year in advance,' Charles would later complain. 'It's so awful to be programmed. I know what I'll be doing next week, next month, even next year. At times I get so fed up with the whole idea.'

But never fed up enough to do anything about it. After Gordonstoun, he went up to Cambridge, just as Mountbatten had said he would. And when he was ordered to take a sabbatical from Cambridge and move to the University College of Wales in Aberystwyth for the summer term of 1969 to learn Welsh in preparation for the Investiture, he meekly went.

He had not settled in to Cambridge straight away. He was accompanied there by the now perennial accusation of favouritism, having gained a C in French and only a B in his much-vaunted history (and that only by learning everything 'by heart', rather than by any flair in his exam work, as Birley, his

Gordonstoun history master remarked, although he did achieve a very creditable pass in his S level paper).

He had little in common with a majority of his fellow students, three-quarters of whom came from state schools, and again he found it hard, as he had done throughout his school days, to make friends. That was partly a consequence of events. Charles went up to read archaeology and anthropology in the autumn of 1967. The following year campuses around the Western world erupted in violence. Faced with the tide of protest over his policy in Vietnam, America's President Johnson announced that he would not stand again. In what almost became a revolution, French students fought pitched battles through the streets of Paris and eventually succeeded in driving President de Gaulle from the Élysée Palace.

Given the strictures of his background, Charles was always an unlikely candidate for the revolutionary barricades. As he made clear after he had put on a false beard and watched that student demonstration on his own campus, he wanted no part of these uprisings that threatened the *ancien régime* he had been trained to represent. And that, as Prince Philip's authorized biographer Tim Heald wrote in the *Daily Express* a few days before the Investiture, was going to make his job 'increasingly onerous. His main support comes from the older age groups. His own contemporaries are generally sceptical about the value, indeed the validity of any hereditary system, let alone a hereditary monarchy.'

If politics formed an inevitable barrier between the Prince and his fellow undergraduates, so did his own reserve. Potential acquaintances no longer had to fight their way past a cortège of bullies making disgusting slurping noises, but people still shied away from him, fearful of being accused of toadying to the student Prince. Those who made the effort were not assured of a warm and grateful welcome; the fear still lingered that he was only being befriended because of who he was.

Added to that was an increasing awareness, if not of his own importance, then certainly of the privilege of his position which allowed him to select with whom he mixed, and then always on his own terms. Since leaving school he had assumed command of his own support group – of advisers and bodyguards and equerries leavened by an occasional contemporary like Hywel Jones, a socialist economics student whose rooms were on the same staircase who stayed up talking politics with him late into the night – and they provided Charles with all the companionship he had come to require.

There were also inevitable restrictions as to where he was allowed to go even when he wanted to join in. Jones, who had read Karl Marx when he was fourteen and was of an age in an era when it was still possible to believe in centralized socialism, persuaded Charles to join the university's Labour club to 'broaden his mind'. R. A. Butler, the former Tory Chancellor, Home and Foreign Secretary, and Master of Trinity, intervened to point out sternly to him the folly of the officially apolitical heir to the throne being seen to align himself with any party.

After the rigours of Gordonstoun, however, it was nothing less than 'marvellous to have three years when you are not bound by anything, and not married, and haven't got any particular job', as he observed. And while he was never going to be able to do more than nibble at the edges of university social life, that was more freedom than he had ever before enjoyed. He joined the Dryden Society, played cello in his college orchestra, and sang in the Madrigal Society. His academic work improved and at the end of his first year he felt assured enough to switch courses. When Butler asked him why he was giving up archaeology and anthropology, two subjects which had so interested him, to take up history and the study of the British constitution, Charles replied: 'Because I'm probably going to be king.'

Butler, one of the most astute British politicians of the post-war era, who many believe should have become prime minister, said that Charles was 'boyish, rather immature, and perhaps too susceptible to the influence of his family' when he arrived at

Cambridge. The university, said Butler, gave him a chance to 'grow'.

He had his own kitchen in his rooms where he could practise the culinary arts he had first tried to master as a young boy in the kitchens at Buckingham Palace without worrying about what others might say (his efforts below stairs at the Palace were not always appreciated: the staff complained that he got in their way and he once dropped a tray loaded with butter, baking powder, two dozen eggs, and sultanas).

He was also able to give outlet to his quirky sense of humour. Laughter was very important to him. 'Were it not for my ability to see the funny side of things, I would have been committed to an institution long ago,' he once remarked. He enjoyed making people laugh. 'It is very useful for getting people to listen to what you are saying,' he said.

It was also a way of currying favour. Shortly before he arrived at Gordonstoun he had discovered the Goons, those surrealistic, nonsensical characters played by Harry Secombe, Michael Bentine, Spike Milligan and Peter Sellers on the long-running radio show. They appealed to Charles 'with an hysterical totality' and he soon learnt to imitate their various voices and to sing the 'Ying Tong Song', 'the only song I do know by heart'. So good were his impersonations that 'When my small brothers heard a recording of the Goons for the first time, they thought it was their elder brother.' He even felt moved to pay tribute to the Goons at his Investiture, telling his somewhat bewildered audience that Wales had produced 'many brave men, princes, poets, bards, scholars, and, more recently, a very memorable Goon' – Harry Secombe.

As in many things, Charles was running several years behind the times. The Goons had gone off the air in 1960, to be superseded by a more cutting and topical brand of comedy, and it was not his singing of 'Solo for a Raspberry Blower' that earned him the grudging approval of Windmill Lodge, but his ability to mimic Bob Whitby's bombast.

At Cambridge he went one step further, and made fun of himself. In his second year he appeared in a comedy revue. Charles gave himself the pleasure of uttering such lines in a Goon-like voice as 'I like giving myself heirs,' much to the mirth of the sell-out audience who had queued for hours to see him. It was, he recalled, a typical undergraduates' show 'full of the most awful sort of groan jokes'. The most memorable picture was of the heir to the throne and all its vast estates sitting onstage in a dustbin.

Such frivolity was not allowed to spill too far over the edge of the stage, however. For all the theatrical levity, the essential gravity of the monarchy had to be maintained. There were rules to be obeyed. And there were always those duties to perform. Butler called them 'balcony jobs' and the Investiture, when the television audience was added in, provided the biggest gallery this or any other prince had ever played to.

Charles had his 'misgivings' which were quickly confirmed by the reaction to his arrival at Aberystwyth. Bombs started exploding. Students tried to saw off the head of the town's statue of the last Prince of Wales. The event was condemned by the students' union. On the personal front Charles again found himself ostracized. 'I haven't made many friends, there haven't been many parties,' he plaintively remarked. Everywhere he went he was faced with jeering demonstrators and obscene graffiti.

He tried to placate the mob with soft words. 'I don't blame people demonstrating like that,' he said. 'They've never seen me before. They don't know what I'm like. I've hardly been to Wales, and you can't expect people to be over-zealous about the fact of having a so-called English prince amongst them and be frightfully excited about it.'

He made speeches calling for 'tolerance and patience' and the 'simple effort to try and understand the other person's point of view and his idealism, and not to condemn it outright'. When he tried to make personal contact, however, he found that, for once, royalty's embrace did not work, and his attempt to talk to the Welsh-chanting demonstrators met with failure.

'I asked this chap who was holding a banner what it meant,' he recalled. 'He just hurled abuse at me. So after I'd asked more questions I gave up. There was no point.'

At that stage in his development Charles was still willing to listen to the other side of an argument and there was no escaping this one, which was being screamed and chanted at him wherever he went. The Welsh, he observed, were 'depressed about what might happen if they don't try and preserve the language and culture which is unique and special to Wales'.

Charles intuitively agreed with many of the protestors' demands. His interest in anthropology had been stirred by what he had seen and the people he had met in Papua New Guinea where another culture was also in retreat. There, people still wore 'magnificent headdresses of Bird-of-Paradise feathers'. In Wales old women still wore the traditional witch's hats. Charles would like to have seen both forms of headgear survive into the future, just as he wanted to see the societies which spawned them withstand the onslaught of Western (or American) cultural influence. 'If something is unique and special, I think it is well worth preserving,' he said.

It was with a genuine commitment, therefore, that Charles went to work in the university's language laboratory for the six weeks allotted him. It was not time enough to learn any language, and certainly not this one, but it did enable him to stand up at the Eisteddfod shortly before the Investiture and deliver a three-hundred-word speech to the Welsh League of Youth in a way that sounded as if he could speak Welsh. Fighting erupted when he started. It ended with rapturous applause. In between Charles had promised to help preserve the Welsh language and paid princely homage to his decapitated predecessor, the unfortunate Llewellyn the Last.

It was a good performance which won just acclaim. The Welsh Nationalist MP, Gwynfor Evans, called it 'amazing. I have never heard anyone who has taken to Welsh so recently master the language so well.' The mayor of Caernarvon, overcome with the sentimentality his countrymen are so noted for, declared, 'When he stood up at the Eisteddfod and started to speak in Welsh, he wasn't a boy. He was a prince. You could have put a suit of armour on that lad and sent him off to Agincourt.'

A suit of armour might yet have come in handy. For if Charles had won round the majority of Welshmen, there remained a hard core of separatists who wanted nothing whatsoever to do with the (English) Royal Family or the Prince they were having foisted on them. Indeed, so seriously did the security forces take the threat to the Prince's life that in the early part of the year a meeting had been held at the Welsh Office to discuss postponing the ceremony. That would in effect have meant cancellation. George Thomas argued against it. No part of Britain, he argued, could be placed off bounds to the Royal Family. The Queen agreed.

It is doubtful if today the security forces would have sanctioned what was ultimately an unnecessary ceremony. In 1969, however, before violence became an endemic trait of British life and parts of Northern Ireland and certain inner cities effectively became no-go areas for the Royal Family, it was still possible to trust to the efficacy of the police.

As Thomas pointed out, it would none the less 'require great moral courage from that young man' to go ahead as Lord Snowdon and the Earl Marshal, the Duke of Norfolk, were planning. The Queen has always been against American presidential-style protection which, she argues, cuts her off from her subjects. That also applied to her son and heir, and most especially in Caernarvon. The honorific of Prince of Wales had been acquired for the English Crown by the force of Edward I's arms. For the most obvious of political reasons, force could not be employed seven centuries later to invest another English prince with the title. Security had therefore to be as low key as possible.

That was not very low, as it turned out. The risk, as the

bombings illustrated, was all too real. There were police sharp shooters hidden in the battlements. Armed plain-clothes policemen moved through the crowds. Police helicopters hovered overhead. On the orders of Commander Jock Wilson of Scotland Yard, who led the Special Branch team guarding the Prince, spot checks were carried out on people arriving by road. An extra 2800 police had been drafted in and Army explosives experts had accompanied the postmen on the morning deliveries. Manholes had been sealed. Frogmen were on underwater guard on the royal yacht *Britannia* which was anchored off Holyhead.

Charles slept the night before on the royal train in a siding 'somewhere in the country'. The police would not say where. Nor would they reveal who was aboard. It would not be the last time that mystery would surround the Prince's activities on a train, though on this first occasion there was no need for speculation – so jittery was the situation that Charles was not allowed into Caernarvon until the day of the ceremony and had to be moved around the countryside for his own protection.

Yet, despite those tensions and the extra pressure it placed on a twenty-year-old who most certainly did not enjoy being put on such public display, Charles bore his ordeal well. And if he looked pale and not a little nervous, who could blame him? Certainly not the tens of thousands of people who converged on Caernarvon for the most spectacular piece of royal theatre since the Coronation. And if they in turn were 'deluding' themselves into thinking that they were witnessing 'an ancient historic ceremony' and not the 'bunk and hocus-pocus' Emrys Hughes insisted it was, then it was a delusion the millions watching on television were prepared to share and enjoy.

This, as one newspaper trumpeted, was 'Britain at its best!'

Prince Philip proudly declared that Charles 'came, saw and conquered the Welsh'.

Sir Winston Churchill's grandson, Nicholas Soames, who joined the Royal Family aboard the *Britannia* afterwards, recalled

95

looking up as the Prince of Wales's standard was unfurled for the first time. 'He asked six or seven of us to spend the night on board after the Investiture and when he came on board for the first time as the Prince of Wales, this fantastic standard burst out on the deck when he stepped on board. It blew out across the deck as the band played "God Bless the Prince of Wales" and it was really, really moving.'

Television and the photographers' long lenses had provided a close-up view of the human touches behind the spectacle. There was the uneasy moment when the Queen lowered the coronet on to her son's head and a look of terror flickered across his face, as though he was concerned for a moment that it was going to fall off. There was his whispered, 'Thank you,' and the Queen's command to him, 'Wave,' and the way he blushed and how when she held his hand so tightly that, when she let go, you could see on colour television where the skin had turned white.

Such intimacies could not help but dispel the remoteness that since time immemorial had been a crucial bastion of monarchy. They stampeded the movement towards treating the Royal Family as show-business or soap opera. And, as strange as it may seem as one hearkens to their more recent complaints about 'press intrusion', it was the Royal Family who authorized the change, on the advice of the man who had just been given overall control of their public image.

In 1968 William Heseltine had become the Queen's press secretary. It would prove to be a pivotal appointment.

Born in Western Australia in 1930, Heseltine was the son of a primary school teacher who had emigrated there from Hull twenty years before. His family claimed descent from the boat-builder who built the *Endeavour* in which Captain James Cook had discovered Australia. His mother was also a teacher and his parents had struggled to earn the money to send him to the fee-paying Christ Church Grammar School in Claremont. Heseltine rewarded their sacrifice by becoming head boy and going on to take a first in Australian history at the University of Western Australia. He then moved to the capital, Canberra, and took a job as a junior clerk in the federal government. There he was spotted by Sir Robert Menzies. At the age of twenty-five he was appointed Menzies's private secretary, a spectacular rise due in almost equal parts to outstanding ability and a Byzantine sense of diplomacy (it is said that he managed to keep his heretical dislike of cricket a secret all the time he worked for the cricket-mad Menzies).

In 1960 Buckingham Palace had asked Menzies to recommend someone for the post of assistant information officer as part of the plan to extend its Commonwealth base. Heseltine asked to be considered. Menzies, as *The Times* observed, 'did the rest'. It would prove to be Menzies's last and most decisive influence on the Royal Family, although not even that sagacious old political war horse could have had any inkling of the forces he had unleashed.

Under the command of Sir Richard Colville, the Palace press office had long worked to the rule that no information was the best information. Press 'releases' were little more than threats of the 'if you bother Prince Charles, we will take him away from school' kind. The Royal Family had traditionally gone along with this less-is-better approach. It was as if they were instinctively aware that too much light could only damage their mystique: when his private secretary Lord Stamfordham urged George V to look a little more cheerful on public occasions, the King replied: 'We sailors never smile on duty.'

But smiles, and their attendant repertoire of handshakes and walkabouts and 'photo opportunities', were what public occasions now demanded in an age increasingly dominated by the rapacious demands of the media. If the Royal Family was to avoid imprisonment in an ivory tower of irrelevance, it had to establish a bridge-head with the general public. That, at least, was the argument propounded by Prince Philip and which he persuaded the Queen to accept. And in Heseltine, whose Australian background freed

97

him from the stifling conservatism that afflicts most courtiers, they had just the man to carry it through.

It was Heseltine who came up with the idea for *Royal Family*, the joint BBC–ITN documentary which took the largest television audience in British history behind the royal scenes and showed an informal year in the life of the Queen and her family. It was the most fantastic piece of eavesdropping of all time.

The Duke of Windsor once remarked: 'The pleased incredulity with which the public reacts to the elementary demonstrations on the part of royalty that they are, after all, like other people is matched only by the public's refusal to accept them as such.' And 'like other people' was exactly what that 105-minute film showed the Royal Family to be. The film, as Heseltine said, 'enlarged and subtly changed the public's ideals of what the Queen and her family are really like'.

There was nothing subtle about the public's reaction and a quarter of a century later Heseltine would be called on to counsel the Queen as to how best to get her family out of the hole he had helped dig. For having been treated to an unprecedented insight to how the Royal Family lived, people wanted more, and then more again. A voracious appetite had been whetted and a whole industry, employing thousands of people and expending millions of pounds, would quickly grow up to feed it. In 1986 when Heseltine was appointed the Queen's private secretary – a job which Queen Victoria's prime minister Lord Rosebery called 'the most important in the public service' – it was a tacit acknowledgement that public relations, as *The Times* noted, had 'moved from the fringe to the centre of the Crown's function'.

The Investiture was part of that process and when it was over Charles flew to Malta to spend a few days of rest in the company of the island's governor, Sir Maurice Dorman.

The Investiture had been a miserable ordeal at times for Charles, but he had done his duty and he had earned his holiday, part of which he spent, as the accompanying press corps duly noted, rubbing sun-tan lotion into the back of Dorman's daughter, Sibella. She was a contemporary of the Prince at Cambridge and the cameras which only a few days before had been focused on events of an official nature, were now being pointed at her and the private life of the Prince she had befriended. For this, too, was part of the process and would soon become the main one, much to the fury of the Royal Family and Heseltine, who between them had unwittingly contrived to set this soon-to-be runaway train in motion.

Sibella's moment in the spotlight was brief. The blood sport of 'royal watching' was still in its infancy and besides, Sibella was not the woman who could claim to be Charles's first 'real' girlfriend. That honour belonged to Lucia Santa Cruz, the daughter of the then Chilean ambassador to London.

Chapter Six

Charles left Cambridge with a passable lower second BA honours degree and some belated experience. That latter was provided for him by Lucia Santa Cruz. Attractive, dark-haired and three years older than Charles, she was helping Rab Butler research his memoirs. She was different from the run of fair-haired English roses that made up Charles's usual romantic fare, not only in looks, but in her high-born Latin-American sophistication which enabled her to embark on an amorous liaison without demanding a wedding ring at the end of it.

That was just as well. The 1701 Act of Settlement specifically prohibited Charles from marrying a Roman Catholic, which Lucia was. It did not, however, prohibit a relationship of the kind the Master of Trinity went out of his way to encourage.

As Butler tactfully put it: 'At the Prince's request, my wife and I allowed Lucia to stay in the Master's Lodge so that they could have more privacy.' There was talk of a key being 'slipped' into Charles's hand. It was important, Butler continued, that Charles should enjoy himself while he could, before the responsibilities of his position closed in on him.

Charles took felicitous advantage of his mentor's considerateness and, while it lasted, his romance with Lucia was passionate and exciting. It was not the precursor of a licentious lifestyle to follow, however. 'Because a girl stays in the same house overnight, well, it isn't a case of "Here we go, hooray and whoopee,"' he once said. 'It simply cannot be like that. In my position I have

to live a rather old-fashioned life, and so do those in my circle.'
In fact, that was rather less to do with the restraints of his royal
position, and much more to do with the temperance of his personal tastes. In that, he was something of a rarity in a family
who had traditionally taken great delight in the pleasures of the
flesh. There was no need to plumb the archives for appropriate
examples. His grandfather's generation sufficed to set the moral
tone. The Duke of Windsor, when he was Prince of Wales, had
snorted cocaine and enjoyed an adulterous affair with, among
others, the aviatrix, Beryl Markham, as did his brother, the Duke
of Gloucester, who ended up paying her hush money. Their
sibling, the Duke of Kent, was a transvestite who had an affair
with the playwright Noël Coward and was caught in bed (or
so court rumour continues to insist) with a Buckingham Palace
footman.

Out of that libidinous generation only George VI behaved in
a manner his subjects would have deemed appropriate. Charles
had inherited his grandfather's sense of decorum. Unlike the
women in his family, he drank only in moderation and he
thoroughly disapproved of smoking. And sex, so it would tran-
spire, was of no great importance or moment. That was not to
say that it did not interest him. He was not a polished performer
but he had plenty of what one girlfriend called 'Hanoverian
enthusiasm' when the occasion arose. But what it was not, as it
is for so many young men, was a consuming preoccupation. Even
in his twenties he was more interested in his work than he was
in his libido; and work, once he left university, meant the armed
forces.

In March 1971, he joined the Air Force as a flight lieutenant
at the RAF College in Cranwell, Lincolnshire. It was all part
of his on-going training programme which, he explained with
unconscious condescension, was designed to teach him more
'about people'. In his mother's youth such knowledge was
deemed unnecessary if not positively harmful and royal children
were kept in isolation. But Britain's social foundations had shifted

since the 1930s and even Charles, whose enthusiasm for history sometimes outstripped his academic ability in the subject, was aware of monarchy's changing role and the regard in which it was held. As he explained shortly before he joined the forces: 'In these times this sort of organization is called into question. It is not taken for granted as it used to be. In that sense one had to be far more professional at it than I think you ever used to be . . . I think one has to be more "with it" than of old, and much better informed.'

But no less protected. There was a limit to how far the heir's brush with normality was allowed to go and, much to his chagrin, Charles discovered that the aeroplanes he was flying had been specially modified for his safety.

In the gesture of breaking out of the cotton wool he was being smothered in, he insisted on being allowed to make a parachute jump. He made it in July of that year from 12,000 feet above Dorset because, he said, 'I'd always wanted to do it because I wanted to see how I'd react.' He found out the moment he stepped out of the RAF Andover and got his feet entangled in the rigging.

'The first thing I thought was, "They didn't tell me anything about this,"' he recalled. 'Fortunately, my feet weren't twisted around the lines and they came out very quickly.' The incident still left him badly shaken. It was, he admitted, 'a rather hairy experience'.

It was the beginning of a spate of supposedly dare-devil activities which included underwater escape practice in a hundred-foot-deep tank and ended with him being mockingly dubbed Action Man after the plastic doll popular at the time. It was a soubriquet Charles detested but it stuck and would dog him throughout his time in the services which, had he been left to his own devices, would have been spent in the RAF.

He did well and, with special instruction, completed the twelve-month course in five which earned him a report that stated that he had 'a natural aptitude for flying'. There was to be no divergence, however, from the course that had been so carefully mapped out for him by the Queen's advisers that evening in 1965 and in September he switched to the Royal Navy.

It was a move he accepted with practised fatalism. In words as diplomatic as he could make them, he said: 'I wanted to go into the Navy, partly for historical reasons, partly because it was a form of tradition in my family, but basically because I felt I had been brought up in the Navy in some ways, heard so much about it. It was the Service I had always known about, having been on the *Britannia* every year as a child.'

Starting at the Royal Naval College, Dartmouth, where his father had first met his mother, he served on the warships *Norfolk*, *Minerva*, *Jupiter* and the aircraft carrier *Hermes* before being given command of the tiny, wooden-hulled minehunter, HMS *Bronington*. In all, he was destined to spend five years in the Senior Service and there were moments of enjoyment.

At Dartmouth he did well in seamanship and navigation which, so Lord Mountbatten observed, 'is all we seamen care about'. There was the sailor's pleasure in travel – to the West Indies, Australia, the Pacific, the Mediterranean. It gave him, he reiterated in that patronizing manner which was becoming a trait, 'a marvellous opportunity to get close to the ordinary British chap if possible'. He finally got the opportunity to learn how to fly helicopters which he found 'very exciting, very rewarding, very stimulating and sometimes bloody terrifying'.

He grew a beard because, as he explained to the future Earl of Bradford who he knew from Cambridge and who was growing one at the same time, he wanted to see 'what my mother will say'. (The answer was not much. The Queen dropped a leaden hint from the great height of her regal position that it might be better if he took it off before the next State occasion.)

For the first time in his life he was allowed out without a detective by his side or in the back seat of his car. And on shore leave in Toulon in the south of France, he was even able to join a party of brother officers on a tour through the red-light area which ended in the kind of nightclub where girls in various states of undress dance on the tables.

But however hard he liked to pretend, Charles was never just another naval officer. He was allowed extra leave to complete his official duties. Courses were tailored to fit his schedule. He was given his own cabin aboard ship. He could have refused these favours if he had wanted to. He never did. He saw no reason why he should; it was what he had been brought up to expect and he accepted them as no more than his due.

What he did object to was the precautions taken to ensure his safety, without appreciating that they were a variation of the privileges of which, in other circumstances, he was quite willing to take advantage.

That made the restrictions no less irksome, however. He was told that the Buccaneer strike aircraft and the Sea King helicopters that his brother Andrew would pilot during the Falklands conflict were too dangerous for him to fly. 'I could have stayed in the Navy, I suppose,' he later said. 'I could have concentrated purely on being a naval officer. But there were difficulties with that because I would only have stayed if I could have gone on flying, which was my main love in the Navy. And it was becoming more and more difficult, because people get into a terrible state about me flying, you know – if I am going to fly myself into a hill, the sea, or whatever.'

When Charles first joined the armed forces there had been the inevitable objections. He had firmly rebutted them. 'It is pointless and ill-informed to say that I am entering a profession trained in killing,' he said. 'I am entering the RAF and then the Navy because I believe I can contribute something to this country by so doing.' But only on a limited scale.

As Britain's post-imperial role continued to shrink, so did the importance of its navy which, when Charles's great-grandfather had served in it, had outnumbered any other fleet in the world by almost two to one but was now getting smaller by the year.

104

The force that emerged after successive governments' budget cuts was by necessity a highly qualified meritocracy which placed increasing reliance on technology, a development which was bound to limit the career future of a prince who had only managed to scrape a pass in O level maths at the third attempt.

There was another restraint and that was the agenda decided on by Mountbatten, the Prime Minister, the Archbishop of Canterbury and those other worthies to provide the future king with experience but which in effect made him a tourist in his own life. It was a programme devised for the best of reasons which produced the worst of results. Because everything was worked to a pre-determined timetable there was no objective other than the immediate one of adding another tick on his curriculum vitae before he moved to the next project; no need for long-term consistency of effort and therefore no real point. His life was to be one long training project for a job he could not inherit until his mother died, a macabre prospect as well as a distant one, given the longevity of the female members of his family.

Had he been a different kind of person, that might not have worried him. 'I could go and play polo all over the world,' he said. But despite all the best efforts of the press to portray him as a playboy prince, that was never a real starter. He certainly played a lot of polo, but he was always looking for something more meaningful to occupy his time, which led him into areas of controversy and added to the ridicule to which his increasingly eccentric intellectual shilly-shallying exposed him.

That only increased his frustration which sometimes crossed into depression. For no matter how many examinations he passed or how many parachute jumps he completed, he always felt he had more to prove. Never was that more obvious than when his brother, Andrew, returned from the Falklands where he had served with distinction on board a Sea King helicopter flying decoy to the Exocet missiles the Argentinians were launching against the British fleet. Andrew acknowledged his fear, Charles his jealousy.

'I was frightened, absolutely,' Andrew recalled, with the honesty of someone who has seen combat. 'I think to a large degree if you're not frightened then you make a mistake.'

Charles, so anxious to be seen to pass muster, complained: 'I never had that chance to test myself. It's terribly important to see how you react, to be tested.' Tests of that potentially fatal kind were never going to be allowed on Charles's itinerary, however. The intention was to train a future king, not kill one. Whatever life might hold for him in the long run-up to the throne, it was not going to include leading his nation's troops into battle in the style of Henry V, the Prince to whom the mayor of Caernarvon had so extravagantly compared him.

As it happens, Charles was secretly quite glad not to have been around to face that definitive test of his manhood. He left the Navy at the end of 1976 and he was glad to be out, for despite all his bravado, he had not enjoyed his time as much as the official record pretends.

His essential insecurity carried through into his work and he was only half joking when he admitted, 'I used to have a terrible time filled with horror and wondering what would happen . . . I always used to get very nervous, especially when I had to bring the ship alongside. My knees knocked so violently I had to tie pieces of sorbo rubber between them to stop them demoralizing the troops.'

He did not settle naturally into the enclosed, matey life on a frigate or a minehunter and his fellow officers, like his school and university contemporaries before them, found him aloof and stand-offish. No one doubted his commitment and his determination to do well, but it was obvious that he preferred life in a palace to the one on offer aboard ship. 'He really did not enjoy going back after he had been home on a few days' leave,' one of the Household remembered. 'He was always very gloomy about having to go back.'

What he especially enjoyed was the company of his great-uncle, Lord Mountbatten. While other men of his age would have looked forward to a round of parties and flirtations, Charles preferred to motor down to Broadlands, the Mountbatten estate in Hampshire, for a few days of chat and gentle instruction.

'It's lovely having him here, we've had so many cosy chats,' Mountbatten said. 'What a charming young man he is.'

Charles's relations with the father he continues to call 'Papa' had not improved much over the years and, while their differences were sometimes exaggerated, the two were never able to forge an easy bond of fellowship. 'I didn't listen to advice from my father until I was in my late teens,' he once observed. And not much afterwards, as it turned out. At Philip's instigation, theirs was and remains a long-distance relationship. Instead of speaking face to face, Philip preferred to communicate with his eldest son by note. It was a routine he had first got into when his children were young and he was so often away. It carried through into Charles's adulthood. Philip would not walk round to Charles's apartments, even when they were both under the same roof. He rarely telephoned. Instead he would bombard Charles with hand-written messages of advice and sometimes of rebuke.

'Prince Philip is a great note scribbler but it did seem a rather strange way of keeping in touch with your son,' one of the Household remarked.

That distance meant that Charles had to look elsewhere for paternal companionship and throughout his twenties he went out of his way to cultivate the friendship of men older than himself. Uffa Fox, Prince Philip's gruffly spoken sailing companion, took an interest in him when he visited Cowes in August. Rab Butler did the same when Charles was at Cambridge.

Another and more cerebral influence was the South African-born writer, Sir Laurens van der Post. A disciple of Carl Jung, van der Post introduced Charles to the Swiss psychiatrist's esoteric notions on the 'collective unconscious' and the importance of dreams, which eventually led to the Prince keeping a record of those he could remember. They teamed up on an African safari in 1977 when he was twenty-eight and van der Post seventy. Ten years later the ancient mystic would lead Charles on a 'spiritual voyage of discovery' into the Kalahari Desert.

One man who might have played a greater part in his life if circumstances had been different was the Duke of Windsor. Charles was fascinated by the great-uncle who had had the courage to behave in a way that he never could. He first visited him at his home in the Bois de Boulogne when he went to Paris in 1970. He returned to see him on a number of occasions thereafter. He also got on well with the Duchess, and continued to correspond with her after the Duke's death in 1972, much to the chagrin of his grandmother, the Queen Mother, who detested the woman she held responsible for her husband's early death (and who, so court gossip insists, married the prince with whom she had secretly been in love but who never returned her affection).

That exercise in bridge-building was expected to pay dividends in the form of the Duke and Duchess's papers and jewellery which the Royal Family confidently expected would be bequeathed to Charles. After the Duke's death, however, the Duchess's affairs came under the control of Maître Blum. A tough French lawyer, she assumed total charge of the Duchess's declining years, with the result that Lord Mountbatten's visits came to an end. Perhaps there was concern that he might have pressurized the Duchess into relinquishing those valuable possessions to the Royal Family.

After the Duchess's death the jewels were auctioned off in aid of charity while the papers, including the Windsors' love letters, were turned into a best-selling book. Charles, Prince of Wales, received nothing from his princely predecessor's estate. It was a sad end to an uninspiring story but Charles never blamed the Duchess. Despite the bitterness engendered by her marriage to the king, and that final, unnecessary estrangement as the Duchess sank ever deeper into the incomprehending twilight of senility, his view was, 'Well, she is family.' It was the Duke, however, who had most impressed him. Even as a frail old man he had a kingly dignity about him which Charles greatly admired.

Women also played a part in Charles's development and the most important ones, like the men, were older than him. The Queen Mother had been a bedrock of affection when he was a boy, though that relationship cooled as he grew older. He was close to Lady Susan Hussey, the Queen's most trusted lady-in-waiting, who is the sister of the politician William Waldegrave and is married to Marmaduke Hussey, then a newspaper executive, later the chairman of the BBC. Ten years Charles's senior, Lady Susan Hussey, as the Prince's former valet, Stephen Barry, noted, was available for long conversations. 'It was to Lady Susan that he talked about his girlfriends and problems,' Barry said. 'She was always at the Palace. Her husband working late hours on his newspaper, she was in no tremendous rush to get home.' She was, Barry concluded, an 'influence'. It is a view others in the Palace shared. Charles was also very fond of Princess Alexandra, who was twelve years older and, like Lady Susan, 'a rather sophisticated type of woman with a charm bordering on being sexual', as one member of the Household described them.

It was Mountbatten, however, who exerted the most powerful influence over his still unformed great-nephew. Charles, always in search of a 'guru' (another term he disliked intensely), promoted Mountbatten to the post of 'honorary grandpapa'. Mountbatten was duly flattered and returned the compliment. When Charles had gone to sea for a long tour of duty he had written: 'I've been thinking of you – far more than I had ever expected to think of a young man – but then I've got to know you so well, I really miss you.'

The relationship continued to bloom after Charles left the Navy. The two men met frequently and would spend long summer weekends alone together at Windsor. Their routine was comfortable and as simple as a retinue of servants could make it. Mountbatten would arrive carrying an old battered suitcase which had belonged to his late wife, Edwina. Unlike most other guests who were put into one of the Shelter Rooms, he would sleep in one of the grander bedrooms just along the corridor from the Queen's sitting room.

The weekend began the following morning with an eight o'clock wake-up call, followed by breakfast in the nursery. Then, if the weather was fair, they would set up camp in a pair of comfortable chairs by the aviary below the wall of the East Terrace, which commands a peaceful, rural view across the lawn towards Frogmore, their papers and brief cases laid out on a couple of card tables. There was always a jug of lemon refresher to hand, a concoction invented by Lord Mountbatten.

Lunch would be a cold picnic of poached salmon and salad. In the afternoon they might go swimming together in the pool in the Orangery, the glass doors of which slide back. Both Charles and Mountbatten were keen on sunbathing, and they would often sit out without their shirts or, if they had been swimming, stretched out on the sunbeds. They would put sun cream on each other's backs. In the evening they would dine informally in the Queen's formal dining room, wearing corduroys and blazers.

These meetings were casual and relaxed and inevitably attracted unfavourable comment. The British aristocracy had long looked down on Mountbatten who they regarded, with considerable cause, as a dynasty builder whose ambition it was to take over the Royal Family. They saw him as a vain poseur, which he was (it was Mountbatten who advised Charles that, since he had all those uniforms and medals, he should wear them, as Mountbatten did). They were irritated by his obsession with his ancestors and his own, often fanciful, pedigree. His alleged bisexuality and the miscegenations of his wife had long been the subject of salon gossip. On a more serious note, the partition of India and the ensuing slaughter of as many as ten million people over which he had presided as the last Viceroy had made him powerful political enemies. The fact that ten years after his death

Antony Lambton, who disclaimed the earldom of Durham but none the less represents a grand aristocratic tradition, could write a book devoted to demolishing Mountbatten's dynastic fantasies is a measure of the hostility he had generated among the upper classes. The Queen Mother, herself the daughter of an earl, shared many of the prejudices her caste held against her daughter's uncle-in-law.

But whatever his faults (and they were plentiful), Mountbatten was also a man of considerable talent. He rose by his own efforts to the rank of Admiral of the Fleet. Of greater significance, he also served as the Supreme Allied Commander in South-east Asia from 1943 until 1947 and the United States, which provided the bulk of the military forces for the war against Japan, would never have allowed its men and treasure to be placed under the authority of an incompetent. That Mountbatten most certainly was not. He was intelligent, energetic, immensely charming and hard-working. And if his pride in his own lineage bordered on the vainglorious, his understanding of royal history enabled him to foretell, with some prescience, what the monarchy's future requirements and pitfalls were likely to be. His advice was also invaluable on other matters: an enthusiastic campaigner for a variety of causes, Mountbatten soon had Charles interested in such diverse projects as the United World Colleges and the plan to raise Henry VIII's flagship *Mary Rose* from the bed of the Solent where it had lain for over four centuries.

With an eye to his physical development, it was also Mountbatten who took it upon himself to write to Charles counselling him to go out and 'sow his wild oats and have as many affairs as he could before settling down'. This was one piece of advice Charles found difficult to follow. Naturally shy, brought up in a matriarchal society, young for his years and emotionally inhibited, he was no princely Lothario. He much preferred the tweedy moorland adventures of John Buchan's Richard Hannay to the sex and snobbery of Ian Fleming's James Bond, and was more interested in holding long and serious conversations (usually about himself) than he was in joining the post-Pill sexual revolution.

The press, of course, were having none of that. He was heir to the throne and that, they decreed, made him the most eligible bachelor in the world. It was yet another image Charles would quickly come to loathe but one he inadvertently kept encouraging. His aunt, Princess Margaret, had warned him that if his attempts at courtship were to have any chance of success they had to be conducted in private. Charles would not listen. In petulant defiance of the reporters who were now making a living out of following him around, he refused to meet his friends behind the Palace walls. If he liked a girl he would invite her to join him at polo. But that, as Margaret had foreseen, inevitably led to another spate of over-the-top speculation which usually put an end to anything before it started.

When he was twenty-seven he added to his problem by saying that 'Thirty is about the right age for a chap like me to get married.' As his birthday drew nearer, so did the attentions of press. 'I've only got to look at someone and the next morning I'm engaged to her,' Charles complained. The list they came up with was long, eclectic and sometimes plain silly. The girls were dubbed 'Charlie's Angels' and at one time or another people seriously – and very foolishly – argued the cases for the singer Lynsey de Paul and the Catholic Princess Marie-Astrid of Luxembourg. In between he dined with actress Susan George (she described the Prince as 'very romantic'); was linked with television-chief-cum-naturalist Lord (Aubrey) Buxton's hearty daughter, Lucinda (always a non-starter; Cindy was not the marrying kind); and enjoyed the company of the attractive American Laura Jo Watkins ('He's a great guy,' she said, but the strictures of royal life were 'unlivable for kids like us').

There were other, more serious prospects, but he was rarely without competition for their affections. In 1973 he saw a lot of the eminently suitable Rosie Clifton, whose father became Standard Bearer, Her Majesty's Body Guard of Honourable

Corps of Gentlemen at Arms. But she was really in love with Lord Vestey's brother, Mark, whom she married two years later.

Charles's pursuit of Lord Manton's daughter, Fiona Watson, was equally unsuccessful. According to legend, that romance came to an end when it was revealed that she had bared herself in the girlie magazine *Mayfair*. In fact, it was the competition that saw him off long before Fiona stripped off for the camera. Charles was 'very cautious and very careful' about committing himself and would often wait until the last moment before asking a girl to join him for dinner. Fiona was not the kind to sit at home waiting for the telephone to ring and when Charles did call she at first dismissed it as a prank before telling him that she already had a date with Gordonstoun-educated Mark Cottrell whom she eventually married. It was the end of an affair that had never started.

Sabrina Guinness, from the banking side of the clan, was another who fell at the first hurdle. Philip and the Queen could be friendly and welcoming, if they had a mind to be (to the amazement of her staff, the Queen enjoyed chatting to Koo Stark who, she insisted, should sit beside her on the sofa at Windsor) or cold and intimidating if they did not, which was the case with Sabrina. Invited to spend a weekend at Balmoral, she travelled north by train and was met at the station by Prince Philip's electric minibus painted in Duke of Edinburgh Green, which the staff irreverently called 'yob green'. When she arrived at the castle fun-loving Sabrina, who once worked in Hollywood as Ryan O'Neal's nanny and whose friends had included Mick Jagger and Jack Nicholson, jokingly remarked that the minibus looked like a Black Maria. 'You'd know all about Black Marias,' was Philip's blunt retort. She knew she was out when she sat down only to be told by the Queen, 'Don't sit there – that is Queen Victoria's chair!' The whole experience, she remembered, was 'terrifying'. The brief relationship, she later remarked, was not intimate.

Part of the problem was one of location. At Balmoral there was no escaping the constant appraisal to which the Royal Family subject their guests. But then that applied just as much to Sandringham, Buckingham Palace and, except for a brief time in high summer, Windsor Castle. Except in the degree of comfort, Charles was not very different from any youth on a council estate who was still living with his parents. He had a choice of royal homes in which to entertain his girlfriends but little real opportunity to indulge in what Stephen Barry called 'very close relationships'.

As the valet pointed out, Buckingham Palace, for all its size, is 'totally unsuitable for anything secret to take place'. Charles's rooms were along a straight corridor which brought them into the full view of everyone on the nursery floor. 'It would have been impossible,' Barry insisted, 'for a girl to have spent any time there without a footman or his policeman or me not being aware she was there.'

It was also the Queen's home. The Queen had a disconcerting habit of going on a tour around the Palace after dinner with her page and, if she thought no one was there, going through Charles's and Anne's rooms to see what she could find, which put a rein on everyone's behaviour.

Barry said: 'If he was meant to be in his bed in the morning when I went to wake him up, he was in bed. Alone.' When Charles was at Buckingham Palace it was still his nanny Mabel he kissed last thing at night and first thing in the morning.

'I sometimes thought the limitations on his privacy were part of the reason for his participation in so many energetic sporting activities,' mused Barry. It might have been Kurt Hahn's asexual vision come to adult fruition – but not quite.

There were always friends' houses where Charles could enjoy weekends of greater privacy than the royal residences allowed him. There was even the very occasional possibility of enjoying the same facilities at home. Most of the time, though, he was content to end his day alone, perhaps after a visit to the opera which would be planned and executed like a command perform-ance. It would always include a formal dinner in the supper room behind the Royal Box, with china, linen, silver and food brought over from Buckingham Palace and footmen to serve it – the kind of lavishness which only the Queen Mother would have dreamt of emulating.

There was no mistaking, though, on whose terms the evening would be conducted. He had to be addressed as 'Sir', and Lady Diana Spencer was deep into her relationship with him before that barrier was lowered. The girl was not collected but had to get herself to the theatre or the opera or, if specially honoured, to Buckingham Palace for a quiet dinner surrounded by half a dozen servants in Charles's apartment. She would usu-ally have to make her own way home again. As in everything else, the girl, whoever she was, had to fit in with the Prince and his interests.

But if that had always been the royal way, so were the gifts that had accompanied an evening out with a royal prince. That was one royal tradition, however, that Charles chose to discon-tinue. There was no present afterwards. Unlike the previous Prince of Wales, Charles did not have accounts with Cartier or Van Cleef and the most a girl could expect was a bunch of flowers and that rarely.

Charles had been brought up to appreciate the price of a dog lead ('Dog leads cost money!' as his mother once famously reminded him) but not the value of the romantic gesture. Unless you happened to be an opera fan, therefore, an evening out with the Prince could be an obstacle course of tedium, which only the determined or the besotted were prepared to tackle.

Chapter Seven

Lady Diana Spencer was the one who claimed the prize but there were other significant candidates before her for the glamorous, but ultimately destructive job – that of wife to the Prince of Wales. Some shied away. Others were taken in, only to be rejected on the basis of temperament or previous associations. All were affected by the experience which surprisingly, strangely, was less intimate than might have been expected.

'I don't know how the idea got about that I'm amazingly successful with women,' he once said. The situation, he insisted, was quite the contrary. 'My constant battle is to escape, and that is sometimes a very difficult thing.'

There was no escaping his responsibility, however, and one after another suitable and not so suitable candidates were paraded into the limelight for public appraisal.

The first girl who looked a likely princess was Lady Jane Wellesley, daughter of the Duke of Wellington and descendant of the general who beat Napoleon at Waterloo. She was beautiful and poised and had known the Prince since childhood. They started walking out together towards the end of 1973. In the time-honoured fashion, Jane, who was twenty-three at the time, insisted, 'There is no romance. We are just good friends,' which was enough to convince everyone that an engagement was just around the corner. When they holidayed together on the Duke's 30,000-acre Molino de Rey estate near Granada, which his famous forebear had been given by the grateful Spanish nation,

116

the announcement appeared imminent and 10,000 people jammed the roads around Sandringham when she spent New Year's Eve there.

In many ways theirs would have been an ideal match. Certainly the Queen thought so. Self-confident in a relaxed, unstuffy way, Jane fitted in well, getting up early in the morning to see the guns off for their day's shooting, joining the Queen for a ride later in the morning, always cheerful and helpful. 'The Queen was very fond of her,' a member of the household recalled.

Jane Wellesley had one fatal flaw. She was intelligent. Having worked in public relations, she went on to make a career for herself in broadcasting which brought her into close contact with media intellectuals like Melvyn Bragg. She could see what restrictions and demands would be placed upon her if she agreed to marry Charles and the idea appalled her. 'I couldn't, just couldn't give everything up to become his wife,' she said.

On another occasion she asked a reporter: 'Do you honestly believe I want to be Queen?' The question was a rhetorical one; she went on to dismiss the whole business with a grand remark of the kind the first Duke would have applauded. 'I don't want another title,' she said. 'I've already got one, thank you.'

Altogether, her romance with the Prince lasted some eighteen months. Their friendship survived the experience and she remained on his reserve list for years afterwards. Charles knew that, should a girl drop out at the last moment (something which happened more frequently than he liked to admit), he could telephone Jane, secure in the knowledge that she would not take offence at the lateness of the call, and ask her to make up the numbers at the opera, which, if she was free, she was happy to do.

Easy-going, undemanding, and conducted at a distance, it was the kind of relationship Charles was able to understand and deal with. He moved into more troubled water with Davina Sheffield, his next important liaison. She was a cousin on her mother's side of Lord McGowan, whose family made its money out of ICI, and on her father's, a descendant from the wrong side of the blanket of the Dukes of Normanby and Buckingham. She was attractive, sexy and immediately flattered by the Prince's attentions. She was going out with the Old Harrovian power-boat racer James Beard. In the wheels-within-wheels of interrelationships that is the aristocracy, Beard's sister Victoria was married to the Earl of Normanton, whose brother Mark was Charles's contemporary at Gordonstoun.

That tenuous connection did not prevent Charles asking Davina to join him for a weekend at Balmoral when she was supposed to be going to Cap Ferrat with Beard – or Davina from accepting. But Scotland, she discovered, was most decidedly not the South of France. In Provence everything was centred around leisurely *al fresco* lunches, and dinners that ran through into the early hours followed by a visit to a nightclub. At Balmoral all was order. The days were spent out of doors. The evenings were rigid in their routine. They began at 7.30 with cocktails prepared beforehand in a large jug by an equerry. The 'full waited dinner' was black tie and long dresses and kilts, eaten at tables of six to eight people. Each candle-lit table had its own page, footman, under-butler and wine waiter. When the Queen ate, her dogs would be at her feet under the table. Afterwards everyone was expected to play gin rummy or bridge. Coffee and liqueurs were served to the accompaniment of the wailing sounds of bagpipes played by a pipe major.

It was very different from life with the handsome Beard, though Davina seemed to enjoy the change. She soon became a regular at these family get-togethers, and started popping up at Sandringham and Windsor, as well as making return visits to Balmoral. She impressed the Queen, an important consideration, by always being up to see the guns off in the morning and joining them when invited.

She excited Charles with her sensuous good looks. She was also very poised. After the Prince and Davina had been swimming off a beach at Bantham in Devon, which he had found when he was training at Dartmouth, she had walked into the men's changing room by mistake. She was surprised there in the nude by a lifeguard named Ray Atkinson. 'It was a great sight,' Atkinson recalled, 'but very unexpected.' Davina, he said, 'didn't bat an eyelid'.

According to Stephen Barry, who had a valet's insight into his master's mind, Charles wanted to marry Davina. Circumstances, however, conspired against her. Beard made sure they did. He had not taken kindly to being dumped in favour of a prince and chose to disclose to a Sunday newspaper that he had once lived with Davina in a cottage outside Winchester. Lord Mountbatten, who held firm views about what was acceptable in a prospective queen, ruled that Davina's 'past' took her out of contention.

By then Davina herself was having second thoughts about the wisdom of a relationship with the Prince of Wales. She was followed everywhere by newspaper reporters who she was left to deal with on her own without the help of a detective or private secretary or the walls of a castle to protect her. At the start she had been cool and collected. By the end she was often reduced to tears and on one distressing occasion spent two hours crying in the loo at Heathrow airport with the press waiting outside to pounce when she reappeared.

It was therefore with feelings of regret leavened with relief that Davina, five foot ten inches tall and eminently desirable, found herself outside Charles's romantic orbit. If she was ever wholly in it, that is. 'I never had a relationship with him; it was a friendship,' she insisted. There is no reason to disbelieve her, if only because it was an extraordinary remark to make if it was not true. But whether she had or had not was of less significance at the time than the way Charles meekly accepted the royal hypocrisy expounded by Lord Mountbatten and accepted one set of morals for men only to reject them for women.

A more urbane man might have chosen to take a more worldly view of the situation. Charles, despite his fondness for Davina, did not. He was summoned to lunch by Mountbatten who gave the heir to the throne the benefit of his interpretation of what was acceptable royal behaviour. Shortly afterwards Charles ruthlessly cut Davina out of his life.

Such severances were achieved in brutal fashion. One day the girl's telephone call would be put through by the Palace switchboard. The next day it would not and that, quite simply, was that. There was no face-to-face confrontation, no chance of a reconciliation, just the impersonal voice of the Palace operator saying that the Prince was not available.

It was not a considerate way to end a relationship but by now a certain imperiousness was to be observed in the Prince who, as a young boy, had been so considerate and eager to please. When he wanted something, he demanded it there and then. If it was not immediately forthcoming he would lose his temper and start shouting. The rages passed as quickly as they flared, and he always apologized to the unfortunate footman or secretary afterwards. But the remorse did not stop it happening again, and with increasing frequency as he grew older.

At the same time he also became rather faddish in his ways. Ever more interested in his health, he gave up drinking milk and cut down on his consumption of meat until he reached the edge of vegetarianism, a dietetic development which so annoyed his mother that, in a rare flash of temperament, she advised him to 'grow up'. He refused to drink coffee and restricted himself to one cup of Lapsang Souchong tea in the afternoon which he enjoyed with a chocolate Oliver biscuit. He started collecting different kinds of honey, favouring first one from the Orkneys, then another from Devon and so on. He would insist on taking his favourite of the moment with him everywhere he went, including on his foreign travels. He insisted on scraping the pot clean and woe betide any unfortunate footman who threw it out before he had decreed it to be absolutely empty.

Such penny-pinching verged on the ridiculous. He lost his temper when the Palace chefs used some overripe mangoes to make ice cream, exclaiming, 'Mango ice cream is such a waste, a waste, never again.' It was as though by some magical royal command mangoes should not rot which, of course, is exactly what they ceased to do; henceforth any fruit that was about to go off was promptly thrown away by the kitchen staff. And while he was forever switching off lights to save electricity, he would also open wide the nursery windows in the middle of winter, heedless of the profligate waste of heat and the power it had taken to create it. The practicalities of life, his staff noted, often passed him by and there was certainly something woolly about a man in his late twenties who still went to bed with a teddy bear.

He became obsessive about exercise. 'If I didn't get the exercise, or something to take my mind off things, I'd go potty,' he said. He followed the programme of Canadian Air Force callisthenics when he arose in the morning. He became a proficient skier. Still in search of his own manliness, he took up steeplechasing because, as he explained, 'It is a great challenge to try to overcome a certain element of natural fear ... going flat out over fences and wondering if you are going to get to the other side in one piece.'

He started organizing his work schedule around polo. 'I feel a hundred times better after a game of polo,' he said. For all his efforts, however (and at one point he was playing three or four times a week), Charles was never a good polo player, despite his flattering four handicap. As someone who frequently played with him explained, 'Polo is a team game and before each match we would try and work out the best way of dealing with the opposition – who would do what, who would pick up which player. Charles would nod, but when we got out on the field it was as if he hadn't heard a word we'd been saying. He didn't do a single one of the things we had spent hours discussing.' It was yet another example of the Prince's increasing self-absorption and it was only by dint of his royal position that he was able to get away with it.

For all his eccentricity, however, there were still touches of the

121

'gentle boy with a very kind heart' his grandmother remembered. Shortly after Davina Sheffield was expelled from his life, Lady Sarah Spencer came into it and she would greatly benefit from Charles's attention.

Red-haired and headstrong, she was invited to join the Royal Ascot houseparty at Windsor in the summer of 1977. The daughter of Earl Spencer and god-daughter of the Queen Mother, Sarah had been forced to make a premature exit from West Heath public school for girls when her youthful taste for strong liquor ended in one drinking session too many. 'I used to drink because I was bored,' she recalled. 'I would drink anything.' It was food, not drink, however, that had become the problem by 1977. In what would soon be revealed as a terrible family trait, Sarah was suffering from anorexia nervosa, the 'slimmer's disease' which is closely linked to bulimia.

Illness was something from which Charles recoiled. Concerned for his own well-being, he went out of his way to avoid anyone who had so much as a cold, while hospital visits were anathema to him. If anyone is late for an appointment, even by just a few minutes, he will always ask: 'Are they ill?' In Sarah's case, however, Charles took a considerate interest in the welfare of this otherwise bouncy young woman who started accompanying him to polo and joined him on a two-week skiing holiday in Klosters. It was at Charles's prompting that Sarah eventually booked herself into hospital for treatment of the disease. Six months later she was able to report that she was 'very much better', and that Charles's encouragement and support had been most helpful.

Charles, she said, was a 'fabulous person' who made her laugh. The inevitable talk of an imminent engagement arose, but once again the relationship had not progressed as far as public and certainly press imagination had taken it. 'I'm not in love with him,' Sarah said. 'I think of him as the big brother I never had.' She continued: 'He is a romantic who falls in love easily. But I can assure you that if there were to be any engagement between

122

Prince Charles and myself, it would have happened by now. I am a whirlwind sort of lady as opposed to a person who goes in for long, slow-developing courtship. Of course, the Prince and I are great friends, but I was with him in Switzerland because of my skiing ability.' In case anyone should miss the point, Sarah declared, 'Our relationship is totally platonic.'

Once again, and on the same grounds, there was no reason to doubt such an emphatic statement – just as there was no reason to question future girlfriend Anna Wallace's private admission that her relationship with the Prince, who wanted to make her his future queen, also never progressed beyond the point of friendship. By the testimony of those he was supposed to be going out with, Charles was having a very fallow time of it.

That did not worry him. It was not as though he was lacking for female companionship.

One muse was the Australian-born Dale Harper, who in 1973 married Lord Tryon, the banker son of the Queen's late treasurer. He is a quiet, reserved English gentleman with a fondness for fishing that Charles shares. She is boisterous, outgoing and with a sense of humour Charles described as 'typically' Australian. Charles first met the woman he promptly nicknamed Kanga on a trip to Australia in the late sixties. They became the best of friends – but, then, so did her husband. Anthony Tryon owned an estate in Wiltshire and a lodge in Iceland, and Charles became a frequent guest at both, shooting pheasant in England and fishing for salmon in the rugged tranquillity of Iceland.

It was friendship of the most relaxed kind and if rumours inevitably circulated about just how close the Prince and his friend's wife really were, then Kanga was flattered enough not to try to dispel them. When Charles visited Australia in the 1970s, the Tryons were often there and Kanga made it her business to act as his unofficial hostess in her home town of Melbourne, organizing parties and nights out at the opera, often helped by generous invitees who would be happy to pick up the bill. Charles became godfather to the Tryons' son, Charles, born in 1976, and Kanga opened a clothes shop in Knightsbridge called by the nickname Charles had given her.

The woman who really enjoyed the Prince's confidence, though, was Camilla Shand, niece of Lord Ashcombe and descendant of the property speculator who made the Duke of Westminster so rich by building Belgravia for him. More intriguingly, she is quite possibly the great-granddaughter of Edward VII and, as such, Charles's second cousin once removed.

The evidence is circumstantial but persuasive. Camilla's great-grandmother was the society beauty Alice Keppel. She was married to the seventh Earl of Albemarle's son, George, who obligingly stepped aside when Edward, then the Prince of Wales, took a fancy to her. Alice had a deep, alluring voice and an obvious sexual magnetism. She smoked with an aplomb befitting a Hollywood actress. As Osbert Sitwell wrote after meeting her for the first time, 'She would remove from her mouth for a moment the cigarette which she would be smoking through a long holder and turn upon the person to whom she was speaking her large, humorous, kindly, peculiarly discerning eyes.' The Prince was captivated. They met in 1898 and their affair began almost immediately. She was twenty-five, he fifty-seven.

Two years later Alice gave birth to Camilla's grandmother, Sonia. Edward took a paternal interest in the child; usually most pernickety about his clothes, he would amuse her by sending slices of hot buttered toast tobogganing down his immaculate trouser legs.

Sonia grew up to marry Roland Cubitt of the building family. Their daughter, Rosalind, married Major Bruce Shand. Their daughter, Camilla, became the wife of Andrew Parker-Bowles and, in imitation of her great-grandmother, the mistress of the Prince of Wales.

Charles first enjoyed her company when he came down from Cambridge in the early seventies. She was not beautiful in the conventional sense – the Shand looks sit better on her brother,

Mark, the rugged adventurer whose conquests included Bianca Jagger, the late president John F. Kennedy's daughter Caroline, and who later married financier Sir James Goldsmith's erotic niece, Clio. But she shared Charles's interests in riding and frequently accompanied him out on the hunt.

Most importantly, she was a good listener. Charles had been taught to keep his hopes and ambitions to himself. As his father had advised, he had learnt to be wary of speaking his mind. It was understandable, therefore, that when he did find someone he could trust enough to talk to, it was very hard to stop him once he got started.

As a boy it had been Nanny Anderson who had fulfilled the role of confidante. She had been supplemented by the Queen Mother and, later, Lady Susan Hussey. Now, in the early bloom of his adulthood, it was Camilla who became his most intimate audience. 'Camilla was like a nanny to him,' one of her family observed. A member of the household explained, 'Prince Charles is a real loner. That's his basic nature and that is why somebody like Camilla is so terribly convenient, because she has got her own organized life and does not depend on him for anything but is always there at the drop of a hat for a little light chat and anything else that might imply.' Given Charles's immaturity, the consequence of an upbringing that had provided him with material comfort but little emotional succour, Camilla might have been an ideal wife for him.

It was a relationship not without its obstacles, however. She was not a virgin, having enjoyed romances with Kevin Burke, the son of aviation pioneer Sir Aubrey Burke, chairman of Hawker Siddeley, and with banking heir Rupert Hambro. She was a year older than Charles, a petty consideration but one that weighed against her at the time.

There was also the fact that she happened to be in love with Andrew Parker-Bowles, a dashing career officer in the cavalry and a notorious womanizer. Charles never asked Camilla to marry him; Parker-Bowles did and she accepted immediately.

125

That legal impediment did not take her out of Charles's royal circle. Parker-Bowles was a friend of Charles. He was also a relation, albeit a distant one: his Aunt Mary, one of the famous four daughters of the Derby-winning baronet Sir Humphrey de Trafford, was married to the Queen Mother's late cousin, Sir James Bowes Lyon.

It was a connection that gave him early entrée into the company of the royal family. He had known both Charles and Anne since childhood. Indeed, he might well have ended up as Charles's brother-in-law. In the early seventies Anne and Parker-Bowles enjoyed a passionate affair. Had he not been a Roman Catholic, the romance might well have ended in marriage. As it was, in 1973 he married Camilla. It was a union that allowed them both the independence to follow their own interests. He would rise to become the Colonel Commanding the Household Cavalry and Silver Stick-in-Waiting to the Queen and, eventually, the director of the Royal Army Veterinary Corps.

Camilla did not take to the role of army wife, much preferring the excitement of the hunting field to the cocktails-and-bitchery of the regimental round. So, while Parker-Bowles pursued his career, in London and sometimes abroad, she settled into the undemanding life of a landed country gentlewoman.

The arrangement appeared to suit both partners. Camilla remained on the closest of terms with Charles, while Parker-Bowles was able to maintain his own friendships. He continued to see a lot of Princess Anne and, when the opportunity arose, to make new friends.

In 1979 Parker-Bowles (the family name is Parker: the Bowles was acquired from a grandmother along with her fortune) was posted to Rhodesia as ADC to Lord Soames, the country's last Governor-General whose difficult task it was to oversee the country's transition from white minority rule to black democracy. While there he struck up a friendship with Louise Gubb, a blonde and beautiful Rhodesian-American photographer who worked for Associated Press. It was an association that led to

Right   Action man in the making, Australian style. (*Hulton Deutsch*)

Below   Action man triumphant: Charles in the RAF. (*Anwar Hussein*)

Above Charles with Lady
Jane Wellesley: the Queen
approved. (*Anwar Hussein*)

Right Sabrina Guinness was
less favoured. (*Topham*)

Left The relationship with
Mountbatten's granddaughter,
Amanda Knatchbull, did not
survive his assassination.
(*Tim Graham*)

Above Charles with his long-time friend and lover, the 'much-maligned' Camilla Parker-Bowles. (*Hulton Deutsch*)

Left Feisty, free-spirited Anna Wallace was too much for Charles to handle. (*Tim Graham*)

Right With his Australian confidante, 'Kanga' Tryon. (*SI*)

A healthy Diana with Princess Grace at the palace ball, shortly before the wedding. (*Anwar Hussein*)

Within six months, bulimia had taken its toll. (*Hulton Deutsch*)

A study in deception: Charles and Diana on their honeymoon at Balmoral.
(*Anwar Hussein*)

Above The carefully nurtured myth of the happy family, still intact in 1989. (*AP/Topham*)

Left The physical challenge of polo has long been Charles's safety valve. (*PA/Topham*)

Highgrove: Charles's home and spiritual retreat. (*Tim Graham*)

A couple apart, together at the Seville Expo, 1992. (*SI*)

Where now for the Queen and heir? (*Martin Keene/PA/Topham*)

one extremely embarrassing social moment when Charles flew in to preside over the independence ceremonies.

Parker-Bowles had been invited to the dinner party beforehand at Government House given by Lord and Lady Soames. So, naturally, had Louise Gubb. Charles's escort that evening was supposed to be a runner-up in the Miss Rhodesia contest. Three days before the dinner, however, Camilla telephoned from England and announced that she would be arriving in Salisbury the following day. Who, people wondered, was she coming to see – Charles or her husband?

Mary Soames was 'askance' but in the time-honoured way, the show had to go on and appearances maintained. 'And pray God the claret be good,' Lady Soames remarked to her husband.

Camilla, the Prince and the army officer carried off the evening with aplomb. As far as they were concerned, there was no loss of honour, no cause for upset, not in these circumstances which suited everyone's purpose – everyone, that is, except Louise who did not understand the rules of this upper-class British game and who, as one who comforted her afterwards recalled, was 'very upset by the whole situation'.

Louise eventually retreated to South Africa. The other three returned to Britain to continue what, in this modern age, would be criticized as the strangest of arrangements but which would have been perfectly understandable to Alice Keppel and the next generation of royal mistresses.

Much to the distress of her family, Parker-Bowles took up with Lord Soames's daughter Charlotte Hambro, the granddaughter of Sir Winston Churchill who later wed Earl Peel – and, by one of those not so rare coincidences, given the propensity of this circle to make love to each other, the former sister-in-law of Rupert Hambro who had once enjoyed a fling with Camilla.

Camilla, meanwhile, continued to make herself available to Charles, an appreciative voice at the end of the telephone, a welcoming face out on the hunting field, an obliging companion at cosy dinners. In the same way that Mrs Freda Dudley Ward, described by Thelma, Lady Furness, as his 'good habit', and Lady Furness herself offered comfort to the Duke of Windsor when he was Prince of Wales, so Camilla provided Charles with the kind of easy-going, undemanding fellowship he desired.

Matters were not progressing so well on the public front, however. Charles, who found it difficult to commit himself to anyone, would happily have carried on as he was, a bachelor increasingly set in his quirky ways. As the heir to the throne, however, it was beholden to him to secure the succession which meant acquiring a wife, and the clamour for him to do so was rising.

As usual, Lord Mountbatten had a solution. It came in the not unattractive form of his own granddaughter, Amanda Knatchbull, also Charles's second cousin. Having married his nephew Philip to the future Queen Elizabeth, it would have been the fulfilment of his all-consuming dynastic ambitions to have married his granddaughter to the future King and he came closer to achieving that coup than is generally known.

Charles had known Amanda since earliest childhood. She had always called him Charles, unlike every other girlfriend who had to call him 'Sir'. She was, as Mountbatten carefully pointed out to Charles, a member of the family, and as such fully understood the responsibilities that went with the job. If Camilla was the ideal mistress, Mountbatten insisted, then Amanda would be the perfect wife. He did everything he could to encourage that notion and under his charming, overpowering influence, the couple started to see each other in a romantic light.

They went on holiday together, to the Caribbean island of Eleuthera where Amanda's parents had a home. Charles asked her to marry him, only to be rebuffed by the remark, 'What a funny idea.'

On Mountbatten's prompting the courtship continued. Charles gave her a gold bracelet. Mountbatten organized a £3000 wardrobe so that she could start looking the part he had in mind for her. Charles became an increasingly frequent visitor to

Broadlands where Amanda just happened to be. They also enjoyed quieter moments together.

When Charles had been up at Cambridge, the Queen had given him the use of Wood Farm on the Sandringham estate. A pleasant house at the end of a tree-lined drive, it had once been the home of George V's epileptic son Prince John, who had lived there until his death in 1919.

When Charles took it over it was refurbished, but only in the simplest manner which enhanced its homely, relaxed atmosphere. Indeed, so taken was the Queen with the house she had ostensibly given away, that she was soon using it herself for long periods of the year. Prince Philip also became enamoured with it and converted a barn which he joined to the house, so adding enough bedrooms to entertain almost the entire family.

Charles still had call on it, though, and when he took Amanda there, they had what was still a comparatively modest house to themselves. They were looked after by Mrs Hazel the cook-cum-housekeeper and Rosa the housemaid, but they only came in during the day; for once there was no accompanying army of gossiping servants. Amanda was put up in the Queen's rooms while Charles had the room opposite where Prince Philip slept when he was there. During the hunting season Charles would drive over to Leicestershire and Amanda would go with him. On other days they would walk along one of the nearby beaches where they would picnic.

Afternoon tea would be served back at the house at five o'clock. After an early evening bath the couple would reconvene for dinner which they served for themselves off the hot plate on the trolley. Often they would take it through to eat off their laps in front of the fire in the sitting room.

No one bothered them. The help had gone home while the detective who accompanied Charles everywhere stayed in his room. They were alone, conducting a courtship in the way in which Charles's aunt, Princess Margaret, had advised him.

129

By the summer of 1979, just after Charles had reached the thirty-year deadline he had set himself, there was a luncheon in the Queen's private dining room at Buckingham Palace. It was attended by the Queen, Prince Philip, Lord Mountbatten, Prince Charles and Amanda Knatchbull. Members of the Household believed that the final arrangements for an engagement to be announced in early 1980 were discussed that day. At the very least, it clearly signified that the romance was well on the course upon which Mountbatten, the dynastic navigator *par excellence*, had set it.

To make sure it stayed there, Mountbatten arranged for Amanda to accompany Charles on a tour to India at the end of the year. Prince Philip put his foot down when his uncle said that he was going to accompany them himself, pointing out that his return to the sub-continent that he had once ruled as viceroy would detract from Charles's presence. When Lord Brabourne, his son-in-law and father of Amanda, agreed with Philip, Mountbatten reluctantly agreed to back out – but only so far. He still planned to accompany Charles and Amanda on the flight after which they would go their separate ways, to meet up occasionally and for a few days at the end of the tour. 'From a purely selfish point of view I must confess I would be very, very sad to have to forgo the great happiness of being with two young people I love so much and showing them the country which means so much to me, but if the price of my selfishness were to spoil the visit for you, then that would be a price I could not even contemplate.'

Mountbatten was never called upon to make that sacrifice. On 27 August 1979, while on holiday at Classiebawn in County Sligo which had come into his possession when he married Edwina, he was blown up by the IRA. Also killed were his fourteen-year-old grandson, Nicholas Knatchbull, and Paul Maxwell, a local Irish boy. His daughter-in-law, Lady Brabourne, died in hospital the next day.

Charles, fishing in Iceland with the Tryons when he heard the news, was overwhelmed and crushed. He broke down in tears, much to the dismay of his father, who maintained the stiff upper lip expected of the military man he had been. This was one occasion, however, when Charles could not have cared less what his waspish-tongued father thought or said.

The IRA announced that Mountbatten had been 'executed' in order to bring 'emotionally home to the English ruling class and its working-class slaves' that the 'war' would continue until they tore out 'their sentimental, imperialist heart'. They had certainly succeeded in tearing the heart out of Charles.

He went to Windsor and spent hours sitting looking out over the countryside from the east terrace where he had spent so many happy, fulfilling hours in Mountbatten's company. He read Psalm 107 at the funeral service at Westminster Abbey, the one which begins, 'They that go down to the sea in ships . . .' His graveside wreath read "To HGF from HGS' (to honorary grandfather from honorary grandson). He delivered the address at the memorial service at St Paul's Cathedral. It was a passionate entreaty delivered with tears in his eyes.

'Does it not seem a cruel and bitter irony,' Charles asked, 'that a man who served under Admiral Beatty in his flagship during the first war, who in the second was torpedoed, mined and finally sunk by aerial bombardment in HMS *Kelly*, who helped defeat the scourge of tyranny and oppression throughout Europe and the Far East and finally ensured that independence should be brought to the continent of India – that a man with such passionate concern for the individual and for progressive thought and action should suddenly and mercilessly be blown to bits with members of the family he adored through the agency of some of the most cowardly minds imaginable?'

Charles's affection for the departed warrior was palpable. He could, Charles acknowledged, be 'ruthless', but his 'infectious enthusiasm, his sheer capacity for hard work, his wit made him an irresistible leader among men'.

Once the eulogies had been delivered and the tour to India

postponed, the Prince went into retreat at Balmoral where he was joined by his cousin, Norton Knatchbull. The two men, who had never been close, despite their time together at Gordonstoun, found common ground in the tragedy. They went over the subject again and again, as they tried to give reason to the utter irrationality of their loss.

Charles's strong religious faith helped him through. So did the memory of Mountbatten's good work; as he noted in his memorial service address, his great-uncle 'was desperately trying to sow the seeds of peace for future generations'.

It was to provide Charles with an example. If there is a guiding principle to his commitments, it is to provide encouragement to the young via such diverse means as the Prince's Trust, the Outward Bound-style Operation Raleigh, and the various youth employment schemes he champions.

What did not survive the assassination was the romance with Amanda.

Had Mountbatten lived, as many in the Household believe, Charles would have married Amanda and the future history of the Royal Family would have been duller but a lot more secure.

Without Mountbatten's indomitable enthusiasm to prop it up and at the same time propel it forward, it withered under the weight of mutual apathy. There simply was not the passion there to carry them through. That had not mattered in the past. Indeed, Queen Mary would have been aghast at the suggestion that a royal marriage was anything more than a necessary and not particularly pleasant act of State. Mountbatten continued to argue that arranged marriages ultimately had a better chance of survival than those built on the shifting sand of love and in that he had the support of Prince Philip who, when appraised of his uncle's plan, remarked, 'Good, it beats having strangers coming into the family!'

Amanda's parents took an altogether more modern view of how best their daughter's life might be lived. She had a right to expect more and Charles, who had no great desire to get married, agreed. They parted on the best of terms, like brother and sister, which was how they had regarded each other before the great matchmaker had involved them in his last and grandest scheme.

Amanda went off to make a life of her own, away from the Royal Family. Charles, meanwhile, continued on his search. His attention was soon taken by Anna Wallace, the high-spirited daughter of Hamish Wallace, who owned considerable estates in the Midlands. They may not have been as close, Anna admitted, as people might have thought but there is no doubt that Charles was besotted by her. He wrote her a large number of letters, invited her to Windsor Castle and Buckingham Palace, introduced her to his family and for a while generally behaved like a man in love.

That did not please Hamish who, like many members of the British upper class, held an ambivalent attitude towards the Royal Family and considered the heir to the throne a less than ideal suitor for his daughter. He refused to buy her a wardrobe befitting a prince's attentions and she had to make do with one Zandra Rhodes frock for grand occasions.

She was none the less flattered enough by Charles's attentions to continue seeing him. She also found his gaucheness endearing, which was just as well because Charles was certainly no James Bond, armed with impenetrable *savoir-faire*.

On one visit to Windsor Anna asked for a glass of champagne. Charles scurried away, only to return with a bottle of brown ale he had appropriated from one of the guardsmen. 'Mummy's got the keys to the drinks cabinet,' he explained.

On another occasion Charles's mood was irretrievably upset by the Incident of the Tablecloth. He was entertaining his date to dinner in the nursery, which, given the signposts of the Prince's psychology, was a great honour that pointed in a significant direction. The evening was ruined before it even began, however, by an over-enthusiastic footman who laid the fine antique table in what one member of the Household called a 'grown-up fashion'.

133

Off came the tablecloth, on went the silver candlesticks and some elegant table mats.

When Charles saw what had been done he sat down, put his head in his hands and started to moan, 'I want a tablecloth.' It transpired that for as long as he could remember, Nanny Anderson had used a tablecloth on that particular table and Charles, who retains an infant's clinging grip on the totems of his childhood, could not bear to see it without one. By then it was too late to do anything about it; dinner was about to be served.

Anna managed to take such setbacks in her elegant stride and the romance appeared to be progressing at a suitable pace. It was, however, very much a one-sided love affair. For while Charles may have lain awake at night pining for this tempestuous, free-spirited woman, Anna most certainly did not stay at home waiting for his telephone call. She continued to see banker Alan Morris, and Lord Hesketh's brother, Johnny Fermoy-Hesketh, who she was destined soon to marry. That inevitably became known to Charles's security men who considered it part of their duty to check on the background and behaviour of anyone Charles took an interest in. It did not require sophisticated bugging equipment or illicit tape recordings to ascertain what Anna was up to; the old-fashioned, less technical but still efficient method of street surveillance served just as well.

At the height of their relationship Anna had moved into an apartment just off the King's Road in Chelsea. Charles visited there only once, when he was invited for dinner. Anna at the time was working as personal assistant to Persian-born Homayoun Mazandi, who later married Lord Renwick. To help the evening along Homayoun lent Anna her cook and butler.

Matters did not work out as they might have, however. The food was delicious, the candle-lit atmosphere romantic, the service discreet, but Charles made his apologies and left before midnight. Anna went out shortly afterwards to see Morris. That did not escape the notice of the security men who had accom-

134

panied the Prince to Anna's home and Charles never again visited there.

There had been other mishaps along the way to the dénouement. There was the well-reported occasion when Anna was said to have angrily hissed at Charles, 'Don't ever ignore me like that again – I've never been treated so badly in my life,' after he abandoned her at the Queen Mother's eightieth birthday party at Windsor Castle. She denied the incident ('I would never be so rude,' she said). But there was no denying that Anna, whose fiery disposition had earned her the nickname, Whiplash, had no intention of playing wallflower while Charles toured the room or, worse, spent much of the evening dancing with Camilla Parker-Bowles, which is exactly what he did at a polo ball at Lord Vestey's Stowell Park in Gloucestershire a few weeks later. She was too independent and too attractive to play second fiddle to anyone, even a prince.

At one point, though, Charles had been hers for the asking. He invited her to Balmoral to meet the Queen. He told her that they would be the only people there. It was the moment Charles intended to ask her to marry him. He never got the chance. She refused to go to Scotland. 'Too tedious for words,' she said afterwards. Charles, used to getting his own way, was humiliated. It would not be allowed to happen again and it did not.

Within a year Charles had married Lady Diana Spencer.

Chapter Eight

Lady Diana Spencer hove into Charles's romantic sights in Cowes in the Isle of Wight in the first week of August 1980. The timing was right and Diana seized her moment with a cunning that belied her years. Charles was still depressed by the failure of his romance with Anna Wallace who had left him with the distinct feeling of romantic inadequacy. Introspective, wary of arguments, unused to being contradicted, he had shown himself incapable of dealing with an independent, emotionally charged woman. Diana looked to offer a tranquil alternative. She was very eager to please. She was attractive in a long-limbed way that was bound to stand out in the dowdy world in which Charles moved. And, no small consideration, she was too young to offer further threat to his bruised ego. Or so it seemed, and Diana went out of her way to maintain the appearance of compliant innocence.

Not everyone was taken in. The Prince's valet, Stephen Barry, firmly declared, 'She went after the Prince with single-minded determination. She wanted him – and she got him!'

Barry would be punished for his perception the moment she was married. In those early days, however, it was still smiles all round as Diana set about ingratiating herself with the Prince.

At the age of sixteen, in a remark that owed more to adolescent fantasy of the kind expounded in her step-grandmother Barbara Cartland's novelettes than Machiavellian plotting, Diana told friends that she was 'out to get Charles'. Within two years, though, the childish dream had hardened into ambition.

In the summer of 1979 Diana went to Scotland to stay with her sister Jane, who was married to Robert Fellowes, the Queen's assistant private secretary. After becoming Diana's own private secretary he would, by vicious irony, be faced with the impossible task of trying to contain the damage his sister-in-law caused within the Royal Family. The Queen had given Fellowes, the son of her Sandringham land agent, a cottage on the Balmoral estate three miles up a lane from the castle. By having Diana to stay he helped create the situation he would later have given his career to avoid.

Diana was there to help look after Jane's new-born daughter, Laura. It was a task that allowed her plenty of free time which she used to wander around the estate. 'You had the idea she wanted to be seen,' one estate worker recalled.

The Prince she hoped was doing the watching was not Charles, who at that time was still heavily ensconced with Amanda Knatchbull, but his brother, Andrew, her intellectual equal who was also her own age. She would later joke: 'Of course, it was Andrew I should have married really.' She had quickly readjusted her sights, however, after that visit to the royal yacht *Britannia*.

Diana had known the royal family since earliest childhood. Her father, Johnny Althorp, the future Earl Spencer, had been an ADC to the Queen, and Diana's early life was spent at Park House, the ten-bedroom Victorian mansion on the Sandringham estate her father leased from the Queen. Built by Edward VII to accommodate the overflow of guests, it stands only 200 yards from Sandringham's back entrance.

The Queen and the Queen Mother exercised their dogs in the field that ran behind the house. Andrew and Edward had played in its nursery and she had been taken up to the big house for tea and parties. She first met Charles, as she recalled, 'when I was still wearing nappies. I've known him all my life.' She was quite literally the girl next door.

But no matter how close anyone might get in the physical sense, the Royal Family always keeps its distance, and boarding school and the move to Althorp House in Northamptonshire on the death in 1975 of her grandfather, the seventh Earl, had taken her out of the royal orbit. She did not rejoin it until 1978 when Jane married Robert Fellowes. Diana was bridesmaid at their wedding and regularly went to stay with them at their new grace-and-favour apartment in Kensington Palace where Princess Margaret and her daughter, Sarah Armstrong-Jones, also lived.

Diana made a point of making friends with Sarah, who was almost three years her junior but happened to be very close to her cousin Charles. It was Sarah who invited Diana aboard *Britannia*.

She did not make a blinding first impression on the Prince. 'She was really just a shy, giggling girl,' as one who was aboard the yacht recalled, 'who was trying to be on her best behaviour.' Charles's interest was mild at most. It was enough, though, to entice Diana back up to Scotland a few weeks later. She again stayed with Jane, and again made a regular point of displaying herself on those walks through the grounds which somehow always brought her before the castle walls. This time the display worked and she was invited to spend four days at the castle.

She used her time well. A member of the Household recalled: 'Most of the ladies do not get up until after the guns have gone out, but Diana was always up at the crack of dawn – if you looked out of your window at a quarter to eight you would see her walking in the garden – and made a great point of being there to see them off.'

It was now that she played her sharpest card. 'She would go around telling everybody how much she loved Balmoral and that it was such a magical place and how she loved it beyond imagination,' the member of the Household continued. Charles started asking her to accompany him fishing. He asked her to join him on long walks through the estate in which she professed such an interest.

Charles, under pressure from both Queen and public to find himself a suitable wife, adores Balmoral. He has an almost spiritual attachment to its glens and mountains which he is delighted to share with anyone who shows the faintest glimmer of interest, so Diana 'knew full well what she was doing by saying she thought it was such a magical place', according to a member of the Household.

On those walks Diana often wore the knickerbockers that became one of her early fashion trademarks. There was no trace, though, of the shyness which became an even more famous one. The bashful, peek-a-boo glances from behind a fringe came later, and then only for the benefit of the press cameras. On that first visit to Balmoral she was outgoing, vivacious, and 'extremely' friendly, to staff and fellow guests alike.

Charles was suitably impressed, as he had every reason to be, for in those early days, before illness and unhappiness took their toll, Diana, everyone agreed, was 'enchanting'. The Queen, so one of her Household remembered, 'would have been much happier if Charles had married Jane Wellesley or Amanda Knatchbull but she had reached the stage when she thought that Diana was better than nobody'. In other words, she did not object, an important consideration in a family where collective approval usually takes precedence over individual desire.

The Queen Mother took a more positive approach. Shortly after that first visit to Balmoral she invited Diana and Charles back for a few days at Birkhall, her house on the estate. It was a grandmotherly intervention and in that she had been encouraged by Diana's own grandmother, Ruth, Lady Fermoy, who was one of the Queen Mother's oldest friends. The two old ladies were both very fond of the gambolling nineteen-year-old and would prove her vital allies in the months ahead as flirtation escalated into a rush towards marriage and Charles, who was never very sure of the wisdom of what he was doing, sought reassurance.

The Queen Mother, who would come to dislike Diana intensely, had no reason at that stage to be anything other than supportive of the young woman whom she had known since birth. And if Lady Fermoy chose to overlook some of the glaring flaws in Diana's character, who could blame a grandmother's indulgence when the future looked so bright?

Princess Anne did not take to her. She would come to refer to her as 'a silly girl'. But Charles was certainly not going to be swayed by the opinion of his younger sister and it was soon obvious that Diana had succeeded, where older and more sophisticated women had failed, in capturing, if not the heart then the commitment of the Prince of Wales. And it was precisely because she was so young and apparently ingenuous that she had succeeded where others had failed. 'She'll keep me young,' he would remark on his engagement day.

Once back in London, Charles started to invite Diana out. It was all very discreet and low key – but for those familiar with Charles's courtship pattern, the signs were obvious. In October he took her to the ballet and paid her the singular honour of inviting her to Buckingham Palace first. She arrived in her Mini Metro just after 6.30 in the evening, drove through the archway into the quadrangle and was shown up in the lift to Charles's apartment on the second floor.

Other girls had been up to his quarters. Indeed, only a few months earlier Anna Wallace had watched the rehearsals for the Trooping the Colour from there. But only Amanda Knatchbull had been given the Buckingham Palace treatment on a date before, so Diana's presence there was quite enough to fuel Charles's staff's speculation.

It was given further impetus when she was invited in November to Wood Farm to celebrate Charles's thirty-second birthday. It was confirmed when she arrived at Sandringham in January. She made a point of going into the nursery and making a great fuss of Mabel Anderson, who was then looking after Princess Anne's son Peter Phillips but remained the emotional lynchpin in Charles's life. And when the guns went out early in the morning, Diana was always there to wave them off with an ingratiating remark about how 'wonderful' Sandringham was.

'She was everywhere, picking up the birds, being terribly gracious and absolutely oozing charm,' a royal confidante remembered. 'And she looked marvellous, very relaxed and quite thrilled with herself.'

The same could not be said of Charles. If Diana was indeed 'home and dry', as one of his staff put it, by January, the Prince remained his usual reserved self. 'He certainly didn't look as though he had just found the most wonderful girl in the world,' a member of the Household said. But, then, that was not what Prince Charles was looking for. As he once explained, he was looking for 'someone whose interests I could share' and who could share his. 'A woman', he continued, 'not only marries a man, she marries into a way of life, a job.' That was especially true in his case and Charles explained in great detail to Diana the demands that would be placed on her if she became his wife. She was left in no doubt whatsoever what her duties would be.

They also discussed the age gap. Diana had at first been concerned by the twelve-year difference but that soon got lost in the excitement of the courtship which was rushing them both along at a speed over which they soon lost control.

The press, on to a circulation winner with this one, had taken to publishing detailed biographies of every woman Charles had said hello to. The public, rising to the journalistic bait, flocked to see him with each contender in the Future Queen of England stakes. He was being subtly chivvied at home too. The Queen would never have dreamt of bursting into Charles's apartment and demanding his immediate marriage, which was one story doing the rounds at the time. Rather, there would be gentle hints of the 'she seems a very nice girl' sort. And a very nice girl was exactly what Diana appeared to be.

There were other pluses on her check list. In the cynical business of vetting a royal bride-to-be such things as family background, education and, in the case of a prospective Princess of Wales, previous form had to be taken into consideration. Diana passed on all counts.

141

The Queen knew all she thought there was to know about the Spencers, who had served the royal family in one capacity or other for ten generations, and regarded them as solid enough stock. On the educational front Diana had been a notable under-achiever (a prize for looking after her pet hamster stands out), but that certainly did not count against her with a family that takes a perverse pride in its anti-intellectualism.

Nor did her romantic experiences offer any impediment to her progress. Expressing a view that was widely shared by the royal family, Earl Mountbatten had advised his great-nephew: 'For a wife [you] should choose a suitable, attractive and sweet-charactered girl before she has met anyone else she might fall for. I think it is disturbing for women to have experiences if they have to remain on a pedestal after marriage.'

Diana had had her admirers. They included George Plumptre, who went on to make a career writing books about gardening, and Old Etonian Simon Berry, a member of the family of St James's wine merchants. They had dined out together in the cheap and cheerful Chelsea restaurants favoured by the upper-class set. Sometimes they would eat at home and Diana, who had attended a Cordon Bleu cookery course, would make scrambled eggs. She had been skiing with Berry and sixteen other friends. She had once been infatuated with a lieutenant in the Scots Guards named Rory Scott and used to take his shirts back to her flat to wash.

There had been no physical conclusion to these relationships, however. As Diana herself declared, there was no past waiting to be exposed because she simply did not have one. Her uncle, Lord Fermoy, put it more gracelessly when he announced: 'She, I can assure you, has never had a lover.' Diana, in other words, was a virgin. And while that, as Sarah Ferguson proved, was not a prerequisite for marrying into the Windsors, it did make the handling of what was becoming a very public courtship that little bit simpler.

Put it all together, and ferment it with Diana's uncanny ability instantly to charm most people she meets, and it made a very attractive package. But all was not as it seemed: as the Royal Family discovered to its enormous cost, the ingredients which looked so appealing at first glance were also the ones that would cause all the problems later on.

There was the underlying emotional inconsistency in Diana's family. Her maternal uncle, Edmond Fermoy, was a manic depressive who shot himself in 1984. Her mother deserted her husband. Her father was subject to uncontrolled outbursts of temper and physically abused her mother. Charles once remarked: 'I was told that before you marry the daughter you should first look at the mother.' It was advice he might have done well to follow.

There was the educational deficit which made it hard for her to see her role in its historical perspective or to comprehend the sequential need, if her marriage was going to be made to work, for a little professional humility.

At the core of these difficulties was her desire for attention and affection. They were her addictions. She craved them, the way a junkie craves heroin. She demanded them from her husband. When he failed to supply them in sufficient quantities, she switched to dealers who could.

Charles, so self-sufficient himself, was incapable of dealing with a problem which at first he did not even recognize. If he had, both he and Diana would have been spared years of unhappiness which culminated in the ridiculous sight of the Prince who had wanted to stay single pleading with the woman who had so wanted to get married not to leave him.

Charles, had he been more fortunate or experienced enough to know how to look, would have found out more about Diana before he took the fateful step of asking her to marry him, but this was one courtship that was never going to expose the fault lines in the characters of the protagonists. Relationships need time and a certain amount of privacy to develop. Theirs had had neither. They were constantly on show and that brought out the best in Diana who had a natural flair bordering on genius for turning the spotlight of publicity to her own advantage.

The Royal Family detested the attention she attracted. During her visit to Sandringham Prince Edward fired a shotgun over the heads of the photographers, Charles told the assembled reporters that he hoped their editors had an unhappy New Year and even the Queen, normally so patient and polite, became irritated enough to shout, 'Why don't you all go away?'

It was a harbinger of worse to come but even then there was nothing the Royal Family could do to stop it. For the public, as they could not fail to note, had fallen in love with Diana. So had the reporters assigned to follow her. She was a journalist's dream (literally so in the case of photographer Kent Gavin of the *Daily Mirror* who complained that she appeared in his dreams every night framed as if in a camera lens). She was obliging, vivacious, photogenic and always helpful. In a letter to *The Times* her mother complained that Diana was being 'harassed' by unscrupulous pressmen who were inventing 'lies' about her.

Frances Shand Kydd completely misunderstood the situation and her daughter's role in it. Rather than discouraging the attention, Diana went out of her way to court it. She never ran so fast from the 'rat pack' of royal reporters that they could not catch up in time to get a quote from her and another photograph for the front pages. The shy look, she found, was particularly popular with the photographers and she gave them lots of it.

She also became friendly with many of the journalists, especially James Whitaker of the *Daily Mirror* whom she invited into her flat for off-the-record chats. It was her early work experience of using the press to her advantage and in private she went to the length of disassociating herself from her mother's remarks. It would have been hypocritical if she had not – it was the press, after all, who, by portraying her in such glowing terms, had all but ensured that Charles would make her his wife. And that was what she was determined to become. Charles, she would quickly discover, was not the right man for her but in that flush of infatuation she was not looking for the defects in her suitor. Charles was her Prince and that was good enough.

She did not have long to wait. At the end of January, Charles flew to Klosters for his annual skiing holiday. Upon his return he invited Diana to join him for dinner at Windsor. It was almost exactly six months to the day since she had walked aboard *Britannia* and it was just before she was due to fly to Australia for a holiday with her mother and stepfather, Peter Shand Kydd. 'I chose the moment so that she would have plenty of time to think about it, to decide if it was all going to be too awful,' said Charles naïvely, as if there really was a chance that Diana was going to say no.

The dinner took place in the middle of the week when the Royal Family is usually in London. Charles insisted on returning to the castle (at no small inconvenience to the entourage of valets and footmen who had to bring the food down from Buckingham Palace) for this significant occasion. The reason was poignant and reveals much about the Prince's character: Charles wanted to propose in the secure surroundings of his old nursery.

Without the help of nostalgia's rose tint, there was nothing particularly romantic about the nursery sitting room at Windsor Castle. It is a large room painted in a pale shade of green with a pale green carpet laid in the old tram-rail style. There is a television set and a fireplace in one corner and set on its mantelpiece is a photograph in a leather frame of the Queen and Philip taken in the 1950s. On the walls hung pictures of Queen Victoria's grandchildren. The sofa was covered in a pink linen material which matched the day cloth on the dining table.

That was changed to white linen for the visit of Diana. After the Incident of the Tablecloth no attempt was made to brighten the room to fit the occasion. There were no candles. The food served was cold poached salmon and salad followed by fresh fruit. There was not even any champagne. Instead Diana and Charles were served Malvern water and lemon refreshers, the concoction

145

of lemon squash and Epsom salts that was supposed to 'keep the Prince regular'.

The wording of the proposal was typically Charles. He recalled saying, 'If I were to ask, what do you think you might answer?'

Yes, was the reply. 'It wasn't a difficult decision,' Diana said. 'It was what I wanted.'

It ended with a kiss, but no more. Charles retired early to his apartment on the top floor of the Queen's Tower; Diana slept the night in a single bed in the Shelter Rooms on the ground floor. There was no backstair creeping and Diana drove herself home the following morning. She left before breakfast.

Even by the mundane standards of royal courtship, it was not exactly an auspicious moment in what the Archbishop of Canterbury would later feel moved to call a 'fairytale' romance.

The engagement was formally announced at 11.00 a.m. on Tuesday, 24 February 1981 (*The Times* had the story on its front page that morning, courtesy of a leak by the former Prime Minister Sir Edward Heath). Charles and Diana were in Charles's office with a few close members of his staff to listen to the announcement on the radio. 'The atmosphere was not very natural,' one who was there recalled. 'The reaction was really rather muted.'

Charles appeared determined to remain calm and unmoved. As he walked along the corridors of Buckingham Palace, receiving the congratulations of the staff, he seemed distant and distracted. 'You might have been wishing him Happy Birthday for all the reaction you got,' one said.

When Diana was asked by a television reporter if she was in love she immediately answered, 'Of course.' Charles paused for a moment before replying, 'Yes . . . whatever that may mean.' Charles did not seem to know. When he put his arm around Diana as they walked down the corridor, 'he might have been with Princess Anne', one member of the Household remarked.

Diana, for whom marriage was all about falling in love, looked 'coy and bewildered', as one observer remembered. 'She certainly didn't seem to be as thrilled as she had been.' She had won the Prince's hand. As she may already have intuitively sensed, winning his heart would prove beyond her. She equated that with undivided attention and that was something Charles would not give, even if he had been able to. He was not like the last Prince of Wales, who had been so besotted with Mrs Wallis Simpson that he had sacrificed his throne to his passion. For Charles, as for his mother before him, duty was far more important than ardour. To him marriage was not an emotional union of the kind poets write about: it was more an act of state than a declaration of the heart. 'Creating a secure family unit in which to bring up children, to give them a happy, secure upbringing – that is what marriage is all about,' Charles once explained. 'Marriage is more important than just falling in love.'

They were the remarks of a prince who had been brought up to believe that the individual must take second place to the institution. Diana did not share her fiancé's sense of dynastic responsibility. She had a little girl's idea of what being a princess was all about and, right from the outset, she found the reality of royal life tedious and restrictive. But there was no escaping it now. Out of schoolgirlish desire and her own decision over that frugal dinner at Windsor Castle, Diana had effectively surrendered her independence. Henceforth her life would be a royal one, with all that entailed.

It began a few days before her engagement. For her own safety, she moved out of her bachelor flat in Earl's Court in West London and into, first, Clarence House as a guest of the Queen Mother, then a few days later into Buckingham Palace where, it was expected, she would eventually reside as Queen Consort.

The woman destined to become the world's most photographed clothes horse arrived with two suitcases. She was nervous. She was soon very lonely. And, despite what she may have expected, she was most certainly not the centre of attention.

It started off well enough, though. Before Charles went to Australia and New Zealand on official royal business he took

Diana to Scotland. They went up on the royal train with Nicholas Soames and his wife, Catherine, to spend a few days at Craigowan, a small shooting lodge on the Balmoral estate. It was a much-needed respite after the hurly-burly of the previous few weeks and as informal as anything that Charles did could ever be. (Whereas Anne really did do everything herself, Charles always needed a retinue of servants on hand to keep the wheels of informality turning.)

Their time was spent walking and picnicking and barbecuing in the log cabin given to the Queen by the people of Finland. The royal party would set off early in the morning in a Land-Rover towing a trailer, which was really a chest of drawers on wheels in which the stainless steel cutlery and plates were kept. After cooking their lunch of steaks, chops and sausages, eaten with a salad prepared by the kitchen staff and clearing up afterwards themselves (a house rule at Balmoral), the afternoons were spent walking or, in Charles's case, fishing. Everyone stayed out until as late as possible, before returning home to bath and change into corduroys for an 8.30 p.m. dinner eaten with more stainless steel cutlery. They usually retired early and, in keeping with Charles's sense of decorum, Diana slept in the bedroom usually reserved for the Queen, while he had the Duke of Edinburgh's dressing room.

Diana was in captivating form and still insisting how 'magical' the place was. It was, everyone agreed, a welcome and relaxing break and the mood was still cheerful when Charles returned from the Antipodes.

The engaged couple were reunited at Balmoral. Charles, Diana noted, greeted her with nothing more exciting than a peck on the cheek. Her spirits were still 'buoyant', however. She readily posed for photographs with the Prince and a golden retriever called Harvey. She wore her shooting 'breeks', a sweater with several white and one black sheep on it, and a smile that was both ready and real.

The idyll did not last. A few days later Diana was back in

London with the gates of Buckingham Palace shut behind her. She was installed in a suite of rooms on (where else?) the nursery floor. Her apartment, which was between Prince Andrew's bedroom and his and Prince Edward's brushing room, where the footmen pressed their clothes and polished their shoes, consisted of bedroom, sitting room, bathroom and nursery kitchen. It was comfortable and cosy but that did not make it a happy time for Diana. This was the period when, in a very informal way, she was expected to learn the royal ropes. She was not a willing pupil. Lady Susan Hussey and Oliver Everett, Charles's assistant private secretary, were assigned the task of tutoring. It was a thankless one.

Diana took an immediate dislike to Lady Susan. She found her intimidating and bossy and went out of her way to avoid her. Everett fared little better. It was his job to teach her how to walk properly in readiness for her marriage and he would parade her up and down the palace ballroom with yards of tissue paper attached to her head and dragging on the floor behind her in imitation of her wedding train.

On the broader front, it fell to Everett to instruct her about the job of wife of the Prince of Wales and future Queen Consort for which she had applied with such enthusiasm and for which she had just been accepted. There is no school for princesses. Trainees have to learn by previous example and, for that reason, Everett gave her James Pope-Hennessy's biography of Charles's great-grandmother, Queen Mary, and Georgina Battiscombe's authoritative account of his great-great-grandmother, Queen Alexandra.

They had both been Princess of Wales, he explained. He told her he thought it would be useful if she read them and learnt how they coped with the role she was about to assume. After Everett left the room Diana threw the books on to the floor where they lay until a footman picked them up. 'If he thinks I'm going to read those silly, boring books he's got another think coming,' she raged. 'I don't need them, and I won't read them.'

She never did read the books, though there was no question in the minds of those who were employed to serve her that Diana needed all the help she could get as she struggled to come to terms with her new position. She found it hard going. Even dealing with the staff caused her difficulties. Well-mannered to a fault, Charles would always end an order with, 'if you don't mind'. It was not a question, simply a courtesy. Diana adopted an altogether more familiar approach. It was not always well received; the hierarchical system applied below as much as it did above stairs. When Diana started to make unwelcome visits to the kitchens, the Yeoman of the Glass and China gave her a sharp lesson in class divisions. Pointing to the door, he declared, 'Through there is *your* side of the house – and through here is *my* side of the house.'

The future Princess beat a blushing retreat, never to return. Other young women might have made a joke out of the incident but Diana was not in humorous mood by this stage. Whatever she had dreamed of, this was not it. She was irritable, bored and desperately lonely. And below the surface, another problem was about to make its destructive presence felt.

Charles was not there to see the change overtaking his fiancée. His New Zealand and Australia tours were followed by one to Venezuela. He went there in his capacity as head of the United World Colleges, which was an international group of sixth form colleges founded by Lord Mountbatten for the idealistic purpose of promoting international peace and understanding. From the end of April through into May he was in the United States where he received an honorary fellowship from the College of William and Mary at Williamsburg in Virginia. When he was in Britain he spent very few evenings with Diana. There was always some official dinner to attend which had been written into his agenda before the engagement.

Diana, left to her own devices, started to complain – that Charles was not paying her enough attention, that the Queen was ignoring her. If true – and the demands of royal duty had been explained to her before she agreed to become engaged – the neglect was neither intentional nor ill meant. Charles had his long-planned schedule to fulfil, as had the Queen, who would none the less have liked to have seen more of her prospective daughter-in-law. The Palace is a working office with bedrooms over 'the shop', as Philip called it. It is not a place for lingering luncheons or cosy chats. And the Queen most certainly was not to be found chatting to visitors propped up in bed on lace pillows, which, so one member of the Palace staff remarked, 'was what Diana seemed to expect'. If her day was never as arduous as it was sometimes portrayed, it kept her busy enough.

She always made time, though, for her children – and by royal definition they now included Diana – who would ring through on the internal telephone and ask if she had anyone with her. If the answer was no, they knew they were welcome to join her for an informal lunch or dinner. That system had been carefully explained to Diana when she arrived at the Palace but she did not once telephone the Queen's page. Concerned, the Queen did the telephoning herself to ask Diana down to her apartment. She soon stopped doing that because, she said, 'She doesn't want to come and have a stuffy old dinner with me.'

But by then Diana was not interested in lunch or dinner or indeed food of any kind.

Chapter Nine

Diana hated herself in her engagement photographs.

'I look hideous!' she said. 'I'm so fat. I'll have to lose weight.'

Charles tried to reassure her. In his stiff, formal way, he told her that was not true, that she was really a beautiful woman. So, in an altogether more relaxed way, did the staff. It made no difference.

'Do you think so?' she would ask before answering her own question. 'I'm so ugly!' she insisted.

She started an exercise programme under the guidance of a private teacher, Nellie Smith, who gave her an hour's session twice a week in the Palace's Bow Room. She also swam regularly in the Palace pool.

But whatever shape she was looking for was not to be seen in the photographs she took such an interest in. In what became an obsession, she looked at them in the newspapers every morning, comparing the different photographs and pointing out the ones she liked. The papers never ceased to compliment her, on her style, her good looks, her inherent chic. Even the black taffeta dress with its plunging *décolletage* that she chose to wear at her first official engagement with Charles – a poetry reading at the Goldsmiths' Hall – earned their approval.

'It was clearly her way of telling the world: "This is me, Diana Spencer. I'm not just the fiancée of the Prince of Wales,"' one tabloid journalist wrote approvingly.

The reaction at the Palace was notably more muted. There

were raised eyebrows when the 'papers were examined the next morning. Diana took umbrage. 'I don't know why everyone is making such a fuss,' she said. 'It's the sort of dress I would have worn anyway.'

But that, as the Palace courtiers tried to point out as gently as possible, was just the point; that it was not 'anyway' any more, that Diana was supposed to be a future Queen of England, and that it was time to cover herself up.

This was one piece of advice Diana did not mind following. She had not felt particularly comfortable in the dress which, despite all her protestations, had not really suited her. And, besides, with her instinctive grasp of what the media wanted, she soon learned that there were other, more subtle ways of attracting attention to herself. A slight change of hairstyle, a new dress or blouse, was certain to set the photographers to their work. No one was immune, and when *The Times* finally put her on its front page she was thrilled. 'I've made *The Times*!' she proudly announced. The last bastion had succumbed to Di-fever.

It was flattery of the most extravagant kind but it was not enough to exorcize her in-built sense of insecurity. For although the world loved Diana, Diana was finding it harder to reciprocate. The more time she spent at the Palace, the more unhappy she became, which found its expression in her comments about other people.

Her hate list was a long one. She railed against the Royal Family, about how unfeeling they were, how they had no emotions. She did not like Princess Anne or her step-grandmother, Barbara Cartland. She moaned about her mother, Frances Shand Kydd, whom she called a 'self-promoter', a judgement at odds with the public perception of her mother. She disliked her step-mother, Raine Spencer, whom Charles, conversely, had quite taken to. On the night before the engagement was announced Johnny and Raine Spencer joined Charles and his fiancée for drinks at Buckingham Palace. It was only a brief visit of no more than half an hour and again no champagne was served. It did produce one memorable line, though, which came when the Spencers were leaving and Charles was helping Raine on with her floor-length coat.

'This is such a nice fur coat,' Charles remarked.

'Oh, yes, it's a little present from me to me,' Raine replied. 'How very generous you are,' Charles fired back. The pair laughed. Diana, however, never saw anything remotely funny in anything Raine said or did. Her father had been most anxious that his children should get on with their stepmother but they had taken an immediate dislike to the woman, with her grand, imperious air, who in their young minds had supplanted their mother. They had sung, 'Raine, Raine, go away,' and many lunches had ended abruptly with Diana and her older sister, Sarah, being sent out of the room as a punishment for their rudeness. Time had not improved the situation. Raine, so Diana insisted, was 'such a conniving woman'.

Even her sister, Sarah, did not escape the outpouring of vitriol which Diana's Palace confinement had triggered. When Diana's engagement was announced Sarah had innocently claimed some of the kudos. 'I introduced them. I am Cupid. It's wonderful news and I am delighted.'

This was technically true. The sixteen-year-old Diana had accompanied her elder sister on a Sandringham shoot when Sarah was the Spencer girl in Charles's romantic sights. There had been an edge of competition between the two since Diana had moved to London and stolen some of the vivacious Sarah's social thunder. Now Diana appeared to have come out on top and, in a childish display of one-upmanship, was determined to let her sister know it. After one afternoon out together, the sisters came back to the Palace and went up to Diana's sitting room on the second floor. Sarah was going to the country that evening and still had a couple of hours to wait for her train. Diana decided that she was not going to use the Palace as a waiting room. She went out into the corridor and instructed a footman to go into the room and inform Sarah that the future Princess of Wales had been called away on important business. A taxi was duly summoned and Sarah, who was once herself tipped to become Princess of Wales, was rapidly shown the door. The staff involved in this subterfuge were deeply embarrassed. They knew for certain what Sarah probably guessed: that Diana had absolutely nothing to do that afternoon.

But then she rarely did have anything to do. When Sarah Ferguson became engaged to Prince Andrew and moved into the Palace as Diana had before her, it was, as one member of staff recalled, 'Champagne all the way. She was throwing it around like crazy and getting frightfully excited about inviting everybody in.' Diana was quite the opposite.

The first few weeks were taken up with having afternoon tea with the female members of the Royal Family. Princess Michael of Kent came and told Diana, 'You are marrying the most important member of the family and I am married to the least important.' The Duchess of Gloucester called by. So did the Duchess of Kent who, much to the bemusement of Diana who was not aware of the Duchess's illnesses, sent her a box of health-food nut bars the following day.

Her mother, who had been conspicuous by her absence until then, began to make daily appearances at the Palace. She would usually arrive in the morning to take Diana shopping. It became part of the routine. Diana would arise at around 8.30 a.m., have coffee followed by a bath, drawn for her by Evelyn Dagley, the housemaid on the nursery floor, and scented with rose geranium from Floris which Charles happened to like. She would rarely eat breakfast before setting off at around ten o'clock with Frances to the General Trading Company in Chelsea, or the design studio of David and Elizabeth Emanuel who had been commissioned to design and make the wedding dress. Under her mother's guidance Diana's wardrobe started to improve and expand. 'Her mother really helped her in that respect, no matter what she said,' one member of the Household said.

There was no one to show off these new acquisitions to.

155

Charles was still away much of the time, and of Diana's own friends there was no sight.

Diana would later complain of the loneliness of Palace life, of how she was neglected by her fiancé and left to herself for long hours of the day. That was more a symptom of her incipient illness, however, than a reflection on Charles, whose round of royal duties increased in the run-up to the wedding but who had given firm instructions that the Palace and its facilities were to be put at her disposal. In line with that directive, the Palace staff were geared up to receive her visitors. There were several chefs on duty and two footmen poised. She could have had dinner parties for a minimum of six people every night and everyone would have been delighted. Instead she spent most evenings by herself, much to the disappointment of the cooks, who wanted to show off their best for her.

The staff, concerned about their under-employment, started dropping hints and eventually Diana was persuaded to invite her former flatmates, Virginia Pitman, Anne Bolton and Carolyn Pride, to lunch. After that, one flatmate a week would be invited round. There were also lunch dates with Sarah Ferguson and Tally Grosvenor, the young Duchess of Westminster. Diana ate very little. She was, she explained, on a crash diet for her wedding.

That was not true. The sad fact was that Diana was already in the early throes of bulimia, the eating disorder that would soon require urgent medical attention, though at the time no one could put a name to what was ailing her.

At lunchtimes when she did not have guests, Diana would go into the nursery kitchen. She would take down a large glass bowl engraved with the EIIR cypher which held just over half a packet of breakfast cereal. She would fill it with Kellogg's Frosties and several chopped bananas, strawberries and sometimes pieces of apple. She would add tablespoons of caster sugar and pour on Windsor Cream, a thick double cream from the Jersey herd at the Home Farm at Windsor. She would then sit down on top of the spin dryer to eat her way through the mess which she washed down with fresh orange juice. When she had finished, she would go to her lavatory, lock herself in and spew up what she had just forced down. This pattern of gorge and regurgitate would happen twice and sometimes three or four times a day.

Questions started to be asked in the Royal Pantry, the department of the royal kitchens responsible for stores. The kitchen staff knew that Diana was not eating but assumed she was lunching out with her mother or friends. Why, demanded the store-keepers who had not been told of the feeding crisis on the second floor, was so much fruit and so many gallons of Windsor Cream being consumed? And why were so many packets of Frosties being devoured? Was Lady Diana having breakfast parties? Suspicion led to argument and when a nursery footman was accused of stealing the packets of Frosties Diana had to go down to the kitchen and confirm that they really were all for her.

Diana's illness had its origin in her childhood. Bulimia is an emotional problem. It is closely allied to anorexia nervosa, which is believed to be caused by the psychological inability to make the transition from the dependency of childhood to the independence of adulthood. According to consultant psychologist Dr Eric Sigman, bulimia is 'not about food' but is the response to the fundamental problem of 'coping with life, avoiding painful issues, reacting to current stress and unresolved problems from the past'. A study by Dr Ulrike Schmidt of the Institute of Psychiatry found that many sufferers had a history of violence in their families.

Diana was eight years old when her parents divorced on the grounds of her mother's adultery. Frances had married a man a dozen years her senior, just as her daughter would a generation later. She had borne him his children and then, like her daughter after her, had grown tired of her older husband. An affair ensued with the married Peter Shand Kydd which resulted in both their divorces.

It was a particularly painful time for Diana. Her father, bewildered and infuriated by his wife's adultery, expressed his torment in a violent manner which was witnessed by their little daughter 'from her hiding place behind the drawing-room door'.

Frances sued on the grounds of her husband's cruelty. Johnny counter-sued on the grounds of her adultery and won the case. Frances and Peter Shand Kydd were ordered to pay £3000 legal costs, a considerable sum at the time, and Frances lost custody of her children.

Diana was traumatized. Psychotherapist Patricia Peters explained: 'Most bulimics have a history of early emotional starvation and it must be remembered that Diana's mother left her when she was very young. Self-esteem is shattered when a mother leaves a child. The depression that follows is an expression of the anger that is turned against the self.'

If Diana was what might colloquially be called a disaster waiting to occur, then joining the Royal Family was a sure way to make it happen. Any set of in-laws takes a little getting used to, but the Windsors are in a class of their own. Self-sufficient and wary of those to whom they are not related by blood, they only welcome people on their own terms. Diana had to adapt herself to a whole ritual of familial quirks. Some were simply foibles of a kind which all families have. Like the way they laid their pudding spoons and forks across the top of the place setting in a way she had always been told was very bourgeois. How, at Balmoral, they used fish knives which were supposed to be the height of pretentious vulgarity. And how at Christmas they all tried to outdo each other in the meanness of their presents.

There was the Queen's trick of leaving her chocolates out on the grand piano in the salon by the front entrance at Sandringham and then peering down unseen from the window in the corridor overhead to see who would filch one. She took a great delight in teasing the embarrassed culprits who could not work out how they had been found out.

And there was also the discomfiting fact that what was permiss-

158

ible behaviour for a member of the Royal Family was forbidden their guests. At Sandringham one year, for instance, the Queen Mother, the Queen and Princess Margaret got through nearly a bottle of gin and a bottle of Dubonnet between them before dinner. When they sat down at table, the Queen Mother could not get her vegetables out of the serving dish being held by the blank-faced footman and on to her plate. Instead, she kept depositing them on the floor, which sent her daughters into fits of giggles. Had anyone other than a member of the family behaved in such a manner, their suitcases would have been packed for them that night and they would have left the house before breakfast the following morning.

It was all very confusing to someone as young and inexperienced and so fundamentally lacking in self-confidence as Diana. Of far greater concern, however, was the emotional sterility of the Royal Family which made them virtually incapable of sharing their emotions with outsiders. Even something as obvious as a birthday is all but ignored. The Royal Family, for whom every month brings its share of anniversaries and dates which must be observed, make light of birthdays.

On 21 July, three weeks before her wedding, Diana turned twenty. Birthdays are very important to Diana. She always sends cards to people whose birthday it is and takes a delight in giving and receiving presents. She was then at an age when they mattered even more and she woke up to hear radio announcers excitedly wishing her many happy returns of the day. On the nursery floor, however, it might as well have been any ordinary working day. There was no shower of cards or the cheering company of people popping by with presents. Instead Diana was left on her own all morning to pace up and down her sitting room and stare aimlessly out of the window. At noon some of the staff took pity on her and invited her into Prince Edward's brushing room next door and presented her with a chocolate cake and a jug of Pimm's, the only drink she liked in the erroneous belief that it was not alcoholic and therefore would not make her drunk.

159

That night she had dinner with Charles who gave her a leather jewellery case engraved with her initials. By royal standards Charles had done everything expected of him and Diana was delighted with the gift. But she wanted something else, something more, although by then it should have been abundantly clear that she was not going to get it with this particular man.

If Charles was not the most attentive of lovers (and he was not), he still made an effort to keep the weekends free if he was in the country so that he could be with her. Reticently and always with a trace of embarrassment, he would sometimes go so far as a kiss or a squeeze of his fiancée's hands. Should she move closer to him, however, he would always move away. Everything had its time and its place and, as far as Charles was concerned, that was some time towards the end of July when they were safely married. Diana, still the *ingénue*, was prepared to put up with that for the moment. What she was no longer prepared to tolerate was what she regarded as Charles's indifference.

Matters came to an explosive head at the end of Ascot week in June. Diana, who was putting on a brave show and doing her best to appear part of the family, had joined the royal house party at Windsor. The week got off to the worst of starts. Shortly after she arrived, she went up to the top floor of the Queen's Tower to the sitting room where Princess Anne was settling her children.

Diana, still only a Lady, bobbed a deep curtsey to the Princess and said, 'Ma'am, how wonderful to see you.'

Anne dislikes pretension and the airs and affectations of protocol. She was prepared to tolerate them in her elder brother who was born royal and is destined to be her sovereign. She found them deeply irritating in his fiancée. She did not reply to Diana's greeting. Instead she glared contemptuously straight through her future sister-in-law. Diana, humiliated and intimidated, fled from the room.

Diana desperately needed the comfort and companionship of Charles, but he was away in the United States and she had to struggle through Ascot week under her own guidance. She found it a trial. All eyes at this most public of royal occasions were upon her. As always she played her part to perfection, smiling at the crowds as she rode down the course in the open carriage, and, later, as she walked through the milling throngs of people on her way from the Royal Enclosure to view the horses in the paddock and then back again. There were the requisite Shy Di glances for the appreciative photographers. But behind that gleaming façade the stress was building. It only needed a little incident to set her off and it was Charles who provided it.

The Prince flew back to Britain on the last day of the royal meet and arrived at the castle just in time for lunch. Diana went down to the Royal Family's private 'dog door' entrance to meet him. When he stepped out of the car she was hoping, against the evidence of previous experience, for a romantic embrace. What she got was a peck on the cheek and the greeting, 'Lovely to see you.' Without waiting for a response, Charles walked on into the castle and up to his room to freshen up for luncheon. He was not being intentionally heartless. He was tired and jet-lagged from the flight. Diana saw it as a deliberate slight.

She was distraught. She fled to her room and collapsed in tears. It was half an hour before she could be persuaded to come out again.

In the afternoon Diana and Charles rode down the course together in an open carriage. The tears had dried, the smile was back in place, and they looked for all the world the picture of a couple deeply in love. It would not be the last time they would be forced to play such a public charade, although by the end of that day it looked as if it very well might have been.

That night was the party to celebrate the birthday of Prince Andrew. He had actually turned twenty-one in February but the Royal Family, increasingly mindful of charges of profligacy and in line with their nonchalant approach towards birthdays, preferred to combine the celebrations with the traditional Ascot ball which had recently been discontinued as part of the Palace economy drive. In other words, it was an excuse for a lavish, white-tie-and-tails knees-up of the grandest kind.

There was dinner for a thousand people. Prince Andrew was seated next to the Duke of Rutland's fun-loving daughter, Lady Teresa Manners, who two years later would be fined £75 for engaging in what would be described in court as a 'passionate embrace' with her male passenger as she drove down the M6.

Elton John was there as a friend of Andrew's but he did not mingle with the other guests. Instead he ate supper by himself in an ante-room while he readied himself for his performance – even a star of Elton John's lustre was nervous about playing in front of this audience. Shortly after midnight he came out on the stage in the Waterloo Chamber where the royals gather every year on the anniversary of Wellington's great victory over Napoleon and where, four decades before, the Queen and Princess Margaret had performed their wartime pantomime. With all his showman's charm, he dedicated his first tune, 'Your Song', to the Queen.

The Queen was relaxed and behaving like a mother at a family party for her favourite son rather than a sovereign on parade, in stark contrast to Charles who was very much on duty and insisted, to the despair of his fiancée, on working the room and making sure that he spoke to as many people as possible. Joe Loss and his orchestra kept the older guests on their feet. The younger crowd congregated in the discothèque where the music was wild. Diana went wild to it. 'She was clearly determined to make a spectacle of herself,' a guest recalled. She behaved as though she had had too much to drink, although in fact she had not touched a drop. Nervous, upset, emotionally drained, she danced frenetically with first one man, then another, and eventually by herself, a crazed figure with a half-vacant look on her face.

Charles looked on in bewilderment before taking himself off to bed. One by one the guests followed suit. But still Diana danced on until, by five o'clock in the morning, she was alone. One of the Household looked out of the window and saw Diana

162

in the quadrangle, a gaunt figure in the half light, exhausted, lost in her thoughts, but still moving in slow, rhythmic time to the music that was now playing only inside her head.

Chapter Ten

In the early hours of 2 June 1981, central London was hit by a violent thunderstorm. The crack of the lightning and the rattle of her window-pane awoke Diana.

Frightened, she crept out of her bed and out of her room and then ran down the red carpeted corridor of the nursery floor, past Andrew's and Edward's bedrooms, past Mark Phillips's dressing room and Anne's suite. From the windows which looked out over the inner courtyard she could see the rain falling and the lightning flashes. She was 'scared', she later said.

Two-thirds of Buckingham Palace away from her own apartment overlooking Constitution Hill she came to the door that led into Charles's sitting room. She ran through it and on into his bedroom where she joined the Prince under his covers. It was the first night she had spent with him and she did not leave his bed until six o'clock the following morning. Despite their closeness, it did not turn out to be the momentous night it could have been, as she indiscreetly informed a number of the Palace staff afterwards. Charles offered his protective arm and told her not to be frightened of the thunder. He treated her decorously – more decorously than she might have wished.

Diana, more innocent but more earthy than her fiancé, had been living under his roof for three months. The idea, or so one of Charles's aides explained, was that the couple should 'get to know each other better'. But that was exactly what Diana felt they were not doing. She saw little of her husband-to-be who seemed more concerned about his job and his 'wretched' duties than he did about her. And because of the nature of royal life, when they did have a chance to be together they were almost always surrounded by staff or, what was worse, members of his family. Even when opportunities like the thunderstorm presented themselves, no use was made of them.

Diana, for whom affection and attention were medicine vital to her deteriorating mental condition, felt neglected. Cut off from her friends, though that was substantially her own fault, bored, lonely, subsisting on a diet of Frosties and double cream, she was moving perilously close to breaking point.

It all became too much for her that night of Prince Andrew's birthday party at Windsor. She did not stop dancing until day had almost reclaimed the night. She then went straight back to her room, and packed up. The police checked her out at 5.30 a.m. when she set off to Althorp, her father's home in Northampton-shire. At that moment she was sick, flustered and had no intention of ever going back. The wedding was only three weeks away. As far as Diana was concerned that morning, it was cancelled. In her anger and despair she had decided that she was not going through with it.

Her father calmed her down and talked her round. Earl Spencer had never fully recovered from the stroke that had almost killed him in 1978. For the rest of his life he found it difficult to talk, and excitement and upset were things he was advised to avoid. However, he had always adored his youngest daughter.

Diana would later complain that she had only ever been a 'nuisance' to her parents, that they had really wanted a boy. It was true that Spencer, anxious to produce an heir to his earldom, had urged Frances to try again after their first son, John, died ten hours after he was born in 1960. And Diana may have been right when she said that, had that infant lived, she would never have been conceived. But it none the less required a profound sense of inferiority to mistake her father's affection for her as

165

anything but deep and genuine. By playing the emotional waif, though, she succeeded in attracting a greater share of his attention and she certainly got it when she arrived at Althorp House in Northamptonshire shortly after breakfast.

She usually 'hated' going to Althorp 'because Raine is there,' she said. At the height of this crisis, however, home was where she had to be, in the company of a father whom she regarded as 'very intelligent . . . much brighter than everybody gives him credit for'. Now she was in urgent need of his advice.

The Spencers are an old family of courtiers who have served the Crown loyally since the reign of Charles I. Now they were about to marry into the ruling house. By the old-fashioned standards of conduct that Johnny Spencer tried to live up to, it would have been an act of gross discourtesy to break off the engagement to the future king only a month before the wedding. And besides, from the point of view of her own happiness, was Diana absolutely sure that that was what she really wanted to do? Had she not assured her father when he told her, 'You must only marry the man you love,' that 'That is what I'm doing!'

After a weekend of second thoughts, Diana made her decision: the wedding would go ahead.

In years to come, after the fairytale had been garrotted by the tapes of illicit telephone recordings, a Gothic tale would be spun around the marriage of Charles and Diana. It would contain the piquant, prurient allegations of betrayal and infidelity and adultery and bugging devices behind the arras. Charles would be transmogrified from winsome prince to wicked ogre who cruelly neglected his beautiful wife and reduced her to tears of unhappiness. Diana, in turn, is presented as either an innocent victim or a schemestress to rival Lady Macbeth. It even had the requisite thunderstorm.

As is more usually the case in such situations, the truth or what can reasonably be accepted to approximate to it, lies not out on the rim of the emotional spectrum, but in the grey middle. Charles could be selfish, but so could Diana. He should have paid

166

her more attention, but as several members of the Household observed, she could have made more of an effort to make herself more desirable, instead of mooching around all day complaining that she was being ignored. 'She handled it badly,' was the unequivocal opinion of a royal servant. 'If she had had a party every night with all her friends, that would have made him pay her more attention.'

Dame Barbara Cartland put the problem down to training or the lack of it. 'Diana didn't know half the things she ought to have known about,' Dame Barbara said. 'My son-in-law had been equerry to the Queen, but Diana was only a little girl at the time and he didn't teach her anything. She did not know all the rules and regulations. It all came as a shock to her and therefore she found it very difficult. She started off on the wrong foot.'

Of one thing Diana had been sure, however, right from the outset of the relationship: she wanted to be Princess of Wales. She was still young enough to believe in happy endings. And Charles, who had no comprehension of the compromises and concessions that go into the making of a successful modern marriage, needed a wife.

It could have been a union of blissful mutual advantage. It became the most publicized marital breakdown in history, but neither was to know that, and on Sunday night Diana quietly slunk back into Buckingham Palace as if nothing had happened. The crisis had passed for the moment, though no one called it that. It was just a case of quite understandable last-minute 'nerves'. For a while it really looked as if they had been cured and Diana was back on form.

Diana had returned just in time for the start of Wimbledon fortnight. A keen tennis player herself, she spent what had previously been her lonely days watching the matches on television. The rest of the Royal Family were about their official business elsewhere in the country and Diana had the Palace to herself (not, of course, counting the hundreds of staff who were in residence all the time). For the first time since the engagement she appeared relaxed and happy. With her detective, Graham Smith, in tow she mounted exploratory expeditions around the Palace. Normally so staid and silent, the stolid London headquarters of the Royal Family echoed to the sound of their laughter as Diana ran down the corridors, jumping on to the sofas.

'I'm jumping on Brenda's sofas!' she shouted, calling the Queen by the nickname bestowed on her by the satirical magazine *Private Eye*. She would leap on to one, leap off, run on a few more yards, leap on to the next one, and so on, down the marble corridor with Smith in pursuit before collapsing at the end in fits of giggles. There was never anything 'grand' about Diana, as the Palace staff remarked.

She had her flatmates in for a lunch party which she gave in Princess Anne's dining room. After they had eaten the girls all practised curtseying to her which was what they would have to do as soon as she became the Princess of Wales. Diana stood there admonishing them: 'Lower, lower, lower!' That was just a mite too low for Virginia Pitman who, larger than the others, overbalanced and almost fell flat on her face, to the immense amusement of the Princess-to-be.

There would still be the occasional emotional relapse, as when Diana burst into tears at polo a few days before the wedding. The Frosties, fruit and Windsor Cream binges were on the increase.

There was also the Incident of the Bracelet.

On the Friday before the wedding Diana found a package addressed to Camilla Parker-Bowles. She opened it and found inside a gold bracelet with the initials G and F engraved on the nameplate. 'Girl Friday' was the name Charles knew Camilla by.

According to the version of events passed on in good faith by Diana's friends, she was so distressed by her discovery and by Charles's later insisting on personally delivering the gift to Camilla that she burst into tears and tried to call off the wedding.

That account does not tally with the memories of those who were with Diana that weekend. It was in the office of Michael

Colbourne, who oversaw the Prince's financial affairs, that Diana discovered the package. He recalled: 'There were certainly no tears. There was no confrontation in the office as has been reported.'

Others agree with his report. It would have been extraordinary, though, if Diana had not shown some signs of strain as the build-up to her wedding gathered pace. Any woman of her age who suddenly found herself in the eye of this media hurricane would have been buffeted by the experience, and Diana, both inexperienced and weighed down by the emotional deprivation of her childhood, was in danger of being blown away. The discovery of Lana Turner behind the counter at Schwab's drug store in Hollywood and her overnight transformation into a film star was as nothing compared to Diana's leap from obscurity to worldwide fame. For much of the time she did not know what she was doing or in which direction she was travelling.

Charles had been of little help. His schedule – it included everything from hospital openings to hospice tours, and always those official luncheons and dinners – left him tired and anxious for bed and a few hours' sleep before setting off the next morning on another round of engagements. Diana, if not quite an afterthought, had to take her place in the timetable. Understandably, she had found that difficult to take.

As the day of the nuptials approached, however, and the world's interest intensified in the twenty-year-old woman who only a few months before had been working as a part-time cleaning lady, so her peace of mind and mood improved noticeably. Rather than sinking into a state of tearful despair, Diana, always so desperate for attention, started to thrive on the ballyhoo being orchestrated in her name.

That did not allay the underlying tensions between the Princess-to-be and her royal in-laws. Two days before the wedding Princess Anne's new-born daughter was christened. Diana was invited but, still smarting from the humiliation of that put-down she had received during Ascot week, refused to go. Not that

169

Anne cared: she would always regard Diana with, at best, indifference, at worst downright irritation.

Charles was more inviting. He said he wanted his fiancée at Windsor beside him. Diana, however, stood firm.

Diana did have the valid excuse in that that night she would be the centre-piece of the pre-wedding ball and she needed the day to get ready. For the sake of appearances it would have been more diplomatic if she had attended, but Charles did not push the issue. He had always attached the greatest importance to his family and he wanted to savour this last occasion when they would all be together before he left to start a family of his own.

It was the last real family occasion without Diana for more than a decade and it was as enjoyable as Charles hoped it would be. The baby was baptized Zara – her name means 'bright as the dawn' – in the chapel at Windsor which so symbolically burned down at the end of 1992. Afterwards the family gathered in the castle's Green Drawing Room for champagne and christening cake. It was a throng of royals and close friends including the former world champion racing driver Jackie Stewart's wife, Helen, and Camilla Parker-Bowles's husband Andrew who were godparents.

The conversation was informal. The Queen, her thoughts on the days ahead, kept asking if the sleeping arrangements at the Palace for Prince Philip's German relations had been taken care of. The Queen Mother said that, although she had never been to Gatcombe Park herself (a surprising admission, as Anne had been living there for almost a decade), she was delighted that Anne had taken a house in Gloucestershire so that she could bring up her children in the country.

Charles went on his usual tour around the room, making sure that he spoke to everyone, but paying especial attention to Mabel Anderson. Charles's beloved nanny, her duties at Buckingham Palace at an end, had gone to work for Anne on the birth of her son Peter in 1977. Two months before Zara was born she had decided that the time for retirement had finally arrived. A second baby, she said, would be too much, as, she admitted, was the

170

informality of Gatcombe where she did not have the private support system of nursery footman, nurserymaid and her own chauffeur which she had enjoyed at the Palace. She had been replaced by Pat Moss, a sturdy Yorkshire woman who was understandably upset that Mabel was there. When Mabel gave Peter a little gift, tears welled as Pat complained that her predecessor was trying to usurp the child's affection.

By then it was time to dash back to London in time to get ready for the evening's revelry. Anne, who was breast-feeding, was trying to get the clothes into the children's cases but only succeeding in wrapping herself in the tissue paper the Royal Family always use for packing. It was a hot and irritable princess who eventually succeeded in herding her brood into the waiting car.

Back in London everything was just as chaotic.

Charles's valet, Stephen Barry, was in a state of high agitation and was to be observed rushing down corridors, his extra thick, Prince-Michael-of-Kent-style tie pulled tight at the neck and puffed out over his chest, his hands flapping and proclaiming in a panicky voice, 'The Prince, the Prince!' (Charles had run out of lemon refresher.)

Philip's German cousins, a fair number of whom would not have been welcome in Britain in the years immediately following the end of the Second World War, had arrived and the inevitable arguments over who had the better rooms had ensued.

Princess Grace of Monaco was being the most difficult. She was to share a sitting room with the Crown Prince of Norway and his wife, Sonja. Prince Harald, great-great-grandson of Queen Victoria, was delighted with the arrangements. The former Grace Kelly, American grand-daughter of a poor Irish emigrant, was not. In a loud, theatrical voice she would say to people she knew, 'Why don't you come upstairs and we can sit in my sitting room – my *shared* sitting room.'

Prince Edward was struggling with his bow tie.

It was a production that owed more to Mel Brooks than the

Earl Marshal. In the grandest of theatrical traditions, however, everything came right on the night. It was the most lavish, the most glamorous ball given by the Royal Family since the imperial heyday of the 1930s. The men were dressed in white tie and tails; the women wore tiaras. There was dinner followed by dancing to music provided by Hot Chocolate, one of the leading pop groups of the day, and a particular favourite of Charles's. The vintage Krug champagne was in spate.

Raine Spencer looked as though she had never had so much fun. Nancy Reagan looked suitably regal, as befitting the wife of the President of the United States. Frances Shand Kydd, tiara neatly in place, chose to waltz to Hot Chocolate's rock and roll rhythms.

Mark Phillips's parents had an especially fine time. Those who marry into the Royal Family are not permitted to bring their own families with them into the regal corral and the Phillipses had never penetrated further than the outer perimeter of their son's new life. Now they had attended a royal christening, lunched and dined with the Queen and were at a ball with all Europe's royalty. And all in one day.

Princess Margaret was a mite 'over trained', as people say in upper-class circles. 'I mustn't climb the curtain, too cruel,' she hesitantly informed one guest. When the Cinderella hour chimed, she wanted to go home. Her children, Viscount Linley and Lady Sarah Armstrong-Jones, who wanted to stay, would disappear into the throng whenever their mother wobbled into sight. 'She needs to go home – I don't!' Sarah said.

Camilla Parker-Bowles was there, firmly – and safely – on the arm of her husband.

It was a spectacular night of majesty and memory. And presiding over everything, the focus of all attention, was Lady Diana Spencer.

She stood beside Charles at the top of the grand staircase to receive the guests, a liveried footman behind her poised to remind her of any names she might have forgotten or had yet

172

to learn. Instead of the taffeta ball gown everyone had come to expect, she was wearing a dress which was simplicity itself. Pale blue, straight, elegant. She looked as beautiful as any princess in her childhood imaginings.

It has been said that Charles slipped away and spent the night with Camilla. That is not true. He danced with Diana and held her close. There were no scenes, no five o'clock in the morning walk-outs, no tears. They looked for all the world, or at least the part of it gathered at Buckingham Palace that night, like a couple in love.

The following day dawned bright and cheerful. Diana, still in the lightest of moods, went to see the Queen who presented her with the love-knot tiara and an emerald necklace. Diana was delighted with the gift. She said afterwards that the Queen had been very sweet and not nearly as cold as she had imagined.

Afterwards Charles and Diana drove down to Windsor and spent the day together sitting in the garden, swimming in the pool, catching the rare browning rays of the English summer. They returned in time for afternoon tea which, by royal tradition, was served at five o'clock.

When that was finished Charles and Diana went into his sitting room. Ten minutes later it was time for her to leave for Clarence House where she was to spend the last night of her spinsterhood. She emerged looking relaxed and even more radiant than she had the night before. If she had any cause for despair – and according to some chapters in this carefully fabricated Gothic fable, she did – then she gave an Oscar-winning performance because no one had seen her look happier since she arrived at the Palace over three months before.

Charles, too, seemed at ease with himself and sure of the future in those final hours before the wedding. In his sitting room that night he listened to the crowd outside sing 'Rule Britannia'. 'It really was remarkable, and I found myself standing in the window with tears pouring down my face,' he recalled.

He awoke early the following morning and dressed in a comfortable pair of old corduroy trousers and a handmade Turnbull & Asser shirt open at the neck. If Mabel had been there he would have strolled along the corridor to the nursery sitting room to join her for breakfast. But the Palace was still overflowing with royal guests from all over Europe. Beds were at a premium; Pat Moss and baby Zara had moved into Diana's apartment, Peter Phillips had slept in his father's dressing room. Nanny Mabel had had to go and stay with friends and because she was not there Charles chose to stay in his own rooms where he breakfasted on cereal, granary bread and orange juice.

Outside the excitement was building. The Mall was full of people, hundreds of thousands, who had gathered to see him make a princess of the young woman whose shy smile, apparent simplicity and English good looks dominated the front page of newspapers and magazines around the world.

By 8.30 a.m. the nursery floor, never a very private place, was humming with scurrying servants, shouting children and the urgent commands of adults hurrying to get ready. The muffled sound of the waves of cheering could be heard on the royal side of the Palace windows and even Princess Anne, usually so calm, got worked up.

At Clarence House, Diana had eaten what for her was a rarity: 'an enormous breakfast,' which, she said, 'I hope stops my tummy rumbling.' She then climbed into what its designers, David and Elizabeth Emanuel, called 'the dress of the century', that glorious confection of ivory silk paper taffeta, hand-embroidered in mother-of-pearl, with a twenty-foot train trimmed and edged with old lace. It was pure romance because, David Emanuel said, 'One needs romance in the climate in which we live.'

Charles had done his bit as well. It was on his insistence that the service should take place in St Paul's and not Westminster Abbey, the traditional venue for royal weddings, because, he explained, the Cathedral could accommodate the three orchestras he wanted. He took a close interest in all the preparations, from making sure that Mabel Anderson had an excellent seat, to checking over the route the cavalcade would drive down on the way back to the Palace. (When told that there might not be enough soldiers to line the longer route, he replied, with Prince Philip-like logic: 'Stand them further apart.')

The day itself went by in a glorious haze. 'I found we were carried along on a wave of enormous friendliness and enthusiasm,' he recalled. 'It was remarkable. And I kept telling myself to remember this for as long as I could because it was such a unique experience.'

Inspired by his sense of destiny, moved by the enthusiasm of the crowds, he elaborated shortly afterwards: 'We still cannot get over what happened that day. Neither of us can get over the atmosphere; it was electric, I felt, and so did my wife. I remember several occasions that were similar, with large crowds: the Coronation and the Jubilee, and various major national occasions. All of them were very special in their own way but our wedding was quite extraordinary as far as we were concerned. It made us extraordinarily proud to be British.'

Weddings are a declaration of hope in the future and this one was seen and shared in by more people than any in history. After the wedding breakfast Charles and Diana appeared on the balcony of Buckingham Palace. The crowd roared its instruction and the new Princess of Wales said to her husband: 'They want us to kiss.'

Charles replied: 'Why not!' They did and the moment was shared by a worldwide television audience of 700 million. No kiss had ever been witnessed by more people.

Casting his serious eye over the occasion, Charles later remarked: 'Inevitably these things don't always last very long. But I think it made one realize that underneath everything else, all the rowing and the bickering and disagreements that go on the rest of the time, every now and then you get a reason for a celebration or a feeling of being a nation.'

175

The moment of celebration was shorter than Charles, than anyone, could have expected. This, after all, was a marriage that was supposed to – that *had* to – last for ever. But the undertow of disharmony was simply too strong and would start to pull the couple down even as the cheers of the crowd were still fresh in their ears.

Chapter Eleven

Charles's memories of his honeymoon are not of the happiest. The first attempt at consummation ended with Diana collapsing, as she later put it, 'in a fit of giggles', which did little for her husband's *amour-propre*. More seriously, her eating disorder had got worse in the confines of the royal yacht *Britannia* on which the couple cruised the Mediterranean for two weeks.

It was a miserable situation – for Diana, but also for her husband. At that stage Charles had never heard of the illness bulimia, but he soon became aware that something was seriously wrong – so wrong, in fact, that when the couple went up to Balmoral to continue their honeymoon in the Highlands, he sought urgent professional medical treatment for his wife.

During the ceremony at St Paul's Cathedral, the Archbishop of Canterbury, Robert Runcie, had felt moved to describe the union between Diana and Charles as a 'fairytale'. He was echoing the thoughts of millions of people. Real life unfortunately does not follow the Walt Disney version. Princesses do not ride off into a Technicolor sunset to live happily ever after. There are those hobgoblins – rows, bickerings, disagreements – to be confronted, the mundane routine of ordinary life to be dealt with and neither a choice of palaces, nor a host of servants, nor even the use of the world's largest yacht could spare Diana that.

Britannia has a complement of over two hundred sailors which made privacy hard to come by. There were picnics ashore in deserted coves, and opportunities to sunbathe on deck (his passion) or swim off the stern (her interest). But the call of duty was never stilled for long. Charles, as royal tradition said he should, insisted on inviting the officers in to dine with them in the evening. When the yacht docked at Port Said at the entrance to the Suez Canal, Egypt's President Anwar Sadat and his wife came aboard for dinner.

But then privacy, as the crew soon noticed, was something the Princess seemed anxious to avoid. The fumbles and farce of that first night had dealt a blow to Charles's romantic dignity, and in consequence their relationship was not as relaxed as it might have been. Rather than lounge about with her husband, Diana preferred to wander around the ship, talking to the crew, drinking Pimm's with the stokers, and, on one occasion, entertaining the ratings with a rendition on the piano of Henry VIII's evergreen composition, 'Greensleeves'. The petty officers had to intervene gently to steer her back upstairs again, where she belonged.

Aggravating everything was Diana's yearning for Frosties or any other cereal, because by then she was not choosy and would have happily eaten anything. It was hard to hide an illness on a yacht, however grand, and the effort made her irritable. She started counting off the days, in the way she had when she was a schoolgirl at West Heath anxiously awaiting with mounting frustration the end of term.

Matters only got worse after they flew back to Britain. They went straight up to Balmoral where they were greeted in the warm and traditional manner. They drove up to the gates of the castle lodge where all the staff had turned out to greet them. There they switched from car to a trap without a pony to be pulled up the drive by the estate workers while the rest of the staff ran cheering alongside them. Prince Philip accompanied the procession on a bicycle.

The couple were put up in the apartment next to the Queen's rooms. They slept in a large Victorian bed. The sofas and chairs in the sitting room had plaid covers. It was the honeymoon suite where the names of previous occupants were scratched on the window sill: Marina and George, parents of Princess Alexandra and the Duke of Kent, and Edward VII's daughter, Maud, who married King Haakon VII of Norway.

Diana was delighted with her reception. But once the arrival was over and she had settled in she found she was no longer the centre of attention as she had been since the wedding. It left her with a sinking feeling of anti-climax to discover that she was now just one royal among many.

The Queen was in residence. The Queen Mother came to stay. Princess Margaret was there with her children, David and Sarah. So were Prince Andrew and Prince Edward. This was a family outing, Diana complained, not a honeymoon. And one on which she was confined to the back of the bus. On her marriage Diana had been elevated to 'Your Royal Highness'. The staff now greeted her with bows and curtseys. But so they did all the other royal ladies and Diana, however important she was to the public, was right at the bottom of the pecking order at Balmoral.

She went into a sulk that became an almost permanent gloom. Her cereal binges became known to the whole staff after a housemaid found vomit on the bathroom floor which Diana did not have the facilities to clean up herself. She refused to join in the customary activities of the estate, preferring to drive off by herself in her silver Ford Escort to buy sweets at the shop in Ballater which she would eat by herself sitting by a waterfall. Even the swimming in the pool excavated for that purpose in the river Dee failed to interest her.

Balmoral was no longer the 'magical' place it had been when she was so eagerly wooing Prince Charles a year before. She now hated it.

There is a long-established routine at Balmoral. The Royal Family are essentially country people who do things the way they have always been done and there was fishing in the early part of the week and shooting on Thursday, Friday and Saturday through until October when grouse gave way to the stalking of stag. In between such rustic pursuits, Charles spent a lot of time painting.

The focus of everything was the picnics and barbecues. There were picnics every lunchtime, no matter how inclement the weather, and barbecues most evenings. It was simply not done to miss them; even the Queen Mother, in her ninth decade, continued to drag herself out on to the hill wrapped in a tartan rug, to join the others eating those chops and sausages they took such pleasure in cooking for themselves.

By the end of the first week Diana was refusing to go. If she made the picnic, she would excuse herself from the evening cook-out because, she said, she wasn't feeling well. She would stay instead in her room and eat a modest supper of baked beans on toast or sausages and mashed potatoes. (At this early stage, it was only the breakfast cereals she binge-ate which she had trouble keeping down.)

That was not popular with the staff, for one of the reasons that the Royal Family went out barbecuing was to give their servants the night off. They left at seven o'clock and as soon as they were gone, the house was closed down. That was not possible with Diana still there.

When the matter was raised with her she said, 'But I'm only having baked beans.' She failed to take into consideration that one of the kitchen staff had to stay on duty to cook them and that someone had then to bring them up to her room and wait around to clear up afterwards. It was, everyone agreed, 'bad form' on Diana's part and the Queen was not amused.

Princess Margaret, who had made a lifetime's habit of doing as she pleased, stuck up for Diana. 'Let her do what she likes,' she told her sister, and the Queen, who dislikes any sort of family disagreement, let the matter rest.

Charles did not. He can be self-absorbed to the point of arrogance but this was one problem he could not ignore. Diana was his wife and as such was expected to perform her duties. One of her first tasks, which was hardly onerous, was to stand at her husband's side for a few minutes for the photo-call Charles had arranged.

Diana had happily posed for the cameras at Craigowan the previous autumn. This time she threw a tantrum and said, No, she didn't want to do it, why should she, you can't make me.

Charles tried to explain that if they agreed to this one session, the press would leave them alone for the rest of their holiday. Diana said she didn't see why she had to do anything. Charles, like his mother, detests any kind of confrontation. This one was unavoidable. But just as Charles started to lose his temper, Diana suddenly switched moods and agreed to the photo-call. The couple were duly pictured beside a stream. It is a study in deception. Charles, still incensed by the argument, looks stilted and cross and anything but the loving husband. Diana, whose unnecessary fit of temperament had caused the argument in the first place, is holding Charles's hand, a happy smile on her face, the picture of a loving wife.

Charles was worried and there was an urgency to his concern. At the Trooping the Colour ceremony that year someone had fired some blank shots at the Queen. The Queen took the misadventure in her regal stride. She remained calm and in charge and gave no indication of the ordeal she had been through. Charles's reaction was very different. At the drinks at Buckingham Palace afterwards people remarked how ashen he looked. In a stunned voice he said, 'That really was a very close shave.'

It took him longer to recover than it did the Queen, even though it was her life that had been threatened. It was as though it had dawned on him for the first time that he could become King – and at any moment. And if the unthinkable were to happen, that would make Diana Queen.

A few days before the wedding he had admitted to friends, 'I wonder if she is going to be able to cope with the pressures.' They assured him that the tears at polo which had provoked his anxiety were a one-off and nothing to be concerned about. That had proved not to be the case. What had been dismissed as an isolated incident was in danger of becoming a habit, and a potentially dangerous one at that for a prince whose wife's every act was subject to ever-increasing scrutiny and analysis.

It was a situation Charles's experience had not qualified him to handle. It was alarming. It was also upsetting. This was, after all, his honeymoon, and Charles still harboured the highest expectations of his marriage. There may have been an element of expediency in it, but like any newly-wed he hoped that his wife would provide him with a lifetime's companionship and love. Instead he found himself dealing with a woman on the edge of a breakdown.

In a desperate attempt to retrieve the situation, Charles called in a doctor. There was no doubting what kind of doctor he was. As Diana herself said, 'He's my psychiatrist.'

He arrived shortly after the Incident of the Photo-call. He stayed at the hotel in nearby Ballater. He came to the castle every morning shortly before eleven o'clock and would be taken up from the Tower door to the Waleses' sitting room where Charles and Diana would be waiting for him. Coffee would be brought in. The doctor would talk to them as a couple for half an hour and then spend another half hour with Diana on her own. He was there, Diana said, to help her cope with the problems of 'joining the Royal Family'.

Surprisingly, given the matriarchal structure of the family she had married into, less so when related to her motherless childhood, the doctor said that one of Diana's problems was that she was living in a male-dominated world. To try and redress the balance, Carolyn Pride, the flatmate who as Carolyn Batholomew would one day reveal that Diana was suffering from bulimia, was invited to Balmoral for a few days. In another move, albeit one that was already written into their schedule, the couple then moved out of the castle and into Craigowan where Diana found the atmosphere more to her liking.

It was not enough, though, to stop her moaning – about how

bored she was, how she wanted to be back in London, how awful Balmoral was. Charles is also inclined to complain a lot but his concerns were most definitely not hers and the couple, only a few weeks into their marriage, were already drawing apart.

The one bright spark on this otherwise louring marital horizon was that by September's end Diana had a more positive reason than bulimia to lock herself in the loo. She was pregnant.

'Naturally I'm absolutely delighted,' Charles declared, when the news was officially announced in November. 'I feel like any prospective father.' Diana, he added, 'is overjoyed as well'.

It was an opinion he soon had to revise. Diana suffered badly from morning sickness. 'She's finding pregnancy harder work than she expected,' Charles admitted.

The same could be said about Diana's relationship with the Royal Family. The Queen, however, was disinclined to blame herself for her daughter-in-law's problems, though she was concerned enough to instruct her press secretary, Michael Shea, to do what his predecessor Sir Richard Colville had done and ask the press to rein back. The Gordonstoun-educated Shea invited the editors of every national newspaper and the heads of the radio and television news programmes to Buckingham Palace and explained to them that the constant media attention was causing Diana distress.

The press, with the egregious exception of the *Sun* whose editor refused to attend the informal get-together, agreed to reduce their coverage of the Princess. But if Diana no longer had to face a barrage of flash guns every time she stepped outside the royal compound, she was not spared the more pressing problem, which was adjusting to being a member of the Royal Family.

The honeymoon at Balmoral had been the first test. Next came Christmas at Windsor which even those born royal found an ordeal. Charles loved it. For a newcomer like Diana it was the beginning of a month of hell. Once again she found herself competing for centre stage with the other royal ladies. There was no illness to hide behind this time. There was no avoiding the Christmas contest. Everyone was on parade and even Princess Anne, whose attitude towards clothes was one of utter indifference, felt compelled to bring her best dresses and make a rare sartorial effort.

The immediate Royal Family arrived two days before Christmas in time to get themselves settled in and organized. The minor royals like the Gloucesters, Kents and Prince and Princess Michael arrived with their children, nannies and maids just before luncheon on Christmas Eve, by which time Diana had collected her first point over her sister-in-law.

Since she was a child Anne had shared the top floor of the Queen's Tower with Charles. Her marriage to Mark Phillips had not disturbed that arrangement. And why should it? She regarded Windsor, more than any other royal residence, as her family 'home'. But now Charles was married and, on his wife's prompting, he insisted Anne give up her room to Diana.

Anne had long since come to terms with her position in the royal family. She was female and as she once said, 'I've always accepted the role of being second in everything from quite an early age. You adopt that position as part of your experience. You start off in life very much a tail-end Charlie, at the back of the line.'

Deferring to her elder brother was one thing. Playing second fiddle to a sister-in-law she held in little regard was quite another. The Queen tried to mollify her by putting her in the State bedroom suite which was usually reserved for Heads of State but that only made matters worse. It was too grand for Anne. She was not comfortable there. Her Christmas had been spoilt.

Princess Michael also had an accommodation problem. The rooms allocated for her nanny, she complained, were not up to standard. When Princess Michael pressed her point the Queen lost her temper. Nanny, the Queen said, had a very nice bedroom and although her sitting room had to be used as the big nursery by all the children to eat breakfast in, there was none the less a comfortable chair to sit in and a television for Nanny to watch.

184

It was the kind of argument that might best have been avoided, but as Diana was discovering, Christmas did have a tendency to bring out the worst in her husband's family.

There was the competition over the Christmas cards to see who had the best or the most unusual photograph of themselves on the front, a practice which was soon widely imitated in London society but then was something only they did. Princess Margaret never took part in that challenge. She never sent anyone a Christmas card, not even her mother. 'I don't believe in them,' she said. One year Prince Andrew went one better and as well as not sending any cards, refused to buy anyone a present. That was no great loss, for the Royal Family, so keen to outdo each other with Christmas cards, went the other way with Christmas presents.

The gifts were exchanged in the Crimson Drawing Room on Christmas Eve and it was the moment when the British penchant for understatement was taken to its logical and ludicrous extreme. Anne would have spent the year combing the stalls of country fairs to come up with a £3 pair of shooting socks or a 50p bar of soap. Princess Alexandra's were slightly better but the extra expenditure was off-set by the wrapping; instead of proper ribbon, all her presents were tied up with odd pieces of wool.

To Diana it looked as though everyone had been engaged in a competition to see who could spend the least money. What made it even more confusing to her was the pride they took in what they bought. The presents were stacked on trestle tables along one wall. After they had eaten tea the guests would take up position beside them. When the Queen gave the nod, everyone would start tearing them open.

That, as Diana discovered, was not the end of it. Once the gifts were opened, they were left on view on their respective tables so that anyone who chose to could compare what the Duchess of Gloucester and the Duchess of Kent, or, more pungently, Diana and Anne, had given each other.

185

This was a game Diana was bound to lose. Equating affection with quality, she took care and time putting together her Christmas presents. The soaps were from Floris, the sweaters cashmere. This was not the done thing: in the enclosed world of Windsor, cheap was beautiful. What should have been a pleasant family occasion was becoming a torment.

Diana was spared any further tensions that night. After dinner in the State Dining Room everyone retired to bed early so that those with children could be awake in time to open the stockings delivered by Father Christmas in his only (non) appearance. The next day, however, was long and arduous.

It began with a calling tray at about 7.30 a.m. followed by Holy Communion an hour later. There was a large family breakfast in the State Dining Room, which was a particular trial for the Queen Mother and Princess Margaret, who were not used to rising much before 11 o'clock, but could not ignore the Queen's three-line whip.

At 10.30 the family walked down to St George's Chapel for big church and then sherry with the Dean of Windsor. By 12.30 everyone was back at the Castle for the much-favoured gin and French or tonic followed by the Christmas lunch, a grand formal affair, with chefs carving giant birds and a great sideboard, since destroyed in the 1992 fire, groaning with cold meats and glazed hams and a boar's head.

If this was the 'Festival of the Family', as George V called it in the first Christmas speech, it was not a family feast. Younger children had to eat their turkey with their nannies in the Queen's private dining room until they were old enough to hold their knives and forks properly and serve themselves off the silver plate the footmen held.

At 3 o'clock the Castle fell still as everyone gathered round a television set in a room befitting his or her status to watch the Queen deliver her Christmas message. This was never a subject for critical comment. No one dared say anything along the lines of, 'It wasn't as good as last year,' or 'I didn't agree with that

186

bit,' or even, 'That was a good speech.' For Diana it was a case of sit in silence and try to look serious.

And so the festival proceeded, with dinner following lunch and Diana being moved around the table so that she sat next to Andrew at one meal, Philip – who at this early stage found his daughter-in-law quite attractive – at another, but never, now that she was married, next to her husband. The Queen, who worked out the *place de table* herself, would not have allowed that breach of Court etiquette.

Charles, who behaved in private with the same condescension he did in public, enjoyed himself. Diana did not. Her conversation, in line with her education, was severely limited and she had yet to master the royal art of making inane small talk. She found the atmosphere stifling. She was not alone in that; there were almost audible sighs of relief when the party broke up the day after Boxing Day and the royal tribe dispersed until the following year.

There was no escape for Diana, however. After Windsor, the caravan of Court rolled across England to Sandringham, the Queen's estate on the windswept northern peninsula of Norfolk.

Bought and rebuilt by Edward VII when he was Prince of Wales, Sandringham exists in an Edwardian time warp. Charles, who behaves like an Edwardian country squire and has money, the social position, and the sense of immutable security to so indulge himself, likes Sandringham. By the decade's end he would be opening up the house and holding his own shooting parties there in a way that would have earned him the approval of his grandfather, George VI.

While his mother had been in Malta doing what she could to keep her own marriage on an even keel, Charles and his four-month-old sister had been billeted with their grandparents in Norfolk. The King wrote, 'We shall love having him at Sandringham. He is the fifth generation to live there and I hope he will get to love the place.' He did, but he could not persuade his wife to share his enthusiasm. Sandringham, like Balmoral, was no longer as 'wonderful' as it had seemed only a few months before.

Diana's ill-humour was not allowed to disturb the royal routine, however. She was a guest in her mother-in-law's home where she was most definitely not the cynosure. If she was a little difficult, well, as the Queen sagely observed, she was pregnant and she was still so very young. The moods, everyone agreed, would pass and in the meantime there was the shooting and the riding to be enjoyed and the rites of the season to be attended to.

One custom always observed was the 'first footing'. Dating from pagan times, it called for a dark-haired man carrying a piece of coal for luck to be the first person to cross the threshold after the chimes of midnight had welcomed in the New Year. As the likelihood of any unexpected guest getting past the security men guarding Sandringham was minimal, the royal family took the precaution of arranging their own good luck.

One of the estate workers' dark-haired sons or, in grander years, a footman in full livery would be sent round from the back to the front door with a tray bearing the coal and some little gifts for the royal ladies. He would ring the front-door bell which was opened by the Queen's page who would lead him through to meet the Royal Family who would feign surprise at his supposedly unexpected arrival. He would go first to the Queen Mother and say, 'May I have the honour to wish Your Majesty a Happy New Year,' to which the Queen Mother would always reply, 'Thank you so much, and a Happy New Year to you, too.' The young man would move on to the Queen and so on down the hierarchical line.

It was all a little confusing to the insecure twenty-year-old who was finding the effort of playing a princess a tremendous strain. She was tired, she was sick, and, after her tumble down the North End staircase, very sore.

According to the version of events favourable to Diana, the fall followed a furious row with Charles during which she threatened to take her own life. In the throes of despair, so the story continues, 'Standing on top of the wooden staircase, she hurled herself to the ground, landing in a heap at the bottom.' It was, or so it was claimed, the desperate act of a young woman at the end of her emotional tether.

Those who saw the incident tell a more mundane story. It was 4.45 p.m. Diana was coming down the staircase for afternoon tea which was served next door in the drawing room. The Queen Mother was at the foot of the stairs, feeding her corgis, including her favourites, Blackie and Geordie. Diana had got to the half landing where she stumbled and rolled on down to land at the feet of the Queen Mother who almost fainted with fright. The dogs barked, the Queen's page came running down the corridor shouting, 'The Princess of Wales has fallen down the stairs!' Staff and family rushed to the scene, to find Diana getting to her feet again.

The North End staircase, which is panelled up to the dado rail, and painted green above it, has some twenty steps. But they are wide and shallow. They lead to the Queen Mother's rooms and even in her nineties she is able to walk up them unassisted. Anyone falling down them was unlikely to suffer anything more than a few bruises which was all that Diana sustained.

Was it 'a cry for help', as Diana's supporters insist, or simply an unfortunate accident? History depends on who is doing the telling, and others who were at Sandringham remember it as nothing worse than an unlucky trip.

Certainly Diana was embarrassed by the episode and apologized to everyone, especially the Queen Mother who had been badly shaken by the incident. Nerves soon calmed, however, and once George Pinker, the Princess's (and the Queen's) gynaecologist who had travelled up from London to check on the unborn infant, confirmed that the baby was all right, everything quickly returned to normal.

That, of course, was exactly what Diana found so stressful and, at the other extreme, so 'boring'. For a young girl who had only recently been enjoying the independence of a flat and a life of her own in London, it was.

Other than hob-nobbing with the Royal Family, Sandringham offers nothing of interest unless the visitor happens to be keen on shooting. That is the estate's *raison d'être*. George V would expend 30,000 cartridges a year and he rarely missed. Nor did his guests, if they had ambitions of being asked back, and 1000 birds per gun per day was not unknown.

'Can this terrific slaughter possibly go on?' the King's private secretary, Lord Stamfordham, asked in 1912. The answer was no. The greater slaughter of the trenches slaked the blood lust of the aristocracy who lost one in every five of the young men it sent to the Western Front. The bags at Sandringham are none the less still among the highest in the land. Over 10,000 pheasant are blasted out of its grey skies every winter, along with assorted numbers of partridge, hare, rabbit, woodcock, snipe, teal, wood pigeon, and wild duck.

Charles has a reputation in the area for being a 'greedy' shot and in 1968 was one of ten guns who brought down an Edwardian 500 birds on the Broadlands estate of the late Lord Mountbatten.

Charles, who like his father has served as president of the Game Conservancy, takes a countryman's view of the sport. 'The Conservancy', he pointed out, 'was the first organization to regard game quite rationally as a "crop", a valuable by-product of the land, which deserved good husbandry as much as corn or cattle.' By the following season Charles had given up shooting. That was at Diana's urging. She had been brought up in the country, as she was fond of reminding everyone, and during her courtship had made a point of going out with the dogs to pick up the birds the men had brought down.

As in so many other things, however, her attitude towards shooting had undergone a complete reversal since that moment in St Paul's Cathedral when she became the Princess of Wales. She complained that the thump of pheasant hitting the frozen ground distressed her (and, given the grotesque size of the Sandringham birds and the size of the bags, there was a lot of thumping to be heard out on the winter fields). She found the shooting lunches, which were held in such less than salubrious places as the corrugated iron polling booth in the nearby village of Anmer, an uncomfortable bore. In the face of such protests and in the attempt to do what he could to accommodate his wife, Charles agreed to forgo one of the great pleasures of his life. He gave the pair of Purdey shotguns he had inherited from George VI to his brother Andrew.

It was an extraordinary act of personal sacrifice and very much out of character. It was a measure of his effort at the beginning to try to make a go of his marriage. It was a clear indication that all was not well between the couple when he took up shooting again a couple of years later (but not with the same guns; Andrew did not give back the Purdeys).

During that first year together Charles was still trying. The couple still shared a bed (a large brass one) and a bedroom, directly above the Queen's first-floor rooms which enjoy a commanding view over the lawns at the rear of the house. He was nothing less than solicitous of his pregnant wife. It was not easy going. Diana was still a troublesome young woman with an over-developed penchant for shopping and a disconcerting appetite for proprietary breakfast cereals. But Charles, trained up to do his duty no matter what his personal thoughts might be, was at that early stage still making a determined bid to make his marriage work.

At 9.03 p.m. on 21 June 1982, ten days before her twenty-first birthday, Diana gave birth to a son in the private Lindo Wing of St Mary's Hospital, Paddington. He weighed in at 7 pounds, 1½ ounces and was named William. For a while afterwards it looked as though Charles's efforts had not been in vain.

Chapter Twelve

If ever a marriage had a chance of saving itself after the birth of a child, it was the Waleses'.

Diana was thrilled. For once, one of her staff remarked, 'She looked as if she had done something right.'

Charles was there at the birth and was humbled by the experience. 'I found it rather a shock to my system,' he confessed. He was, he said, 'relieved ... delighted ... overwhelmed ... over the moon'. His happiness was obvious and genuine, as was Diana's.

'There was a contentment about her,' noted her friend Carolyn Bartholomew. There was also an air of welcome relief. The pregnancy, with its endless bouts of morning sickness, had been a difficult one, while the birth itself had been very painful.

Charles had done what he could. 'I think it is a very good thing for a husband to be with a mother when she is expecting a baby,' he said, and he had been as good as his word.

Diana had been helped by Betty Parsons, the former nurse and midwife who had assisted the Queen when Prince Edward was born, and she had made a point of involving Charles in the process, explaining the equipment, giving him antenatal books to read, showing the Prince how to relax by deep breathing. Brought up in the most old-fashioned of ways himself, he was enthusiastically embracing the 'new man' ethics.

When Diana finally went into labour, Charles was so well trained that he was able to join her in following Betty's advice to 'Pick up your surf board and ride it like a whale,' and then to 'Doggy, doggy, pant, pant' (pant, pant, blow, blow). He stood by her side, her hand in his, whispering encouragement.

It required more than soft words to help Diana through, however. Like so many first-time mothers, she had wanted to have a completely natural birth, without anaesthetic or any artificial assistance, but the pain of labour had proved too intense. Her contractions began on the evening of Sunday, 20 June 1982. The baby was not delivered until 9.03 the following evening, by which time she was exhausted. It had been worth it, though. On this occasion Charles really did speak for both of them when he announced, 'The birth of our son has given us both more pleasure than you can imagine. It has made me incredibly proud and somewhat amazed.'

The public, who had gathered in their hundreds outside the Lindo Wing of St Mary's Hospital in London's Paddington to hear the announcement of the birth of an heir to the heir to the throne, greeted those sentiments with a resounding cheer. Everything seemed to be as it should be and for a moment appearances did not deceive. Both Charles and Diana took immense and natural pride in what they had produced and, momentarily, in each other. With luck, a little more forbearance and a lot more effort it might have provided the foundations upon which to build a successful marriage. It was not to be. The ill-feeling was already damming up within them. That was not something either of them found easy to confront, given the lack of real intimacy in their relationship.

Diana had been a virgin when she married her Prince that summer's day in 1981. They hardly knew each other, and the honeymoon had not been a success. She had become pregnant within two months and had then suffered nine months of being racked by morning sickness. With the arrival of the baby, Charles found himself pushed even further out of his wife's mind and life. As if these were not difficulties enough for any newly weds Diana fell victim to post-natal depression soon after her son was born.

193

Charles's idea of marriage as a combination of 'the physical *and* the mental', as he put it, was rapidly proving to be neither. Driven out of the marital bed by his wife's seemingly chronic ill health, he quickly discovered that he had little chance of making any headway in serious discussion with the woman he had so precipitately turned into a princess. If he disagreed with something she said, she simply shouted him down – a devastatingly effective tactic against someone who had never been allowed to raise his voice in argument.

One of the earliest disagreements was over the upbringing of the little boy they christened William. Diana was most insistent that no child of hers should be handed over into the care of nannies – and certainly not Nanny Mabel Anderson who Charles was so keen to have. 'A mother's arms are so much more comforting,' she said. In that she appeared to be reflecting the mores of modern society. The undercurrent, however, had less to do with Diana's considered views on contemporaneous child-care than with her own, unhappy upbringing.

After her mother left home, Diana had been placed in the care of a succession of nannies, who came and went as if through a revolving door. Janet Thompson was her nanny for two and a half years. Diana, she recalled, 'wasn't easy. Some children will do as they are told immediately. She wouldn't. It was always a battle of wills.' Some nannies – mostly young girls with little training or aptitude and answerable to a father with little understanding of how to treat women or children – administered ready discipline. One nanny beat Diana around the head with a wooden spoon. Another banged her and her brother Charles's heads together. In retaliation, which she often got in first, Diana would stick pins in their cushions, locked one in the bathroom and threw another's clothes out of the bathroom window.

It was an unusual upbringing in that, while parents whose attitude towards their offspring bordered on indifference were common among the British aristocracy, it was rare for a child to be deprived of the continuity and love of a nanny. Charles, whose

194

relationship with his own parents had never strayed much past the distant, had first Nanny Lightbody, and then Mispy and Nanny Anderson to turn to for affection. Diana had enjoyed no such anchor and was understandably determined to give any child of her own the devotion she had been denied. Charles was not going to disagree with her on that point and, in the face of her insistence, agreed not to bring Nanny Anderson back from Gatcombe where she had been looking after Peter Phillips, but to employ Barbara Barnes instead.

The forty-two-year-old daughter of a forestry worker, Nanny Barnes had previously worked for Princess Margaret's close friend, Colin Tennant, the unconventional Lord Glenconner who owned the Caribbean island of Mustique. She came with his highest recommendation. 'She is a natural with children,' Glenconner said. 'She has a genius for bringing out the best in them. They're never bored. She has all the traditional values to the highest degree, but is perfectly up-to-date.'

With great tact, Barbara declared, 'I'm here to help the Princess, not to take over.'

Charles also insisted on playing his part. He took an earthy pleasure in playing with his son, taking him into the bath with him and helping to change his nappies. 'It isn't only a woman's job to bring children up, it's a man's job as well,' he said.

On 15 September 1984, Diana gave birth to another boy who, on her insistence, was named Harry. Charles had wanted a girl, but was soon very much taken with the little boy who proved to be more like him in temperament than his elder and more highly strung son, William. Charles again attended the birth. 'I wouldn't have missed being present when William and Harry were born,' he said. 'Husbands who turn up later only see a baby which might have been picked off a supermarket shelf for all they know.'

Diana was not so impressed. A lot of what Charles said was now starting to annoy her and his remarks about children and how best to bring them up were particularly grating. 'My husband knows so much about rearing children that I've suggested

195

he has the next one and I'll sit back and give advice,' she remarked sarcastically.

A divergence of parental aims was one of the causes of the edginess that was seeping into their relationship. Charles saw parenthood as a responsibility: his job, he said, was to ensure that his children grew up to be rounded, well-adjusted people who would be capable in their turn of shouldering their obligations.

'I would like to bring up our children to be well mannered, to think of other people, to put themselves in other people's positions, to do unto others as they would have done unto them,' he explained. 'At the end of it, even if they are not very bright or very qualified, at least if they have reasonable manners they will get much further in life than by not having them.' It was a princely objective, and the best way to achieve it, Charles believed, was by tried and tested means: this 'new man' was first and foremost a prince.

'There were some experts who were very certain about how you should bring up children,' he said. 'But then, after twenty years, they turned round and said they'd been wrong. Well, think of all the people who followed their suggestions!'

One of those experts whose books had heralded the more permissive approach to parenthood was Dr Benjamin Spock, who happened to be a distant relation of Diana's and whose techniques she embraced wholeheartedly. She regarded parenthood as an end in itself (William, she declared, 'comes first – always'), while for Charles it was the means to an end.

His whole life had been a training programme designed to prepare him for the responsibility of kingship. That objective had taken precedence over everything, including any notion of personal happiness. It was not a life he wanted for his sons – like his mother before him, he wished above all else that they could enjoy the privilege of a 'normal' childhood – but it was certainly not a genotype he could ignore. To be brought up royal had been his fate. He staunchly believed it would be his sons' and he wanted them equipped by experience to handle their situation, as he had been.

That sense of being royal carried through into everything he did. Sometimes he carried it so far that even his own family found it hard to take. Shortly after their marriage, for instance, Princess Anne invited Charles and Diana across from Highgrove to a buffet dinner party at Gatcombe to meet 'the locals', who included the Duke of Beaufort and the Parker-Bowleses. It was a black-tie affair but that did not detract from the ambience of friendly informality which so characterized Gatcombe Park.

Anne put disco tapes on the sound system, turned the volume up full blast and set the evening's tone by breaking into the can-can. 'Everyone was very relaxed,' said one guest. Everyone, that is, except the Prince and Princess of Wales 'who sat like dummies on the sofa'.

The Waleses left shortly after 10.30 p.m. and the atmosphere instantly lightened. Afterwards Anne remarked with some irritation that the 'one thing I really resent about it is the way my brother came to my house and treated my party like an official engagement!'

The incident was echoed some years later when at the last minute someone dropped out of a Gatcombe shooting party. When it was suggested that it might be a good idea to ask Charles, who had taken up shooting again by then and, after all, lived nearby, Anne replied that the Prince was 'far too grand' to accept a spontaneous invitation.

It is an attitude that further distances him from the rest of his family. Andrew and Charles are too dissimilar ever to have much in common. Charles is introspective and intense while Andrew is hearty and, when he is not playing golf, content to lounge in front of the television. As for Edward, the fifteen-and-a-half-year age gap between him and Charles is too great to bridge. As a consequence, Charles rarely sees his brothers apart from on those family holidays when everyone is expected to be on parade, and at official occasions. Anne who, because she lives so near to

197

Highgrove, sees the most of him, regards him as being spoilt and not as in touch with the real (non-royal) world as he might be.

Not even the Queen has been spared the chill generated by Charles's lordly stance. She will frequently take a detour to call at Gatcombe and see her daughter and grandchildren. So will Prince Philip, who takes an especial delight in his daughter's company. No one ever stands on ceremony during these impromptu visits; a telephone call beforehand to see if Anne is in and has no appointments is the only forward planning required. But neither the Queen nor the Duke of Edinburgh ever drops by at Highgrove where the staff wear a specially designed livery, which includes the Prince of Wales feathers. It is simply not done. One does not 'drop in' on the heir to the throne, even if one is the Queen oneself.

'The Queen has a natural soft spot for her son but is mystified by him like everyone else,' one member of the Household remarked.

But however difficult or aloof Charles might be, he certainly knew the fundamental rules of royal behaviour. Diana did not. Behind the gracious, caring and rather vulnerable public image lay a stubborn streak which often caused her to overstep the boundaries of regal propriety. What made it so difficult for Charles was that she seemed to have no intention of learning the royal ropes as he understood them.

The problem at its essence was one of status and the attention it conferred. Despite her honorific of Lady, Diana had enjoyed no special privileges as a schoolgirl or in her brief working career as kindergarten-assistant-cum-charlady. Now, at a signature on a marriage certificate, she was a Royal Highness and that *was* a privileged position. Overnight, people she had known all her life were required to bow and curtsey to her and address her as 'ma'am' (to rhyme with jam, never with smarm), just as Charles was always called 'sir'. The difference was, Charles was used to it. Diana was not and it quickly went to her head. The staff with whom, only a few months before, she had been so eager to mix bore the brunt and anyone who suggested that she was not fulfilling her duties in quite the manner expected of the wife of the heir to the throne was certain to incur her antipathy.

'She seemed to believe that only the Queen had the right to tell her what to do,' one member of her staff recalled. And that was something the Queen had no wish to do. It was therefore left to courtiers like Oliver Everett to try to keep the Princess under control. It was an unequal contest and one by one Charles's closest advisers and staff either left or walked out.

Stephen Barry was one of the first to leave. He had been valet to Charles for twelve years. He went shortly after the wedding. 'I needed a change,' he explained diplomatically. In fact, Diana had made his life so unbearable that he had no alternative but to resign.

'She was simply beastly to him,' one of the Household recalled. 'When she saw him coming down a corridor she would dive into the nearest room so that she wouldn't have to speak to him. It was very childish but it hurt Stephen enormously.'

Oliver Everett, who had had the impertinence to give her the books he thought might help her in her role as Princess of Wales and which she had hurled to the floor, went close on his heels. He had given up a promising future in the Foreign Office to join the Waleses' staff and Charles would for ever afterwards feel guilty at the way this consummate public servant's career was ruthlessly brushed aside.

The exodus turned into a stampede. Out, for one reason or another, went chauffeurs, footmen, valets, police bodyguards, factotum Michael Colbourne, and butler Alan Fisher, who had once worked for Bing Crosby and found working for the Waleses 'wasn't what I expected'. In an interesting insight into Diana's attitude towards sex at the time, there was also a turnover in maids. She would suddenly, and for no discernible reason, take it into her head that one or other of the women who looked after her was a lesbian and then refuse to have anything to do with her. Most notable among the departures was their private secretary, Edward Adeane. He had taken up the post with the Prince in 1979. Educated at Eton and Cambridge, he was a courtier in the most traditional mould. His father, Sir Michael, later Lord Adeane, had been principal private secretary to the Queen. His great-grandfather was Lord Stamfordham, who had been private secretary to Queen Victoria and then to the Duke of York, later George V. In Adeane's family, royal service was a vocation and it was widely assumed that he would stay with the job until old age claimed him or Charles inherited the throne.

By 1985 some forty members of the Household had left – an astonishing number in a world where jobs are usually for life. Diana's brother, Charles Althorp, defended the clear-out. She had, he insisted, done no more than 'get rid of the hangers-on who surrounded Charles'. That only further irritated the departing staff, many of whom had worked for the Royal Family for years and, in some cases, generations. They blamed Diana. The Princess, they declared, was impossible to deal with or work for.

Charles had increasing cause to agree with them. Even their home was the subject of contention. In August 1980, just a few days after the beginning of his romance with Diana, Charles bought Highgrove for £750,000 from Maurice Macmillan, the bibulous son of the former Prime Minister. A Georgian house set in 410 Gloucestershire acres, it stands in the heart of good hunting country and is within easy reach of the polo at Cowdray Park, Cirencester Park and Smith Lawn, Windsor. It was run-down and overlooked from the main road, but Charles loved it.

Diana, though, hated it; in his effort to win her round, Charles put her in charge of the redecoration from the day they became engaged. It was a daunting task for such a young woman. Highgrove is not very grand by royal standards, but it is still a substantial house with four main reception rooms. On the recommendation of her mother, who had used him twice before on her London homes, Diana employed the South African

Dudley Poplak. The end result was not what Charles, whose notion of good decoration was based more on the sentimentality of an old tablecloth than the aestheticism of a curtain tie-back but who was no artistic illiterate, had in mind for a country house. The floors, with the exception of the hallway, were covered with fitted carpets, not the polished wood he would have preferred. Every cushion had a *frou-frou* frill on it. It was, as one professional observer scathingly remarked, more like the penthouse suite in a Park Lane hotel than a family home in rural Gloucestershire.

Diana professed herself happy with the finished result of what she had overseen, but it was not enough to make her like the house any better. Where she really wanted to live, she said, was in Park House, her childhood home next door to Sandringham, which had just come back on the leasing market. Highgrove, she insisted, did not suit her and no sooner had she moved in than she was saying, 'Oh, we're probably going to move. I don't like this house.'

It had cost very close to £100,000 to bring Highgrove up to standard and Princess Anne was only one of those who found Diana's wasteful attitude offensive. But, then, a lot of what Diana was doing was starting generally to jar. Her spending sprees, which were a symptom of her bulimia, had reached legendary proportions. Her treatment of her husband, a sign of her marital unhappiness, had become a nagging ache in his life. She would tease him by flirting with the more handsome Palace footmen, many of whom were (and are) gay and all of whom found her attentions embarrassing and decidedly unroyal. If that failed to induce the jealous reaction she wanted – Charles had the maddening habit of asking if everything was all right and then walking away to his own bedroom – she would explode in rage.

Diana did not enjoy opera and, once she was married, rarely agreed to accompany Charles on his outings to Covent Garden. Charles saw no reason to forgo one of his greatest pleasures and often went with friends to the Royal Opera House. His guests included such seasoned companions as Camilla Parker-Bowles and her husband. Diana would stay at home at Kensington Palace, seething with indignation at what she regarded as his effrontery in going out without her. Her temper grew worse as the hours passed and by the time Charles arrived home she was often in a towering, door-banging fury.

Consumed by suspicion, she would accuse him of preposterous liaisons with the most unlikely people Those eruptions would be followed by long periods of remorse. The damage would be patched over, promises would be made and the couple would carry on, sometimes for months. Indeed, at times they looked as if they really were the ideal couple of popular expectation.

Diana made a point in those early years of watching Charles play polo and often embraced him warmly afterwards. In another small but touching gesture of affection, she took a close interest in what he wore, buying him ties and advising him on the cut of his suits. Charles had never been noted for his dress sense before Diana appeared in his life. His clothes had been staid, with the emphasis very much on country tweed and traditional bespoke tailoring. Diana perked him up. She encouraged him to wear Italian-made Ferragamo ties and casual, slip-on shoes as well as conventional lace-up brogues. She stirred his latent interest in clothes – so diligently repressed by Bob Whitby, his house-master at Gordonstoun.

It was most noticeable in his suit jackets, made for him by Anderson and Sheppard of Savile Row, whose other clients included Fred Astaire and the fictional Saint. Where before they had been single-breasted and shapeless, they became double-breasted, more form-hugging and always with a *pochette* cavalierly displayed in the breast pocket. By cutting them longer, the tailor succeeded in hiding the Prince's pear-shaped figure. And turn-ups, always a bit of a problem for the Windsors (George V had coldly enquired of his eldest son if it was damp in Buckingham Palace when he had the temerity to wear them in the King's presence), finally gained the stamp of royal approval. The boy who had so ludicrously been named as one of the world's best dressed men had grown up to deserve the accolade. That was Diana's doing.

Charles, in turn, performed something of a Professor Higgins on her. He pushed her to make speeches, encouraged her taste for classical music and, eventually, against all the odds, got her interested in opera. But just when it looked as though they might have overcome their early problems, some apparently trivial incident would waylay them and set them off on another one-sided shouting match.

This marital deterioration was not something of which the public was much aware. On tour and at official engagements, Diana appeared charming and accommodating. The rapport she established with her ever-widening circle of admirers was real and rewarding. There was no reason for her to be otherwise: both needed each other. As Princess Anne observed: 'The Princess of Wales has obviously filled a void in the media's life which I had *not* filled, but I never had any intention of filling it.'

Shortly after it was announced that Diana was pregnant, the couple had paid an official visit to Wales where she had been a resounding success. Her easy manner enraptured the crowds who gathered to see her. She established an instant and unaffected empathy with people that would eventually take her to the top of the royal popularity polls. All she had to do was smile, wave, kiss a child, hug a mother, and people roared their approval. This was lifeblood to Diana, which no one then wished to deny her.

The Royal Family functions best on the wave of public approval and Diana's arrival had been a tonic. There were, none the less, formalities that had to be observed. This was monarchy, not show business. There was more to the job than a cheering throng and an improved sense of self-worth. Being royal is not the same as being famous and most of the receptions, dinners and openings they attend, however worthy they may be, are mind-numbingly dull.

There is also the matter of protocol. In the interests of the institution itself, the heir to the throne has to take precedence over his wife, just as the sovereign takes precedence over the heir. It could not be otherwise if, in a democratic age, kingship was to retain its position at the top of society's pyramid.

It was a precept the Queen Mother had instinctively grasped. When her husband, a shy man of indifferent health afflicted with a bad stammer, was told that his brother intended to abdicate and that he was about to become king, he broke down and sobbed with fear, much to the dismay of his mother, Queen Mary. Had it not been for his wife, it is doubtful if he would have been able to carry on, much less see his nation through the trauma of the Second World War. The dominant partner in their marriage, George's queen, Elizabeth, pushed her reluctant husband into the foreground where he belonged by right of birth.

Diana, conversely, had no interest in playing second fiddle. The Queen had been made to curtsey to her own grandfather and grandmother, even in private. Charles had been taught to bow to his grandfather, George VI. Such suffocating formalities had been eased over the years, but a certain respectfulness was still expected. Diana refused to give it. Behind their backs but in front of the staff she called the Queen Brenda, Princess Margaret Yvonne and Prince Philip became Keith. Prince Edward, meanwhile, was Nig-nog when he was not Cled, derived from Peter Phillips's corruption of Uncle Ed.

If such irreverence was essentially harmless, it was also indicative of Diana's approach to being royal, which carried through into the way she played the hand of public popularity. She had not consciously gone out of her way to enchant her mother-in-law's subjects but once they were under her spell, she had no intention of doing anything to break it. Charles, so used to being the focus of attention, was at first amused, then bemused, then irritated at the way his wife now commanded the centre stage. In Wales he took this sudden ebb of the interest he aroused in good stead. When he saw someone vainly waving a bunch of flowers in Diana's direction, he politely asked, 'Do you want me to give those to her?'

204

But as Di-fever continued to grow, his remarks acquired a more acerbic edge. 'I'm going to have to get used to looking at the backs of photographers,' he demurred. Where before he had willingly gathered a bouquet for her, he now complained, 'I'm just a collector of flowers these days.' In exasperation, he would eventually protest, 'She's not here, there's only me, so you'd better go and ask for your money back,' which only made matters worse. As well as suffering the indignity of being upstaged, Charles was now being made to appear petulant. Diana did nothing to spare her husband his embarrassment. Quite the contrary: once she had learnt the trick, she took a malicious delight in stealing his limelight.

This was illustrated most graphically several years later when the marriage was in terminal decline. In 1988 they toured Australia together. They paid a visit to a music college where Charles, under protest, agreed to play a note or two on the cello. It was too good an opportunity for Diana to miss. While Charles was still playing she strode across the stage, sat down at the piano, lifted the lid and struck up the opening theme of Rachmaninov's second piano concerto. Every camera swung round to follow her, leaving Charles beached and abandoned in his humiliation. It was a cruel and calculated piece of one-upmanship performed by a maestro.

It was not just her husband off whom Diana was prepared to score points. In a way that few would have dared, she was also prepared to upstage her sovereign, though not without taking the precaution of pleading either ill-health or innocence. In November 1982, Charles and Diana were both expected at the annual Festival of Remembrance at the Royal Albert Hall, two minutes' drive from the Waleses' London home at Kensington Palace. At the last minute Diana, in the throes of a tantrum, refused to go. A row ensued, with Diana, as always, doing most of the shouting. Putting duty before his wife as he was bound to, Charles went on ahead by himself.

'Diana's not very well,' he explained to his family, who by this stage knew what the matter was.

But, fraught and distressed as she might have been, Diana did not wish to miss the occasion. 'I'm exhausted, but how can I let people down?' she asked her hairdresser, Kevin Shanley. She eventually arrived at the Royal Albert Hall fifteen minutes late and, in clear breach of royal protocol and simple good manners, after the Queen.

She did the same thing, though more subtly, at the State Opening of Parliament two years later. Diana chose that moment to put up her hair in a classic chignon. By then she was fully aware of how, by adjusting the length of her dress or the cut of her jacket, she could steal every fashion-page headline. By choosing to change her hairstyle so dramatically she was guaranteed the front page.

It was an audacious, breathtaking act of scene stealing. The State Opening of Parliament is one of the most formal occasions on the royal calendar, the moment when the sovereign's theoretical political power is on parliamentary display. By turning it into a fashion photo opportunity Diana was making a mockery of the institution her mother-in-law embodied.

Shanley, who refused to do the style and left it to his assistant Richard Dalton, saw it as an unsuccessful hairdo. 'I knew it wouldn't suit her,' he scoffed afterwards. 'Her hair wasn't long enough but Diana got her own way – and at what a cost. That one hairstyle ruined everyone's fantasy of her.'

It did not. By then nothing could: her position as the world's favourite cover girl was all but inviolate. Princess Margaret, however, saw behind the coiffure and understood its real purpose. Of all the Royal Family, Margaret had been the most supportive of Diana and had always stood up for her when her childish outbursts had tested everyone else's patience. She even had a certain sneaking admiration for the way Diana had struggled to maintain her own identity in the face of the voracious demands of her new-found station. Margaret had faced a similar situation after Elizabeth became Queen and, in her effort to assert herself, had deliberately worn whatever colour dress her sister was wearing, much to the irritation of Philip, who went red-faced reminding her of her position in the constitutional pecking order.

What Margaret had never done was challenge the Queen at such a formal and solemn occasion as the Opening of Parliament and she was outraged by Diana's action. If Elizabeth was prepared to give Diana the benefit of the doubt, her sister was not. 'How could you let her make such a *fool* of you?' she asked the Queen.

Diana was also making something of a fool out of her husband and there is strong belief in his own family that if he had been firmer in the beginning, many of the later difficulties would have been avoided. But Charles was either too accommodating, too timid, or, as many of the Household staff maintain, too weak, to call Diana to order. Instead he did what he usually does when faced with a crisis beyond his immediate control. He turned away from it.

As his marital frustration mounted and the family life in which he had initially placed such great store became ever more fraught, he started looking for other sources of fulfilment.

Chapter Thirteen

The position of heir to the throne comes without job description or prescribed duties. 'There is no set role for me,' Charles has observed. 'It depends entirely what I make of it.'

There are periods of melancholia when doubt overwhelms him and he seems intent on doing absolutely nothing. Those phases can last for several months. But they pass, and the Prince, who has an unquenchable enthusiasm for new ideas and projects, will return to the fray, intent on getting some new scheme off the ground, or some inventive opinion out into the public arena.

If he is not as intellectually incisive as he has been led to believe, he still has a solid educational basis on which to build his life. His interests are eclectic and range from alternative medicine to architecture, organic farming and the problems of the inner cities.

Much of what he says finds a ready and attentive audience. He reflects the fears of many parents when he says: 'Do we have to tolerate an incessant menu of gratuitous violence on both cinema and television? Those of us with children are very concerned by the appalling lack of restraint shown by those who make such films and videos, and define their so-called art by insisting on the absolute necessity of portraying real life.'

He articulates the concern of his younger brothers' generation when he addresses the greenhouse effect and says: 'We thought the world belonged to us. Now we are beginning to realize that we belong to the world. We are responsible to it *and* to each other. Our creativity is a blessing, but unless we control it, it will be our destruction.' The environment, he argues, is a precious, finite commodity which man is abusing. 'Like the sorceror's apprentice causing havoc in his master's home when he couldn't control the spell which he had released, mankind runs a similar risk of laying waste his earthly home by thinking he's in control when he's clearly not.'

His remarks about architecture in particular have struck a general chord. In the fifties and sixties Britain had undergone a cosmetic face-lift performed by incompetent surgeons. Ancient town centres had been torn down and replaced with sky-scrapers built of concrete and glass and devoid of character or intrinsic merit. Terrace houses with front doors and back-yards had been demolished to make way for soulless tower blocks, built on the false premiss that an outlook on to the 'garden of the sky' would compensate for the absence of neighbours and community. The result was a sociological Sahara. Charles took the scythe of royal authority to the self-satisfaction of Modernism. 'A large number of us', he told the members of the Royal Institute of British Architects at their 150th anniversary dinner in the appropriately ancient Hampton Court, 'have developed a feeling that architects tend to design houses for the approval of fellow architects and critics – not for the tenants.' A good architect, he continued, should be 'concerned about the way people live – about the environment they inhabit and the kind of community that is created by that environment'.

His advocacy of such alternative therapies as strict diet and bio-feedback in which the patient brings his immune system into play by imagery techniques also reflects a growing popular interest.

He has been prepared to back his beliefs with action. In 1976 he created the Prince's Trust as 'my fighting arm' to help disadvantaged young people, especially those who belong to ethnic minorities and those who live on the drab housing estates he so despises, to set up businesses of their own. Its motto was 'make their dreams come true' and in just over a decade the Trust's income rose from £250,000 a year to over £2 million. It came to be supported by such pop luminaries as singers Phil Collins and Bob Geldof – who organized the Band Aid relief fund for Ethiopia and whom Charles particularly admires.

In 1985 he set about turning Highgrove into an organic, herbicide-free estate, starting with the Fourteen-Acre Field at the Duchy Home Farm. He brought a missionary zeal to the project: 'In farming, as in gardening, I believe that if you treat the land with love and respect (in particular, respect for the idea that it has an almost living soul, bound up in the mysterious, everlasting cycles of nature) it will repay you in kind,' he wrote in *Highgrove, Portrait of an Estate*. There are, the Prince argues, sound ecological arguments in favour of the change. Pesticides have dramatically reduced the insect population, which in turn has led to a steep decline in such insect-eating birds as the skylark and the grey partridge, while the wryneck and the cirl bunting are almost extinct. Wild flowers are also in retreat in many low-land areas. Mankind, the Prince wrote, is in danger of destroying the 'almost sacred relationship with the miraculous living cycle of birth, growth, maturity, death and decay. By our arrogant denial of the almost mystical relationship between tillage and worship (as if we were too sophisticated and clever for such a primitive and irrelevant concept) we have very nearly destroyed the cultural element of farming in Britain.' He sees it as his duty to show by personal example that there is a viable alternative to the factory farming which has become the commercial norm since the end of the Second World War.

There is an element here of a rich man indulging a hobby. Organic farming is a comparatively costly way of growing food. It produces only about half the yield per acre compared to conventional methods and English Nature recently announced that its conservation benefits 'remain to be proved'. But with an income of approximately £3.5 million from the Duchy of Cornwall landholdings Charles can afford to indulge his experiment.

And by exploiting his royal name for all its worth and adroitly selling his produce under the Duchy of Cornwall's Original label, he is at least assured of a high market price. By 1993, 650 of the farm's acres had been converted to organic methods, with the rest of the 1113 acres due to go the same way before the end of the century.

Architecture is also an area where Charles has declared his determination to put his ideas into practice. In 1989 he announced plans to build a village of his own on Duchy of Cornwall land at Poundbury in Dorset as an antidote to the vast housing estates 'mushrooming around our cities with no sensitivity whatsoever'.

When he first started to involve himself in these issues back in the seventies, his intention was to confine himself to a few well-chosen words dropped discreetly into the appropriate ears. 'I can only go muddling along pursuing the sort of things I think are right and true, and hope there is a result,' he said, adding, 'I always feel I should be somewhat reticent, otherwise you end up thinking you are more important than you are.'

By the mid-eighties he had come to enjoy the effect he could create. The experience went to his head and he was soon declaring, 'I like to stir things up, to throw a proverbial royal brick through the plate glass of pompous professional pride and jump feet first into the kind of spaghetti Bolognaise which clogs this country from one end to the other.' Buildings he did not like became carbuncles. The august British Medical Association headquarters was likened to 'the celebrated Tower of Pisa – slightly off-balance'. The would-be warrior Prince had found his battleground. His cause: to defend traditional British life from the worst ravages of progress. It was a noble ideal, but by taking on powerful vested interests he was certain to provoke a backlash.

The architects were especially virulent, accusing him of architectural illiteracy and comparing his support of the neo-Georgian to the structural Fascism of Nazi Germany. Even his own father, who enjoyed the previous generation's belief in technology and

211

the inevitable benefits of 'progress', weighed in against him by observing that not everyone wanted to live in an environment that was a sterile reproduction of some previous age.

Charles, fearful of confrontation and closeted with lieutenants often selected for their ability to agree with him, was stunned by the venom of the reaction. Put to the test, he sulked. Richard Rogers, one of Britain's leading architects, tried to arrange a clear-the-air meeting with the Prince. After his appointment was cancelled for the third time, Rogers angrily declared, 'This is the reason that in the past some countries beheaded their kings.'

Charles, having refused to talk with Rogers, went on radio and huffily exclaimed: 'I often wonder if it is sensible to say anything nowadays. Sometimes it is dangerous to open my mouth at all.' He added: 'It would be much easier to lead a quiet life ... But if, you know, they'd rather I did nothing about it I'll go off somewhere else.' That was an overreaction. Much of what he said met with general approval. What he failed to appreciate was that, by saying it so forcefully, he was certain to generate vocal opposition. He was also steering perilously close to the eddy of politics.

According to a member of the Household, Charles 'absolutely loathed and detested Mrs Thatcher' who, he believed, was causing deep and dangerous divisions of wealth in Britain; and he wrote to his mother expressing that view. It was a view that the Queen who, like her son, inclines towards the Liberal Democrats, shared; in 1986 the *Sunday Times* carried a detailed account, based on an off-the-record briefing from her then press secretary, Michael Shea, of the distress she felt at the government's apparent lack of compassion for the underprivileged. The furore caused by the article was a stiff reminder of the constitutional convention which obliges members of the Royal Family to keep such opinions to themselves.

By involving himself in such contentious issues as the future of Britain's decaying inner cities and youth unemployment, Charles generated another controversy. That was in no small measure the fault of his advisers. According to Earl Mountbatten's secretary, John Barratt, Edward Adeane was 'boring, dull and lacked a sense of humour'. But he was confident enough to say no to the Prince. It is unlikely that, had Adeane still been in the royal employ, Charles would have been allowed to make the fool of himself he did in 1991 when, having criticized other motorists for driving gas guzzling 'monsters', he then insisted on taking a Bentley, clocking in at a generous eleven miles to the gallon, on a visit to Czechoslovakia. Adeane knew his way around the Establishment's inner alleyways and he knew how to get things done. So did his successor, Sir John Riddell, and Major General Sir Christopher Airy who came after him. Unfortunately, they were unable to hit on a close relationship with the often testy Prince, who used them more as factotums than senior aides. Airy, who only lasted ten months in the job, was particularly bemused by his royal employer. Airy had served as an officer in both the Grenadier and Scots Guards. Charles, in contrary mood, had taken against the Guards which, he proclaimed, were bastions of élitism; without any sense of irony or the ridiculous, one of the most privileged people in the world continually declared, 'I can't bear privilege!'

Barbara Barnes would have been equally perplexed by that remark. In a case of history repeating itself, she had left her royal employer, as had Nanny Lightbody a generation before her, when William started school, and for very similar reasons. Helen Lightbody had run into problems with Prince Philip. Barbara found Charles a more status-conscious employer than he liked to pretend. She attended Lord Glenconner's lavish sixtieth birthday celebrations on Mustique in 1986. Photographs of her at the party appeared in a magazine, and she left shortly afterwards. The Prince had set views of a nanny's place and it was not at smart parties to which he had not been invited.

Others, too, found dealing with the prince's egocentricity more trouble than it was worth. Charles, anxious to keep himself informed on everything from the latest in computer technology to left-wing politics, makes a habit of inviting experts in whichever field currently interests him to join him in forming an informal discussion group. David Mlinaric, one of the most talented interior decorators of his generation who, by genuine coincidence, was in charge of the £16 million refurbishment of the Spencer family mansion overlooking St James's Park, was persuaded to join a committee on design. When he discovered that Charles only wanted a rubber stamp to his own ideas, he quietly resigned.

As the restraining hand of tradition and ability was loosened, so a new set of advisers moved in to counsel the Prince. Their ideas were not always up to scratch. Even such a committed royal apologist as the former arts minister, Lord St John of Fawsley, was eventually moved to remark that his counsellors included 'a number of cranks'.

That was reflected in the efficiency of Charles's office. The increasingly Green Prince frequently proffered his ideas to the Department of the Environment and then complained of obstructionism when his suggestions were not acted upon. When Lord Hesketh became a junior minister at that department, he decided to call Charles's hand. Instead of rejecting the Prince's proposals, as others had done, Hesketh praised them and said that of course they would be taken up – provided that the Prince's office made all the arrangements. The bluff worked: Charles's office increasingly lacked the organizational abilities to put all his ideas into practice.

Projects that had already been announced sometimes failed to materialize. The Poundbury village had not been started four years after Charles first gave it the go-ahead. That was partly the consequence of market forces: the downturn in property prices at the end of the eighties had brought the commercial viability of a new village into financial question. But that was not the only problem facing the project. To Charles's immense surprise, the local planning authorities objected to what one councillor dismissed as the 'Tuscan-style' design, which they felt

214

inappropriate to Dorset. The police opposed the project on more mundane grounds. The warren of alleyways central to the original plan, they said, made an ideal hunting ground for muggers. It was a problem of urban planning of which Charles had no practical experience.

These setbacks inevitably placed Charles on the wrong side of the credibility gap. There appeared to be an element of the gadfly in the way he flitted from one project to another without waiting to see anything through. Diana reinforced that impression when she mentioned his famous Highgrove garden and said, 'He will get bored with it and take up something else. He's like that.'

There was also a serious presentational problem. He was not, he insisted, 'interested in the occult' and had never tried to contact Lord Mountbatten by seance. But he did speak to his plants. 'I examine them very carefully and occasionally talk to them, which I think is very important – they do respond in a funny way,' he said. 'And, of course, if they die I feel deeply saddened by that.'

At the same time, his views on spirituality (most obtusely expressed in his pronouncement 'that deep in the soul of mankind there is a reflection as on the surface of a mirror or a mirror-calm lake, of the beauty and harmony of the universe') were skirting the rim of incomprehensibility.

The press inevitably seized on the more incongruous aspects of his behaviour. His trips to the Kalahari elicited derision. When he ventured to the Hebrides to spend a few days living with a poor crofter, the *Sun*'s headline read: 'A-loon Again'. The Prince, rather than being a force for change, was in danger of becoming a subject for ridicule.

In the seventies there had been talk of sending Charles to Australia or possibly Canada as Governor-General. It revived again in the following decade. In 1988 it was suggested in political circles that he might be appointed Governor of the colony of Hong Kong. That was always going to be a non-starter: Britain was in sensitive and sometimes aggressive negotiations with

215

Communist China over the future of the colony, which could not be entrusted to someone as naïve and inexperienced as Charles.

According to Margaret Thatcher's press secretary, Bernard Ingham, the discussion about any future job for the Prince of Wales never got past the 'desultory' stage; Charles may have disliked Mrs Thatcher but she had power of patronage, and she regarded the future king as a light-weight. The heir to the throne, whose real job was contingent upon the death of his mother, was effectively being denied any gainful employment to occupy the intervening years. That only served to confirm the lingering sense of his own worthlessness that had been written into his psychological making as a boy.

Chapter Fourteen

In the autumn of 1990 Prince Charles was on the verge of a nervous breakdown. His friends – they included his extra equerry Nicholas Soames and his cousin, Norton Knatchbull, now Lord Romsey – jokingly dismissed it as a 'midlife crisis'. In private, however, there was concern that he was suffering from what one friend called 'clinical depression'.

The superficial cause was the injury he had suffered while playing polo at Cirencester Park in June. He had taken a bad tumble from his pony and broken his right arm in two places. One spectator claimed to have seen a bone 'sticking out horribly at the elbow'. The break had failed to knit satisfactorily and the arm had to be rebroken. A metal pin was inserted and bone grafted from the hip to help the mending process.

To compound matters, it had been whispered that during the first operation in the Cheltenham General Hospital, where Charles stayed for three days ostensibly as a National Health patient, part of his tendon was caught in the fracture, causing him excruciating pain. This was corrected in the second operation, performed by consultant surgeons John Webb and Christopher Colton who were chosen personally by the Prince. The delayed shock, it was said, was enough to produce severe depression.

But it was not just the pain in his arm that was troubling him. There was the even more excruciating matter of the heart.

For the past three years Charles had been conducting an increasingly open affair with Camilla Parker-Bowles. Her family and friends knew what was going on. So did Diana. 'Sundays are for Camilla,' he had baldly told his wife – or so some of Camilla's friends reported. What that meant was that Diana was expected to return to London on Sunday evenings, leaving Charles free to be with Camilla.

It was a situation to which Diana took extreme and understandable exception, and one which, in her own mind at least, had been brewing from the outset of her marriage.

Shortly after her wedding Diana had asked one of the royal equerries at a dinner party in Scotland: 'What am I going to do about his women?' Jealous by nature, she resented her husband's continuing fondness for Lady Tryon and Camilla Parker-Bowles. There was no hint at that time, however, that the Prince was doing anything other than maintaining highly valued friendships. As the equerry recalled, it was their influence rather than anything else Diana objected to. It was a problem she easily resolved: by ensuring that Camilla and Kanga were not invited to any event that she was attending, Diana effectively excluded them from the royal circle.

Charles initially went along with his wife's wishes and appeared to be making the effort to be the faithful husband his marriage vows pledged him to be. It would have been extraordinary if he had not. He could be selfish and arrogant, but he was not cruel. A religious man, he places great stock in the oaths he swears. He regarded marriage as one of his princely duties, and whatever private misgivings he might have had about taking a wife he neither loved nor desired, he had been brought up to put duty before self. The dishonesty and deceit of adultery did not come easily to him, at least not in the beginning.

In the version of events put about by Diana's friends in the dying days of the marriage, Charles had fallen straight out of the honeymoon bed and into the arms of Camilla Parker-Bowles. By then, however, time scales were being shifted to create optimum effect. In an earlier report, he was supposed to have remained faithful for only the first two years of his marriage, while in the first account he actually managed to make it through to 1987 before embarking on his extramarital detour.

There was more than pedantry to the dispute over the timing. If Charles had been seeing Camilla during his courtship and throughout his marriage to Diana, then he can be fairly depicted as a heartless, immoral blackguard who drove a young and innocent girl to the brink of suicide. But if he behaved in an honourable fashion for the first years of his marriage, then Diana must shoulder a greater share of the responsibility for her own and her husband's subsequent misery. The Queen, who kept a concerned if discreet eye on the situation, had little doubt as to what the true situation was. Camilla, she said, has been 'much maligned'.

What was not in dispute was Charles and Diana's incompatibility which had so quickly manifested itself in arguments and quarrels. For one thing, Diana had no interest in Charles's intellectual pursuits. If Charles mentioned Rudyard Kipling's *Just So Stories*, Diana would say, 'Just so what, Charles?' When he entertained his architectural friends, she would go out to play bridge with her own circle. Engrossed in her own anxieties, she was not always sympathetic to his problems. The fault for this growing estrangement was certainly not all Diana's, however. Charles, as even his greatest admirers will concede, can be pedantic, imperious, and, surrounded as he is by fawning courtiers who laud his every utterance, convinced of his own wisdom. He believes in following his 'intuition' even if it runs against the available facts. He also had a developing contempt for his wife's intellectual abilities which he found ever harder to camouflage.

This only exacerbated her health problems. She had remained under medical care: since the ill-fated honeymoon at Balmoral a succession of doctors and psychiatrists had been called in to treat her. The Jungian psychotherapist Dr Allan McGlashan, who was a friend of Sir Laurens van der Post, had concentrated on trying to analyse her dreams; David Mitchell was more concerned about her relationship with her husband; Maurice

Lipsedge of Guy's Hospital in London was called in to treat her bulimia. There were others, including her own physician, Michael Linnett. None had been able to give the Princess a lasting mental equilibrium. She was unable to conquer her bulimia; and despite anti-depressants, she was increasingly prone to temper fits, punctuated by tears. The more she came to appreciate the potency of her royal position, the more she slackened the rein on her temper and the more distant and self-absorbed Charles became.

By the mid eighties they were in constant dispute. Charles continued to take an interest in what Diana did, but on the professional rather than personal front. It was Charles, for instance, who ruled that under no circumstances was Diana going to take part in *It's a Royal Knockout*, the 1986 television fiasco organized by Prince Edward, which reduced the younger royals to the ranks of second-rate comedians and provided a foretaste of the *annus horribilis* to come.

The Queen Mother was incensed by the programme. Afterwards she had Andrew, Edward and Anne in to see her and made them promise that they would never, ever, take part in anything like that again. Her face 'white with rage', as one of her staff recalled, she reminded her grandchildren of the Abdication and the danger that had posed to the monarchy. She told them: 'The King [George VI] and I spent years and years building up the reputation of the monarchy and you, in one evening, destroy it.'

Diana was very angry when Charles would not allow her to appear on the show but became 'very smug', as one observer recalled, when she discerned how much trouble it had caused. She was 'thrilled' by the embarrassment of Sarah, whose over-boisterous performance had attracted most of the flak; the two women had long been friends, but in the devouring world of the Royal Family, they soon came to see each other as rivals. She did not thank her husband, though, for getting her out of a derisory situation she had been so keen to get herself into. As far as Diana was concerned, it was just another example of the way he was always trying to hold her back, to dominate her, even if on this occasion he happened to be right. It was an unreasonable attitude, but by then their relationship was becoming one of mutual irritation.

The children were another obvious bone of contention. Diana, whose hostility towards the family into which she had married was becoming more ingrained with each passing year, started to use them as a weapon against her in-laws. She ignored Prince Philip's entreaties and refused to have Princess Anne as godmother to Harry. (Anne countered by organizing a rabbit shoot on the day of the christening.) Charles, a king-in-waiting but not master in his own house, tried to explain the royal point of view but was overruled, as he was in most matters pertaining to his sons' upbringing – from the way they dressed (he preferred them to wear traditional children's clothes while their mother favoured jeans and American T-shirts and, on one ridiculous occasion, overcoats that matched hers) to the food they ate ('The things that are bad for them, just like all children,' Diana conceded).

She had been as good as her word, however, in matters of affection and was very much a hands-on, arms-round mother. Charles was more remote. He was very like his own parents in that he refused to centre his life around his sons. This was most obviously illustrated when William was rushed to hospital in Reading after being hit on the head with a golf club. He was transferred to the Great Ormond Street for Sick Children in London where the doctors decided to operate on his fractured skull. Diana stayed at his side throughout. Charles left to attend a performance of Puccini's opera *Tosca* at Covent Garden with a party of European Community officials. It was, he insisted, his duty. It was also a difference in attitude. Diana, who always found children easier than adults to get on with, spent as much time as she possibly could with her sons. Charles admitted, 'I love William and Harry dearly, but sometimes I just have to get away from home to get some peace.'

In the autumn of 1987 he did just that, and for much of September and all of October, but for one day, he went into retreat at Balmoral, leaving Diana and their sons in London. No amount of behind-the-scenes pleading by the press office, the private secretaries or the Queen herself could lure him south again. He had simply had enough of the rows which had become an almost daily occurrence.

Charles, whose own temper losses were always brief, desperately tried to avoid those confrontations with his wife, but there was no escaping Diana. When he walked out of a room, she would follow him, 'screaming hysterically', as one of the staff recalled. She would slam any handy door, then open it and slam it again. She would walk the length of the bookshelf, punching the books and shouting at the top of her voice, 'No, Charles, no, no, I won't, Charles, no, no,' or, 'I will – and there is nothing you can do to stop me!'

It was impossible to say what the spats were about, for in sad truth they had become arguments for arguments' sake. A remark, often just a look, was enough to set them off. Sometimes it was that she wanted to go back to London. At other times it was that she wanted to stay in the country. If Charles wanted to eat lunch outside under the trees, Diana would insist on having it indoors. If he wanted to take his sons to polo, she would insist on taking them back to London.

'There was hysteria and tears,' one witness recalled. 'Almost everything he wanted to do at that stage, she didn't want to do. She actually seemed to *enjoy* rowing.'

Charles would wring his hands in despair and say, 'Diana, please, you're not being fair.' That only seemed to make the situation worse. 'Don't you dare speak to me like that!' she would shriek.

According to Charles's former polo manager Major Ronald Ferguson, Diana had the stronger personality of the two and she usually came out on top, with Charles giving way, a pained look of helpless desperation on his face. If he did not – and there was the odd occasion like *It's a Royal Knockout* when even Charles felt compelled to stand firm – Diana would storm out of the house.

The most venomous quarrels took place at Highgrove and after one especially vocal eruption, Diana drove off into the Gloucestershire countryside, slewing the car from one side of the road to the other in her temper. The police set off in frantic pursuit, but she made it half-way across the county before they managed to catch up with her.

Camilla appeared like a rock of sanity in this Sargasso of hysteria in which Charles found himself entangled. Despite his wife's injunction against her presence, he had kept in touch with her after his marriage and the two had continued to meet on the hunting field and, periodically, at dinner parties at the houses of friends. As his marriage continued its disintegration and hers cooled after the birth of her two children, they turned to each other for comfort.

Camilla, one of her friends observed, 'was his only hope for a bit of enjoyable "quality life"'. She gave him support and encouragement. She would tell him, 'I'm so proud of you,' and when he demurred and said he was not worthy of such support, she would reply, 'As usual you're underestimating yourself.'

It was flattery and affection of a kind he had craved all his life, coupled with a loving intimacy he had never enjoyed with Diana. The depth of their feelings was revealed in an unauthorized recording of a telephone call they made to each other on the night of 18 December 1989.

With all the enthusiasm of a star-struck lover, Charles says, 'I want to feel my way along you, all over you and up and down you, and in and out . . . particularly the in and out.'

Camilla is equally ardent. 'Oh, darling,' she tells her paramour, 'I just want you now . . . desperately, desperately, desperately.'

It was happiness that could only be snatched at. Camilla saw little of her husband who was away in London most of the week, but she remained none the less still married to a Roman Catholic who did not believe in divorce, while Charles, as future Defender of the Faith and Supreme Governor of the Church of England, was bound by the moral parameters of his position. They could swear their love for each other, but there was never any question, not then, even when their affair was at its height, of them ever setting up home together. They had to make do with hurried visits to the homes of obliging friends. A night was a stolen luxury to be savoured and remembered.

Because they saw so little of each other, the affair retained its burning intensity longer than it might have had they been with each other all the time. However vulgar the ambition, only a man in the throes of nascent passion would want to be reincarnated as a tampon.

It did not take Diana long to work out what was happening. Camilla never overnighted at Highgrove, but she was there often enough when Diana was absent to arouse suspicion.

Paul Burrell, the Highgrove butler, inadvertently helped Diana to keep informed of what was going on. He had started out as footman to the Queen, who had taken a liking to him, and on whose prompting he had married Maria, one of the Buckingham Palace housemaids. When Maria produced a son she was immediately befriended by Diana who started to spend long hours chatting to the young mother at her flat in the Royal Mews.

When the Waleses decided they needed a butler in the country, Diana was most insistent that Burrell be offered the job. The Queen was most reluctant to let him go, offering him a house in Windsor and private education for his children in an effort to try to keep him. As usual, however, Diana had her way and the Burrells moved to Gloucestershire.

Given Diana's continuing friendship with Maria, it was inevitable that the news that the Prince was entertaining Camilla at Highgrove would quickly reach the Princess at Kensington Palace. Maria would innocently say that her husband was being kept busy, Diana would put two and two together and next time she met Charles would say, 'I hear you've been seeing that woman again,' precipitating another round of rows. The shouting was not as one-sided as it had been. Exasperated by what he considered her unreasonable attitude, Charles had discovered the strength of his own voice and started yelling back. There was a reason for his anger, for by 1988, a full year before his own relationship with Camilla was caught on tape, it was clear that he was not the only man in his wife's life.

The first rival for her attention was James Hewitt, an officer in the Life Guards who in 1988 had been seconded to teach Prince William to ride at the Combermere Barracks near Windsor. According to Lance Corporal Malcolm Lette, the Millfield-educated Hewitt's personal-valet-cum-groom, the bachelor soldier and the married Princess soon became the closest of friends. Diana, Lette recalled, 'started sending him presents and buying him things, always in a flash carrier bag – Harrods or other big stores'. One morning he saw Hewitt and Diana disappear into the riding school. He looked inside where he saw 'the pair of them in the corner. I wasn't quite sure what I saw, but they were certainly cuddling'.

As Emma Stewardson, his former girlfriend who was outraged at being two-timed, later revealed, Hewitt had visited the Princess at Highgrove when he had told her he was on duty. Charles was not there at the time.

There were other, more secret meetings. For a while Hewitt rented a room at a house in West London. Diana paid several clandestine visits there. It was an extremely dangerous game that, inevitably, did not go undetected.

Hewitt had a commanding physical presence which was often remarked upon by his brother officers, and Diana continued to see the handsome officer after he returned from serving as a tank commander in Kuwait during the Gulf War. Charles's relatives formed their own opinions about the friendship. 'There is no doubt about what Diana saw in James,' one of Charles's royal cousins said. After the sterility of their marriage, Diana, now a mother of two and approaching her thirtieth birthday, had

225

discovered the excitement of being the object of a young man's adept attentions.

Their relationship, however, never recovered its intimacy after Diana learnt that Hewitt had been more boastful about how well he knew her than discretion allowed. It did not take her long to find someone to take his place.

Diana had known James Gilbey since her bachelor days in her flat in Coleherne Court in Earl's Court. A car dealer by trade and educated at Ampleforth (as was Parker-Bowles), he was the great-nephew of Monsignor Alfred Gilbey, the only priest in Britain sanctioned by the Pope to say the Mass in Latin. She had been reintroduced to him at a dinner party given by the Duke of Norfolk's daughter, Carina, who is married to television presenter David Frost. They started seeing each other, first for lunches at San Lorenzo, run by the Italian-born Mara Berni and her husband Lorenzo, who own a number of properties near to their fashionable Knightsbridge restaurant, then in more surreptitious circumstances.

The Bernis are a social institution in London and count many of their customers, including Mick Jagger and Princess Margaret, as their personal friends. Mara, a friendly, embracing woman, has acted as mother confessor to two generations of young women and Diana quickly started to turn to her for advice and help. Soon she and Gilbey were carrying on their lunchtime discussions not in the restaurant but at a house nearby. One night in October 1989, she was photographed emerging from Gilbey's rented one-bedroom flat in Knightsbridge's Lennox Gardens at 1.15 in the morning.

On New Year's Eve 1989, thirteen days after Charles and Camilla's call had been listened into, Gilbey and Diana were recorded in private telephone conversation. He called her Squidgy and told her over and over again how much he loved her. She asked if he was playing with himself and said, 'I don't want to get pregnant.' Gilbey assured her that would not happen but Diana persisted. 'I watched *EastEnders* today. One of the

226

main characters had a baby. They thought it was by her husband. It was by another man.' Diana later confirmed to friends that the tape was genuine.

There was something decidedly Dada-esque about the leading character in what had become a real-life soap opera watching a television version of the genre and then relating it to herself. By that stage in the royal melodrama, however, most of the major players were only managing to hang on to reality by the tips of their fingernails.

Three-quarters of a century earlier the situation would have been handled with discretion; as Camilla's great-grandmother Alice Keppel remarked as she surveyed the shambles of the last Prince of Wales's affair with Wallis Simpson, 'We did things better in my day.' In Edwardian Britain the 'overriding consideration', the American historian Barbara Tuchman observed, of the upper orders 'was to prevent any exposure of misconduct to the lower classes'. They had usually succeeded. They no longer could. The advent of the long lens, the directional microphone and sophisticated but relatively inexpensive telephone bugging equipment had put paid to that. There was no keeping the lid on these affairs, the broad details of which had found their way into the gossip columns long before the publication of first the 'Squidgy', then the so-called 'Camillagate' tapes, the choicest bits of which were faxed around the world the moment they were published.

With a worldliness that belied her own sheltered upbringing, the Queen was upset, not so much by the adolescent *mots doux* contained in the tapes, as by the marital unhappiness that had led up to them. Charles was less sanguine. Under the tutelage of such 'gurus' as Sir Laurens van der Post, he had been trying to achieve a spiritual equilibrium which others, more derogatorily, regard as Eastern philosophical fatalism.

It had stood him in good stead when his friend Major Hugh Lindsay was killed by an avalanche while skiing with him in Klosters in 1988. 'We shall all miss dear old Hugh quite enormously,' he wrote to a friend. 'But the reason I survived and he didn't is just one of the wonders of our existence.' It proved less effective in helping him to cope with the barrage of criticism now being aimed in his direction which, combined with the patent unhappiness of his home life, was proving an intolerable strain.

The fall from his polo pony had brought his plight into sharp and extremely painful focus. It was the sense of guilt – of having failed his family and himself – with which he found it so difficult to come to terms. It took four months before he was willing to undertake any official engagements, and for some considerable time afterwards his friends continued to worry about his mental health.

As he admitted to Camilla, he was 'not very good' at positive thinking. He felt as if he was being strangled in a tangle of nots: this was *not* the image he wanted for himself or the royal family; *not* what he wanted for his sons; *not* what he wanted in a marriage; *not* what he wanted for Camilla. He was, he complained, a prisoner in his own life. And he did what he always did when faced with a situation he could not control – he walked away from it.

Unable to face Diana's endless haranguing, he spent as little time with her as possible. Friends of Diana recalled their embarrassment when they were with her in the sitting room at Kensington Palace and Charles walked in unexpectedly, took one look at his wife, and walked straight out again without saying a word. The looks exchanged between husband and wife were of unbridled hatred.

The couple still went to Highgrove at weekends but after dinner on Saturday nights Charles would drive off to spend a couple of hours with Camilla. 'It was an escape. He couldn't bear to sit with Diana any more,' one Household member recalls.

That drove Diana into apoplexies of rage. She slammed doors, kicked walls, and burst into tears. Between 1987 and 1990 the rages, according to those who saw them, 'were frightening. Her face turned a bright, bright red.' But only in private. In public both Charles and Diana tried to act as if nothing was the matter and quite often got away with it. There was a natural and understandable desire on the part of those they were appearing before to wish them well and to dismiss as malicious calumnies the stories that had come to dominate the front pages of the more popular newspapers.

Those performances could be quite eerie. The couple could be in the middle of a furious row when they were informed by an equerry or a secretary that it was time to leave. The shouting would suddenly stop as quickly as it had started. Diana would say, 'Come on, Charles, people are waiting for us,' and they would set off for their engagement looking for all the world and the waiting cameramen like a reasonably happily married couple. The moment they got home again, the row would pick up where it had left off and continue until Charles managed to make his escape or Diana went to bed, exhausted.

But there was a limit to how long even these practised performers could keep up the charade. The act started fraying around the edges when the couple visited India in February 1992. On a previous trip to the sub-continent, Charles had visited the Taj Mahal, built by the seventeenth-century Moghul emperor Shah Jehan as an eternal monument to his love for his consort, Arjunand Banu Begum. 'One day,' Charles promised, 'I will come back and bring my wife with me.' In the event his wife went by herself while Charles stayed in New Delhi to address a meeting of local businessmen. It was a photo opportunity which Diana, mistress of pictorial symbolism, used to her advantage, turning first her back to the waiting cameramen, then giving them a plaintive smile.

In Jaipur Diana again underlined the rift by deliberately turning her cheek away just as her husband was about to kiss it. Charles, his lips floundering in mid air, ended up pecking at her earring.

These public rows were very damaging to the image of the monarchy. There was also the danger that William and Harry would be wounded in the verbal crossfire. Harry seemed to take it all in his stride: 'laid back' but brave and adventurous, at the age of two he had caught the professional eye of his aunt, Princess Anne, who believes he has the talent to become a top rider and has taken a close interest in his progress. The feeling in the Royal Family is that his easy self-confidence will see him through the crisis in his parents' lives.

William is another matter. The distress of his mother, whose side he took, upset him more than it did his brother. He became introverted and at one point found it difficult going to the bathroom, which was seen as a symptom of his unhappiness. It was a situation which clearly could not continue indefinitely.

But what to do about it? The obvious answer was for Charles to give up Camilla, Diana to end her extramarital friendships and for the pair of them to try to make a go of their marriage. At the very least they should stay together for appearances' sake. This was the solution Charles favoured. Diana, however, would not co-operate. She wanted to live her life 'honestly' – as also, it transpired, did the Duchess of York, whose own marriage was heading towards dissolution, albeit for different reasons.

Sarah and Andrew had been in love in a passionate, physical way that Charles and Diana never had. Long after their break-up Sarah would protest that they still were. The restrictions of royal life, however, and the constant pounding she had taken from the media and, more invidiously, the Palace courtiers had exacted its toll. The Queen's private secretary Sir Robert Fellowes, whom Sarah called 'Bellows', would arrive each morning in her suite at Buckingham Palace with a handful of unfavourable stories clipped from the morning newspapers and declare, 'We didn't do very well yesterday, did we, ma'am?' She complained that Andrew, the husband she rarely saw, was not supporting her in these confrontations and after five years decided that she had had enough. She wanted out.

So, by then, did Diana. The two women, once friends, now competitors, but united in their marital gloom, egged each other on when they were together at Balmoral. It was a fraught time. They all but ignored their husbands, and insisted on joining their royal cousins, David, Viscount Linley, and George, the fourth Marquess of Milford Haven who is the son of Prince Philip's late companion in excess, in whatever they were doing. This caused embarrassment to Milford Haven and Linley who, as junior members of the 'Firm' ('My son isn't royal,' Linley's mother, Princess Margaret, once declared. 'He just happens to have the Queen as his aunt'), would have preferred to have kept well out of the way of the conjugal fall-out.

That proved an impossibility in a family which places such store on propriety yet was facing the impending failure of two of its most celebrated marriages. This was a calamity that called the credibility of every member of the royal clan into uncomfortable question. So concerned was the Queen by the damage this looming catastrophe would cause the monarchy that she overcame her natural reluctance to involve herself directly in disagreeable matters and called on her daughters-in-law to exercise caution. There was little she could do to enforce her writ, however, for events were rapidly running out of the Royal Family's control. It was Diana and Sarah, supported by the buttress of media attention, who now had the power to set the itinerary. Sarah acknowledged as much when she jokingly suggested to Diana that as she intended to leave her husband and as Diana planned to follow suit, why not make it a joint exit?

There was a breathtaking recklessness to that proposal. It was not one that was ever going to appeal to Diana, though. The Princess had absolutely no intention of sharing centre stage with the Duchess. No matter how unhappy she might be, Diana was not going to surrender her position without first ensuring that her departure would be at a time of her choosing and on her terms.

The Duchess's separation had provided Diana with a warning of the dangers that lay ahead. On the day that it was announced in March 1992 that the Yorks were to part, Charles Anson, the

Queen's press officer, gave a briefing to senior journalists in which he spelt out that henceforth Sarah was not to be regarded as a member of the Royal Family. The Duchess was shocked by the ferocity of the reaction. So was the BBC's court and diplomatic correspondent, Paul Reynolds, who went on radio to report, 'The knives are out for Fergie at the Palace.'

Sarah was soon complaining that she was being subjected to a campaign of emotional and financial 'terrorism' by the Palace advisers as they sought to distance her from the Royal Family. There was even a suggestion in court circles that she be stripped of her honorific, Her Royal Highness.

Diana was determined that she would not suffer the same treatment. She demanded care and control of her sons, plus the guarantee that she would retain all the perks and privileges of her royal status. Those negotiations inevitably involved more arguments.

Yet even at this eleventh hour, Charles was prepared to save his marriage. He was very aware of the damage to the Royal Family its breakdown would cause. He acknowledged to friends that his relationship with Diana would never be a loving one, but in many heated conversations spread over several months he pleaded with Diana to try to make a go of it, if only for appearances' sake, for the good of the children, for the good of the monarchy.

Andrew Morton's *Diana: Her True Story* put paid to that. The book revealed that Diana suffered from bulimia. It alleged that Charles had been conducting an affair with Camilla throughout his marriage. It alleged that the Prince's heartless conduct had driven his despairing wife to attempted suicide. Charles was stunned by the ferocity of the charges levelled against him and outraged by the part his wife had played in bringing them to print. He saw it as an act of the grossest betrayal.

The Queen, desperate to hold her crumbling family together, tried to view matters objectively. She called Diana to Buckingham Palace and pleaded with her to reconsider. Philip forcefully reminded her of where her duty lay. Sir William Heseltine, back on holiday from Australia where he had retired after leaving the royal employ in 1990, had long consultations with the Queen about how best to handle the problem which he unwittingly had helped to create all those years before. Diana – tearful, insecure but playing the professional victim for all she was worth – wilted under this heavy royal pressure and reluctantly agreed to stay on, if only for another few months.

It did not last that long. Charles would not allow it to. After eleven years of argument, desperation, depression, farce and humiliation he had finally had enough of Diana.

He telephoned his mother. He told her, 'Don't you realize she's mad? She's mad!'

Then he hung up the telephone on the Queen.

Postlude

On 9 December 1992, Prime Minister John Major rose in the House of Commons to announce the separation of the Prince and Princess of Wales.

Charles was delighted. He had tried almost to the end to hold together the splintered fragments of his marriage. A separation leading to inevitable divorce was against everything in which he had been brought up to believe, but when it happened he looked as though he was experiencing what one member of his staff described as a 'surging sense of relief'. He had been freed from the millstone of a wife he had never loved who transparently no longer loved him, who upstaged him and shouted him down. She had brought him to the verge of nervous collapse. Now she was gone and he felt, he said, as though he had been 'unshackled'.

He set about expunging all traces of her from Highgrove, into which, he says, 'I have put my heart and my soul.' Out went the frilled cushions and the fitted Wilton carpets, to be replaced with tartan curtains, bleached wool and sisal carpets which gave the house, he explained, 'a really good country look'. In another symbolic gesture, he brought out of retirement his old nanny, Mabel Anderson, whom Diana had refused to employ. It is into her care that William and Harry are put when they pay their weekend visits to their father.

His staff were delighted by the transformation which came over him. They had not seen the Prince so happy in years.

The Queen, too, was cheered. She was at Wood Farm on the

Sandringham estate on the day of the announcement. She did not watch the Prime Minister deliver it on television. Instead she did what she always does when she is agitated and turned to her dogs for comfort. She kept taking off her coat and boots, drying the dogs and then putting on her coat and going out again. Her page, mistaking her distraction for distress, ventured to say that he was very sorry about what had happened. Without hesitating, the Queen replied, 'I think you'll find it's all for the best.'

From Charles and Diana's personal perspective it undoubtedly was. They had run into serious trouble before the honeymoon was over and had been clawing at each other's throats ever since. The previous few months had seen an escalation in hostilities to the point where they could not bear to be in the same room together. That had an unavoidable spill-over effect on the running of the royal business enterprises, and their tours of India and Korea – which the Buckingham Palace courtiers had tried to insist showed how close they were – degenerated into circuses when it became patently clear they could not stand the sight of each other.

Being married to Charles, Diana told her friends, was a 'nightmare'. He was, she alleged, a heartless, selfish man who was bad with his children and took cruel delight in tormenting her with the blatancy of his affair with Camilla Parker-Bowles. Marrying Diana, Charles retorted, was the 'worst mistake' he had ever made. He said she was unstable and not to be trusted. Only the sensitivity of his position as future king had kept them together this long. Now, given the threat to their mental health and the damage caused by Diana's accusations against him, there was little point in continuing with the farce.

Charles had spent much of that autumn trying to persuade his mother of this and, in violation of everything he had ever been taught, had actually lost his temper with her. The Queen, he said, was 'out of touch'. Still the Queen counselled caution but in the end she was forced to concede that, given the depth of animosity, separation really was 'for the best'.

And so, for a while, it proved. That Christmas the Royal Family, no longer able to use Windsor Castle which is closed for renovation, gathered at Sandringham. The Duchess of York was not there. Banned by Prince Philip from staying in the big house, she had been relegated to Wood Farm and was only allowed to join the main party for afternoon tea. Diana stayed away altogether, preferring to spend the holiday in the company, not of her brother as was reported, but of Lucia Flecha de Lima, the wife of the Brazilian ambassador.

Charles and his family were delighted. The familial harmony which had been strained first by the Duke and Duchess of York's marital discord then that of the Prince and Princess of Wales had been restored. It was, everyone agreed, the best Christmas they had had since 1980.

'It's just like old times,' the Queen declared.

Christmas was not nearly so pleasant for Camilla Parker-Bowles. At the first sign of trouble the Royal Family, a self-contained unit complete unto itself, circles the wagons and laagers in. Camilla, however, had no royal edifice behind which to hide, no security officers to protect her. The publication of her taped conversations with Charles had exposed her as the Prince's lover. Her Wiltshire home was besieged by reporters and photographers. Escape became imperative, which was why, a few days later, the bedraggled figure of the mistress of the future King of England was to be seen trudging wearily across several muddy ploughed fields.

The affair was no longer burning with quite the same intensity it once had. After so many years, they had settled down into a routine that was more cosy than carnal. 'They are more friends than lovers now,' one of Camilla's closest friends said in early 1992. The emotional crisis Charles had experienced in 1990 had put a distance between them, while the mounting press speculation with which they had increasingly to contend had necessitated an even more judicious approach to their clandestine rendezvous. But the affair was by no means at an end. They still continued to meet. Should Charles go to Tuscany to paint some watercolours, for instance, Camilla would be discovered holidaying conveniently nearby. It was a friendship on which Charles had come to depend. For almost half his life she had been his confidante and, when occasion allowed, his impassioned refuge. She had encouraged and comforted him and, in her brisk, nanny-like way, had helped organize his life.

Now, suddenly, she had been cast loose. It was not her lover who was waiting for her in the lane two miles away, but a friend. Charles was not on hand to give her any support at the moment when she needed it most. He had not even telephoned her. Instead of the Prince, she had to enlist the services of her daily cleaner who, dressed in headscarf and dark glasses, had driven out of the front gate in Camilla's car to draw off the waiting pressmen and give her the chance to get out and away to Wales where she went to stay with friends 'until the rumpus dies down'.

It never would. Camilla Parker-Bowles was a branded woman whose affair had become the stuff of scandal. As a result she had been shut out of her lover's life. It was the way it had to be.

In private conversation the Archbishop of Canterbury, George Carey, has gone so far as to indicate that he sees no religious reason why, if Charles chose to divorce Diana and marry again, he should not ascend the throne. The 103rd Primate of All England added that the Coronation Oath would have to be modified before Charles could swear it in all integrity but went on to say that he felt Charles should not be treated differently from his future subjects, almost half of whose marriages now end in divorce.

Charles was not willing to put the Archbishop's commendably Christian attitude to immediate test. With the monarchy in a crisis partly of his making, Camilla was left to fend for herself while he went back to the family business of official engagements and charity work. He announced that he was cutting back on polo. That was a diplomatic way of divesting himself of the services of his unofficial polo manager Major Ronald Ferguson, whose own extramarital escapades were proving increasingly embarrassing.

Like Camilla, Ferguson had loyally served the Prince for over two decades. Like Camilla, he was peremptorily dismissed. The Major was deeply upset. Once again Charles was compared to Henry V – not to the valiant victor of Agincourt but to the newly crowned king who, in Shakespeare's *Henry IV*, puts expediency before friendship. Ferguson likened his dismissal to the scene in which an unsuspecting Falstaff joyfully approaches his old friend only to be rebuffed by the denial, 'I know thee not, old man. Fall to thy prayers.'

Like that previous Prince of Wales, Charles was attempting to put his past behind him. He let it be known that his work schedule would increase, that he would henceforth be concentrating on what he had been trained from earliest childhood to do, which was to be a prince.

But, however hard the Royal Family might care to pretend, it could never be like the old times again. Diana would see to that. She wanted out of the Royal Family into which she had so unhappily married but had no intention of surrendering either the status or the attention it had brought her – as her presence at the State banquet for President Soares illustrated. Nor did the public want her to go.

She continued to act as a magnet to the cameras. In May 1993 she joined Charles at the service at Liverpool to commemorate the battle of the Atlantic. It was a blustery day when the wind played havoc with hats and hemlines. To avoid any mischance, the Queen weights her frocks if the weather looks tricky. Diana did not. The inevitable happened. As she went on her twenty-minute walkabout, a photogenic smile always in place, the breeze kept catching her skirt and lifting it skywards. 'I wouldn't have worn this skirt if I'd known it was going to be windy,' she insisted.

Her ability to outshine the family was given its most spectacular illustration on 2 June 1993. It was the fortieth anniversary of the Queen's Coronation. The Queen awoke that morning to find the morning newspapers dominated not by happy remembrances but by her wayward daughter-in-law. The night before Diana had addressed a conference run by the charity Turning Point. She had talked of the 'desperation and loneliness' felt by so many women, of their 'enormous courage' as they battled with post-natal depression, violence at home, 'in a haze of exhaustion and stress'; how many 'cannot cope' and are forced to resort to the 'mother's little helpers' of tranquillizers, sleeping pills and anti-depressants. Once again the Queen who had reigned for forty years, a pillar of doughty womanhood determinedly going about her duty with never a complaint, had been upstaged.

Diana dismissed the timing as immaculate coincidence. To others it was nothing less than a naked exercise in the media power which Diana, free of any constitutional responsibility, had come to exercise. It was the apogee of a development which had begun twelve seemingly innocent years before. She was the loose cannon on the deck of royalty.

The Queen and the Queen Mother lay much of the blame for this at Charles's imperious doorstep. If only, they argue, he had been possessed of either the strength of character or the emotional sensitivity to steer Diana out of her traumas, their marriage might have been saved – and with it the reputation of the family he was born to serve. It was a task that proved beyond him, as Diana proved to be a woman beyond his understanding.

Only Charles seems untouched by the catastrophe of events. Freed from the distracting influence of a wife whose company he found intolerable, he threw himself into a schedule of good works which kept him busy from early morning until late every night. In the furore that followed the announcement that his marriage was at an end, some commentators questioned his fitness for the throne, while others went so far as to suggest that he should renounce his right to the succession in favour of his eldest son, William. Charles – aloof, self-possessed, isolated by birth – ignored the clamour and stuck to the task he has set himself, which is to try to improve the quality of life in the

239

Britain he may one day reign over. He remains desperately concerned about pollution and youth unemployment and one of his constant complaints is the seeming inability of successive governments to tackle those problems. The Prince's Trust, he maintains, is often capable of getting more done than the official agencies.

How much he will really be able to accomplish in the long run remains to be seen. As the memories of Britain's imperial splendour yellow into history, so does the credibility of the rich, remote monarchy. The certainty which sustained it through the century's tribulations is no longer there and the next few years will undoubtedly be difficult ones as Charles and the rest of the Royal Family attempt to adjust to the irresistible undertow of change.

Charles, well-intentioned, hard-working, conservative and old-fashioned, will continue to do his duty as he sees it. It is what he was bred for. But it is Diana, with her brittle glamour and uncanny ability instantly to relate to ordinary people, who has taken over the public's affection.

Perhaps the future really does belong to her, as the Queen so fears.

Bibliography

Barry, Stephen, *Royal Service* (Macmillan Publishing Co., NY, 1981)

Dempster, Nigel, and Evans, Peter, *Behind Palace Doors* (Orion, 1993)

Hall, Unity, *Philip: The Man Behind the Monarchy* (Michael O'Mara Books, 1987)

Heald, Tim, *The Duke* (Hodder and Stoughton, 1991)

Holden, Anthony, *Charles* (Weidenfeld and Nicolson, 1978)

Hyman, Ronald, *Empire and Sexuality* (Manchester University Press, 1991)

Junor, Penny, *Charles* (Sidgwick and Jackson, 1987)

Lambton, Antony, *The Mountbattens* (Constable, 1989)

Menkes, Suzy, *Queen and Country* (HarperCollins, 1992)

Morrah, Dermot, *To Be a King* (Hutchinson, 1968)

Morton, Andrew, *Diana, Her True Story* (Michael O'Mara Books, 1987)

Seward, Ingrid, *Diana* (Weidenfeld and Nicolson, 1988)

— *Royal Children* (HarperCollins, 1993)

Wales, HRH Prince of, and Clover, Charles, *Highgrove: Portrait of an Estate* (Chapmans, 1993)

Whitaker, James, *Settling Down* (Quartet Books, 1981)

Index

93–6, 98; lack of control of his life, 87–8; at Cambridge University, 88–9, 92, 100; at University College of Wales, 88, 92–3; sense of humour, 91–2; girlfriends, 99, 100, 112–15, 116–20, 122–3, 133–5; attitudes to sex, 100–1, 111–12; in RAF, 101–3, 104; in Navy, 103–6; plays polo, 105, 121–2, 237; relationship with Lord Mountbatten, 106–7, 109–11; courts Diana, 115; diet, 120–1; self-absorption, 120–2; temper, 120; dislike of illness, 122; friendship with Camilla Parker-Bowles, 124–8, 135; relationship with Amanda Knatchbull, 128–30, 132–3; and Lord Mountbatten's assassination, 131–2; Diana determines to marry, 136–7, 138–46; proposes to Diana, 145–6; engagement, 146–51, 152–7, 159–63, 164–5; Diana tries to break engagement, 165–6; present to Camilla, 168–9; Zara Phillips's christening, 170–1; pre-wedding ball, 172–3; wedding, 174–6; honeymoon, 177–83; at Balmoral, 178–81; doubts Diana's suitability to be Queen, 181–2; causes of marriage breakdown, 166–7, 194, 201–3, 207, 220–7; Royal Christmases, 187; gives up shooting, 190–1; and his sons' births, 192–3, 195; disagreements over children, 194–7, 221; relations with his family, 197–8; and Highgrove, 200, 210–11, 215,

234; love of opera, 201–2; clothes, 202–3; and Diana's popularity, 204–5; interests, 209–15; advisers, 213–14; affair with Camilla, 217–19, 223–5, 228, 232, 235, 236–7; polo injury, 217; suffers clinical depression, 217, 228; rows with Diana, 222–3, 225, 228–9; telephone call taped, 223, 227, 236; separation from Diana, 7–8, 232–3, 234–6; possibility of remarriage, 237

Eisteddfod, 93–4
Eleuthera, 128
Elizabeth, The Queen Mother:
nanny, 12; and Princess
Elizabeth's childhood, 13;
and Princess Elizabeth's
marriage, 20; and Charles's
childhood, 27, 65–6, 109;
concern at Gordonstoun's
effect on Charles, 62–3;
detests Duchess of Windsor,
108; prejudiced against
Mountbatten, 111; eightieth
birthday party, 135; attitude
to Diana, 139–40; at
Balmoral, 179, 180; Royal
Christmases, 186; New Year
celebrations, 188; supports
her husband, 204; and *It's a
Royal Knockout*, 220
Elizabeth II, Queen: childhood,
12–14, 38; character, 14;
marriage, 18, 19–21, 25–6;
Charles's birth, 21–3; and
Charles's childhood, 10–11,
14, 26–8; surname, 25;
becomes Queen, 27; and
Charles's education, 33,
34–5, 38, 41–3, 48, 63;
Coronation, 36; creates
Charles Prince of Wales,
45–6; Prince Andrew's birth,
47; emotional distance from
Charles, 48; Investiture of
Prince of Wales, 83–4, 94,
96; relations with the media,
98; and Charles's girlfriends,
113, 114, 117, 118, 130; at
Wood Farm, 129; relations
with Diana, 139, 141–2, 151;
nickname, 168, 204; wedding
gifts to Diana, 173; at
Balmoral, 179; blank shots
fired at, 181; Royal
Christmases, 184–7;

Christmas broadcasts, 186;
relations with Charles, 198;
Diana upstages, 205–7,
238–9; political views, 212;
and Camilla Parker-Bowles,
219; and Charles and Diana's
separation, 8–9, 231, 232–3,
234–5; fortieth anniversary of
the Coronation, 238–9
Elphinstone, Lady, 12
Emanuel, David and Elizabeth,
155, 174
English Nature, 210
Eton, 57, 63, 64
Evans, Gwynfor, 93–4
Everett, Oliver, 149, 199

Falklands War, 104, 105–6
Farebrother, Michael, 40
Farrer's, 25
Fellowes, Lady Jane, 137, 138
Fellowes, Laura, 137
Fellowes, Sir Robert, 137, 138,
230
Ferguson, Major Ronald, 222,
237–8
Ferguson, Sarah *see* York, Sarah,
Duchess of
Fermoy, Lord, 142, 143
Fermoy, Ruth, Lady, 139–40
Fermoy-Hesketh, Johnny, 134
Festival of Remembrance,
205–6
First World War, 18, 75–6
Fisher, Alan, 199
Flecha de Lima, Lucia, 236
Flynn, Errol, 24
Fortnum and Mason, 24–5
Fox, Uffa, 107
France, 103–4
Free Welsh Army, 86
Frost, Lady Carina, 226
Frost, David, 226
Furness, Thelma, Lady, 128
Fürstenberg, Princess Ira von, 24

International Monetary Fund,
   85–6
IRA, 86, 130–1
ITN, 98
It's a Royal Knockout, 220–1, 223

Jagger, Bianca, 125
Jagger, Mick, 68, 113, 226
Jaipur, 229
James II, King, 22
John, Elton, 162
John, Prince, 129
Johnson, Lyndon B., 89
Jones, Hywel, 90
Jung, Carl, 107
Jupiter, HMS, 103
Juvenal, 59

Kalahari desert, 76, 108, 215
Kelly, Sergeant, 35
Kennedy, Caroline, 125
Kensington Palace, 138, 228
Kent, Prince Edward, Duke of,
   184
Kent, Prince George, Duke of,
   101, 179
Kent, Katharine, Duchess of,
   155, 184, 185
Kent, Princess Marina, Duchess
   of, 33, 179
Keppel, Alice, 124, 127, 227
Keppel, George, 124
Keppel, Sonia, 124
Klosters, 227
Knatchbull, Amanda, 128–30,
   132–3, 137, 139, 140
Knatchbull, Nicholas, 130
Knatchbull, Norton (Lord
   Romsey), 62, 132, 217
Knight, Clara (Alah), 12–13
Korea, 235

Labour Party, 60, 90
Lachman, Frau, 67
Lambton, Antony, 111

Lennon, John, 58
Lette, Lance Corporal
   Malcolm, 225
Lewin, Lord, 19
Lewis, Isle of, 55
Liberal Democrat Party, 212
Lightbody, Helen (Charles's
   nanny), 10–11, 17–18, 28–9,
   30, 36, 37, 48–9, 195, 213
Lindsay, Major Hugh, 227–8
Linley, David, Viscount, 172,
   179, 231
Linnett, Michael, 220
Lipsedge, Maurice, 219–20
Llewellyn-ap-Gruffydd, 85
Llewellyn the Last, 93
Lloyd George, David, 85, 87
Loss, Joe, 162

Macbeth, 69
MacDonald, Ramsay, 16
McGlashan, Dr Allan, 219
McGowan, Lord, 118
Macgregor, Stuart, 79
Macmillan, Maurice, 200
Madrigal Society (Cambridge),
   90
Major, John, 234
Malta, 98–9
Manners, Lady Teresa, 162
Mansfield, Jayne, 55
Manton, Lord, 113
Margaret, Princess, 13, 20, 58,
   112, 130, 162, 172, 179, 180,
   185, 186, 204, 206–7, 226,
   231
Marie-Astrid, Princess of
   Luxembourg, 112
Markham, Beryl, 101
Marlborough House, London,
   28
Mary, Queen, 13, 25, 28, 38,
   132, 149, 204
Mary Queen of Scots, 34
Mary of Modena, 22

249